MEN'S HEALTH TODAY 2006

MEN'S HEALTH TODAY

2006

Custom Bodywork from Head to Toe!

Edited by Deanna Portz, Men'sHealth Books

RODALE

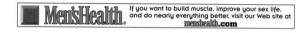

Notice

This book is intended as a reference volume only, not as a medical manual. The information given here is designed to help you make informed decisions about your health. It is not intended as a substitute for any treatment that may have been prescribed by your doctor. If you suspect that you have a medical problem, we urge you to seek competent medical help.

Mention of specific companies, organizations, or authorities in this book does not imply endorsement by the author or publisher, nor does mention of specific companies, organizations, or authorities imply that they endorse this book, its author, or the publisher.

Internet addresses and telephone numbers given in this book were accurate at the time it went to press.

© 2006 by Rodale Inc.
Interior photographs
Page 1 by Svend Lindbaek; page 47 by Sally Ullman; pages 65—71 by Beth Bischoff; page 87 by Diego Uchitel; page 127 by Augustus Butera; page 167 by Hilmar; page 203 by David Sacks/Getty Images; page 229 by Nicholas Eveleigh; page 239 by Stefan Nyvang; page 267 by Peter Berson; page 269—271 by Joseph Cultice

Men's Health is a registered trademark of Rodale Inc.

Printed in the United States of America
Rodale Inc. makes every effort to use acid-free ∞, recycled paper ♻.

ISBN-13 978—1—59486—357—8 hardcover
ISBN-10 1—59486—357—1 hardcover

Book Design by Drew Frantzen

2   4   6   8   10   9   7   5   3   1   hardcover

RODALE
LIVE YOUR WHOLE LIFE™

We inspire and enable people to improve their lives and the world around them
For more of our products visit **rodalestore.com** or call 800-848-4735

Men's Health Today 2006 Staff

EDITOR: Deanna Portz

CONTRIBUTING WRITERS: Daniel Amen, MD; Mark Anders; Matt Bean; Nicole Beland; Brian Boyé; David Brill; Steve Calechman; Leigh Cole; Kate Dailey; Tanya DeRosier; Doug Donaldson; Kathryn Eisman; Christian Finn; Jessica Fischbein; Liesa Goins; Brian Good; Jim Gorman; Siski Green; Erin Hobday; Mikel Jollett; Ian Kerner, PhD; Colin McEnroe; Tom McGrath; Gordon McGuire; Myatt Murphy, Hugh O'Neill; Peter Post; Scott Quill; Phillip Rhodes; Lauren Russell; David Schipper; Lou Schuler; Heidi Skolnik, MS, CDN; Ian Smith, MD; Larry Smith; Ted Spiker; Michael Tennesen; Amy Jo Van Bodegraven; Greta Van Susteren; Mark Verstegen, MS; Sara Vigneri; Sara Wells; John R. White, Jr, PharmD; Mike Zimmerman, David Zinczenko, Tom Zoellner

INTERIOR AND COVER DESIGNER: Drew Frantzen

PHOTO EDITOR: Darleen Malkames

PROJECT EDITOR: Lois Hazel

COPY EDITOR: Jennifer Bright Reich

LAYOUT DESIGNER: Linda J. Smith

PRODUCT SPECIALIST: Jodi Schaffer

Rodale Men's Health Group

SENIOR VICE PRESIDENT, EDITOR-IN-CHIEF *MEN'S HEALTH*: David Zinczenko

MEN'S HEALTH EXECUTIVE EDITOR: Zachary Schisgal

SENIOR MANAGING EDITOR: Chris Krogermeier

VICE PRESIDENT, ART AND DESIGN/BOOKS: Andy Carpenter

MANAGING ART DIRECTOR: Darlene Schneck

PRESIDENT, EDITOR-IN-CHIEF: Tami Booth Corwin

SENIOR VICE PRESIDENT, RODALE DIRECT: Gregg Michaelson

SENIOR DIRECTOR, PRODUCT MARKETING: Janine Slaughter

ASSOCIATE DIRECTOR-ONLINE: Matthew Neumaier

SENIOR MANAGER MULTIMEDIA PRODUCTION SERVICES: Robert V. Anderson Jr.

PAGE ASSEMBLY MANAGER: Patricia Brown

CONTENTS

INTRODUCTION

OVERHAUL THE MAN IN THE MIRROR

There's a show on the TLC network called *OverHaulin'*, geared just to guys. Each episode, a crew of expert mechanics and custom body shop designers dupe an unsuspecting vehicle owner into thinking his junker has been stolen. Then, in the 7 days that follow, they transform the mass of metal—from fender to tailpipe—into the owner's dream car.

This book is *Men's Health*'s version of that show, except that what we're overhauling gets parked on your couch instead of in your garage. Oh, and you're in on the plan.

In these pages, we give you all the motivation and know-how to overhaul your body from head to toe, not to mention every other aspect of your life. All you have to do is read on and pick and choose which tips and shortcuts apply to you.

For starters, you'll lose your spare tire for good, simply by building your diet around our 12 power foods. Then you'll put more horsepower under your hood with our 100 ways to muscle up.

Along with fast cars, men have been accused of liking fast women. Yet when it comes time to igniting things between the sheets, many women are often stuck in first gear while you're car lengths ahead. Like driving on unbalanced tires, this can lead to a bumpy ride—in the bedroom, that is. Which is why we provide 40 passion pointers for revving her engine—so you'll both be running at the same pace in no time. Who knows, maybe you'll even return to the days when you used the backseat for more than Junior's car seat.

Speaking of Junior, we even include an entire section to help you become the dad you wish yours had been to you. You'll find four easy ways to connect with your kids, a game plan for raising a good sport, and six strategies for making sure your kid has a conscience. Are mealtimes a mess? Try our five tactics for getting him to clean his plate. Does bedtime tire you out? Have silent nights in no time with our six tricks.

All this, plus cutting-edge medical advice to beat everything from headaches to diabetes, career-improving strategies to help you succeed at work, and grooming and style secrets that'll make you the sharpest-dressed guy in the crowd. The keys to the new-and-improved you are in this book. Just take a look in the mirror before you start taking these life-changing tips for a spin, because when you're finished with *your* overhaul, you may not recognize the guy staring back at you.

Deanna Portz

ONE

LOSE YOUR GUT

READ UP ON IT

The Abs Diet

Let others lose. You are going to gain. Muscle tone, better health, a great sex life . . . Abs are just the start

By David Zinczenko

You have abs.

Yes, you.

When you think of abs, you may think of Brad Pitt or Janet Jackson. Your cynical side may also think of airbrushing, starvation diets, and an exercise regimen so time-consuming it would violate labor laws. Your conclusion: You have a better chance of scaling Mount Everest in a Speedo than you do of developing great abs.

But as the editor-in-chief of *Men's Health* magazine, I know you can have the midsection of your dreams. Listen: I analyze health and fitness information the way brokers analyze the market. And I've talked to and heard from thousands of folks who have shared their weight-loss success stories with *Men's Health*. So I've seen the plus side of the equation. But I've lived the negative, as well. I know what it's like to feel fat.

As a latchkey kid growing up in the early '80s, I made every mistake in the book. I ate fast food instead of smart food. I played video games when I should've been playing outside. By the time I reached age 14, I was carrying 212 pounds of torpid teenage tallow on my 5-foot, 10-inch frame. But I got lucky. When I graduated from high school, I enlisted in the Naval Reserve, where the tenets of fitness were pounded into me, day after day after day. Soon after I graduated from college, I joined *Men's Health* and learned the importance of proper nutrition and—just as important—the health threats inherent in carrying around too much fat in your gut. If you have a bulging belly, it means your internal organs, including your heart, are literally packed in fat. It's like renting a room to an arsonist.

Whether you want to change your body to improve your health, your looks, your athletic performance, or your sex appeal, this plan—which I call the Abs Diet—offers you a simple promise: It can transform your body so you can accomplish all of those goals. It won't just enhance your life; it will save it.

Here we lay down the nutrition plan that will cut your body fat. And in "Seven Days to a Six-Pack" on page 61, we teach you all the exercises you need to change your life (and the size of your pants).

Start here: The following guidelines are your six-pack, to go.

THE ABS DIET QUICK GUIDE

Most guys who are embarking on a new mission begin with one fundamental question: When do we eat?

Good question. Most diets are all about what foods you'll cut out. This one is all about what you'll include. And that's good news, because if you want to emerge on the other side of this plan with a new body, you must have the flexibility and freedom to keep yourself from getting hungry and the knowledge that you can eat well no matter what.

So let's ring the dinner bell.

Guideline 1: Eat Six Meals a Day

Didn't I tell you this isn't about deprivation?

We're so used to hearing people talk about eating less food that it's become weight-loss doctrine. The new philosophy I want you to keep in mind is "energy balance."

Researchers at Georgia State University developed a technique to measure hourly energy balance—that is, how many calories you're burning versus how many calories you're taking in. The researchers found that if you keep your hourly surplus or deficit within 300 to 500 calories at all times, you'll best be able to change your body composition by losing fat and adding lean muscle mass. People with the largest energy imbalances (those whose calorie surpluses or shortfalls topped 500 calories from hour to hour) were the fattest, while those with the most balanced energy levels were the leanest. So if you eat only your three squares a day, your energy levels are all over the place. That kind of eating plan is great—if your dream is to be the next Chris Farley. But if you want to look slimmer, feel fitter, and live longer, then eat more often. Simply alternate your meals with snacks (we give you a ton of food suggestions on the pages that follow), and you'll keep your stomach full, which will reduce the likelihood of a diet-destroying binge.

Guideline 2: Drink Smoothies Regularly

A blender may be the ultimate weight-loss power tool. Smoothies—blended mixtures of milk, low-fat yogurt, whey powder, ice, and other good stuff—can act as meal substitutes and potent snacks. They require little time; the berries, flavored whey powder, or peanut butter will satisfy your sweet cravings; and their thickness takes up space in your stomach. A University of Tennessee study found that men who added three servings of yogurt a day to their diets lost 61 percent more body fat and 81 percent more stomach fat over 12 weeks than did men who didn't eat yogurt. Researchers speculate that the calcium helps the body burn fat and limits the amount of fat your body can make. So drink an 8-ounce smoothie for breakfast, as a meal substitute, or as a snack before or after your workout.

Guideline 3: Know What to Drink—And What Not To

There are many ways that alcohol can get you into trouble, and not just at the intern luncheon. Alcohol doesn't make you feel full or decrease the amount of food you'll eat. But it does encourage your body to burn as much as 36 percent less fat and make you store more of the fat you eat. And it can inhibit your production of testosterone and human growth hormone—two hormones that help burn fat and build muscle.

Okay, so water isn't exciting, but drinking about eight glasses of it a day has a lot of benefits. It helps keep you satiated (often what we interpret as hunger is really thirst). It flushes the waste products your body churns out when processing protein or breaking down fat. And it transports nutrients to your muscles, to keep your metabolism clicking. Otherwise, the best drinks you can have are low-fat milk and green tea (or, if you must, no more than two glasses of diet soda a day).

Guideline 4: Focus on the Abs Diet Power 12

The Abs Diet encourages you to focus on (not restrict yourself to) a generous market basket of food types—the Abs Diet Power 12—to fulfill your core nutritional needs. These foods are so good for you, in fact, that they'll just about single-handedly exchange your fat for muscle (provided you've kept your receipt). Just as important, I've designed the Power 12 to include thousands of food combinations. (You'll find a few here and more at www.menshealth.com/absdietchallenge.) The more of them you eat, the better your body will be able to increase lean muscle mass and avoid storing fat. Just follow these simple rules of thumb.

- Include two or three of these foods in each of your three major meals and at least one of them in each of your three snacks.
- Diversify your food at every meal to get a combination of protein, carbohydrates, and fat.
- Make sure you sneak a little bit of protein into each snack.

(continued on page 17)

ABS DIET POWER 12

And now, here are the Power 12. Feel free to eat along as you read.

THE ABS DIET POWER 12 KEY

How to read the key: The icons demonstrate which important roles each food can play in maintaining optimum health.

Builds muscle
Foods rich in muscle-building plant and animal proteins qualify for this seal of approval, as do foods rich in certain minerals, such as magnesium, linked to proper muscle maintenance.

Helps promote weight loss
Foods high in calcium and fiber (both of which protect against obesity), as well as foods that help build fat-busting muscle tissue, earn this badge of respect.

Strengthens bone
Calcium and vitamin D are the most important bone builders, and they protect the body against osteoporosis.

Lowers blood pressure
Any food that has potassium, magnesium, or calcium and is low in sodium can help lower blood pressure.

Fights cancer
Research has shown a lower risk of some types of cancer among people who maintain low-fat, high-fiber diets. You can also help foil cancer by eating foods that are high in calcium, beta-carotene, or vitamin C. In addition, all cruciferous (cabbage-type) and allium (onion-type) vegetables earn the cancer-protection symbol because research has shown that they help prevent certain kinds of cancer.

Improves immune function
Foods with folate, the mineral zinc, and vitamins A, B_6, C, and E boost the body's ability to resist disease.

Fights heart disease
Artery-clogging cholesterol can lead to trouble if you eat foods containing primarily saturated and trans fats, while foods that are high in monounsaturated or polyunsaturated fats will actually help protect your heart by keeping your cholesterol levels in check.

1. Almonds and Other Nuts

(eaten with skins intact)
Superpowers: Building muscle, fighting food cravings
Secret weapons: Protein, monounsaturated fats, vitamin E, folate (in peanuts), fiber, magnesium, phosphorus
Fight against: Obesity, heart disease, muscle loss, cancer
Sidekicks: Pumpkin seeds, sunflower seeds, avocados
Impostors: Salted or smoked nuts (high in sodium, which can spike blood pressure)

These days, you hear about good fats and bad fats the way you hear about good cops and bad cops. One's on your side, and one's going to beat you silly. Oreos fall into the latter category, but nuts are clearly out to help you. They contain the monounsaturated fats that clear your arteries and help you feel full.

All nuts are high in protein and monounsaturated fat. But almonds are like Jack Nicholson in *One Flew over the Cuckoo's Nest*: They're the king of the nuts. Eat as much as two handfuls a day. If you eat 2 ounces of almonds (about 24 of them), it can suppress your appetite—especially if you wash them down with 8 ounces of water.

For a quick popcorn alternative, spray a handful of almonds with nonstick cooking spray and bake them at 400°F for 5 to 10 minutes. Take them out of the oven and sprinkle them with either a brown sugar and cinnamon mix or cayenne pepper and thyme.

2. Beans and Other Legumes

(including soybeans, chickpeas, and pinto, navy, kidney, and lima beans)
Superpowers: Building muscle, helping burn fat, regulating digestion
Secret weapons: Fiber, protein, iron, folate
Fight against: Obesity, colon cancer, heart disease, high blood pressure
Sidekicks: Lentils, peas, bean dips, hummus, edamame
Impostors: Refried beans, which are high in saturated fats; baked beans, which are high in sugar

Most of us can trace our resistance to beans to some unfortunately timed intestinal upheaval (third-grade math class; a first date gone awry). But beans are, as the famous rhyme says, good for your heart; the more you eat them, the more you'll be able to control your hunger. Black, lima, pinto, navy—it's your pick. They're all low in fat, and they're packed with protein, fiber, and iron—nutrients crucial for building muscle and losing weight. Gastrointestinal disadvantages notwithstanding, they serve as one of the key members of the Abs Diet cabinet because of all their nutritional power.

In fact, if you can replace a meat-heavy dish with a bean-heavy dish a couple of times a week, you'll be lopping a lot of saturated fat out of your diet and replacing it with higher amounts of fiber.

3. Spinach and Other Green Vegetables

Superpowers: Neutralizing free radicals (molecules that accelerate the aging process)
Secret weapons: Vitamins including A, C, and K; folate; beta-carotene; minerals including calcium and magnesium; fiber
Fight against: Cancer, heart disease, stroke, obesity, osteoporosis
Sidekicks: Cruciferous vegetables like broccoli and brussels sprouts; green, yellow, red, and orange vegetables such as asparagus, peppers, and yellow beans

ABS DIET SUCCESS STORY

"Four pounds a week . . . gone for good."

Name: Paul McComb
Age: 28
Height: 5'9"
Starting weight: 180
Weight 6 weeks later: 155

Once Paul McComb left college and gained some weight, he figured the extra heft was his to keep for life. But when he walked into a nutrition store and stepped on a scale that told him how much he weighed (180 pounds) and how much he should weigh (155), something changed: his attitude.

So McComb went on the Abs Diet—and lost 25 pounds.

He made significant changes by doing such things as eliminating his four or five daily Cokes and skipping the midnight chips. He says the transition was easy. "The Abs Diet had me eating six times a day, so I didn't feel like snacking on chips," he reports.

McComb says the key to his success was planning meals around the Abs Diet Powerfoods so he wasn't tempted by vending machines and snack bars. He'd eat turkey on multigrain bread for lunch, have whole-wheat pasta or chicken for dinner, and snack on peanut butter and chocolate milk. He was happy that he didn't have to count calories, watch carbs, or give up the foods he loves. "Understanding the Powerfoods concept and how these foods work together helped me eat—a lot—and still watch the weight come off."

Impostors: None, as long as you don't fry them or smother them in fatty cheese sauces

You know vegetables are packed with important nutrients, but they're also a critical part of your body-changing diet. I like spinach in particular because one serving supplies nearly a full day's vitamin A and half of your vitamin C. It's also loaded with folate—a vitamin that protects against heart disease, stroke, and colon cancer. Dress a sandwich with the stuff, or stir-fry it with fresh garlic and olive oil. Broccoli is high in fiber and more densely packed with vitamins and minerals than almost any other food.

If you hate vegetables, hide them. Puree them and add them to marinara sauce or chili. The more you chop, the less you taste, and the easier it is for your body to absorb nutrients.

4. Dairy Products

(fat-free or low-fat milk, yogurt, cheese, cottage cheese)
Superpowers: Building strong bones, firing up weight loss
Secret weapons: Calcium, vitamins A and B_{12}, riboflavin, phosphorus, potassium
Fight against: Osteoporosis, obesity, high blood pressure, cancer
Sidekicks: None
Impostors: Whole milk, frozen yogurt

Dairy is nutrition's version of a typecast actor. It gets so much good press for strengthening bones that it garners little attention for all the other stuff it does well. Just take a look at the mounting evidence that calcium is a prime belly-buster. A University of Tennessee study found that dieters who consumed between 1,200 and 1,300 milligrams of calcium a day lost nearly twice as much weight as those taking in less calcium. Researchers think the mineral probably prevents weight gain by increasing the breakdown of body fat and hampering its formation.

Low-fat yogurt, cheeses, and other dairy products can play a key role in your diet. But I recommend milk as your major source of calcium. Liquids take up lots of room in your stomach, so your brain gets the signal that you're full. Sprinkling in chocolate whey powder can help curb sweet cravings.

5. Instant Oatmeal

(unsweetened, unflavored)
Superpowers: Boosting energy and sex drive, reducing cholesterol, maintaining blood-sugar levels

Secret weapons: Complex carbohydrates and fiber
Fights against: Heart disease, diabetes, colon cancer, obesity
Sidekicks: High-fiber cereals like All-Bran and Fiber One
Impostors: Sugary cereals

Oatmeal can propel you through sluggish mornings, and you can down a bowl a couple of hours before a workout to feel fully energized by the time you hit the weights, or eat some at night to avoid a late-night binge. It couldn't be easier to prepare—just add water. Buy the unsweetened, unflavored variety, and use other Powerfoods such as milk and berries to enhance the taste.

Oatmeal contains soluble fiber, meaning it attracts fluid and stays in your stomach longer than insoluble fiber does. It also works like a bouncer for your body, showing troublemakers the door. For example, soluble fiber helps remove LDL cholesterol from your circulatory system.

Another cool fact about oatmeal: Preliminary studies indicate that eating oatmeal raises the levels of free testosterone in your body, boosting your sex drive and enhancing the body's ability to build muscle and burn fat.

6. Eggs

Superpowers: Building muscle, burning fat
Secret weapons: Protein, vitamins A and B_{12}
Fight against: Obesity
Sidekicks: Egg Beaters, which have fewer calories than eggs and no fat, but just as much of the core nutrients
Impostors: None

For a long time, eggs were considered pure evil, and doctors were more likely to recommend tossing eggs at passing cars than throwing them into omelet pans. That's because just two eggs contain enough cholesterol to put you over your daily recommended value. Though you can cut out some of that by removing part of the yolk and using the white, more and more research shows that eating an egg or two a day will not raise your cholesterol levels. In fact, we've learned that most blood cholesterol is made by the body from dietary fat, not dietary cholesterol. That's why you should take advantage of eggs and their powerful makeup of protein.

The protein found in eggs has the highest "biological value" of protein—a measure of how well it supports your body's protein need—of any food. In other words, the protein in eggs is more effective at building muscle than is protein from other sources, even milk and beef. Eggs also contain vitamin B_{12}, which is necessary for fat breakdown.

7. Turkey and Other Lean Meats

(lean steak, chicken, fish)
Superpowers: Building muscle, improving the immune system
Secret weapons: Protein, iron, zinc, creatine (beef), omega-3 fatty acids (fish), vitamins B_6 (chicken and fish) and B_{12}, phosphorus, potassium
Fight against: Obesity, mood disorders, memory loss, heart disease
Sidekicks: Shellfish, Canadian bacon, omega-3-rich flaxseed
Impostors: Sausage, bacon, cured meats, ham, fatty cuts of steak like T-bone and rib eye

A classic muscle-building nutrient, protein is the base of any solid diet plan. Turkey breast is one of the leanest meats you'll find, and it packs nearly one-third of your daily requirements of niacin and vitamin B_6. Beef, another classic muscle-building protein, is the top food source of creatine—a substance your body uses to make new muscle fibers. Look for round or loin cuts (code for extra-lean); New York strip is less fatty than prime rib.

(continued on page 14)

ABS DIET SUCCESS STORY

"I cut my body fat in half in just 6 weeks."

Name: Bill Stanton
Age: 40
Height: 5'8"
Starting weight: 220
Weight 6 weeks later: 190

Bill Stanton, a security consultant, had been pumping iron since he was 15. But even with his rigorous weight training, he kept getting fatter: By the time he reached 40, he had ballooned to 220 pounds on his 5-foot-8 frame. Why? Because Stanton's diet and exercise routine consisted of doing bench presses and squats, then finishing the night with chicken wings and booze.

"My pants were fitting me like a tourniquet, and it was like I was in a bad marriage. I was living comfortably uncomfortable," Stanton says. "The Abs Diet challenged me to get on the program, step up to the plate, and step away from the plate."

After following the Abs Diet for 6 weeks, Stanton lost 30 pounds—and has cut his body fat from 30 percent to 15 percent.

"I work out at Sports Club LA, where people are really focused on looking great," he says. "Even there, guys and girls come up to me. One guy said, 'You are kicking butt. Everybody sees that transformation. You're inspiring a lot of people.'"

Stanton has changed his physique so dramatically that he's even been accused of taking steroids. "I take that as a compliment," he laughs.

POWER EATING WITH THE POWER 12

What's better than eating one belly-busting food? Eating five in one dish. These five recipes can get you through day 1 of your new mission to find your abs. Go to www.menshealth.com/absdietchallenge to satisfy yourself for day 2 and onward.

Halle's Berry Smoothie
(number of Powerfoods: 4)

³/₄ c instant oatmeal, nuked in water or skim milk

³/₄ c skim milk

³/₄ c mixed frozen berries

2 tsp whey powder

3 ice cubes, crushed

Blend all ingredients in a blender. Makes 2 8-ounce servings.

Per serving: 144 calories, 7 grams (g) protein, 27 g carbohydrates, 1 g fat (0 g saturated), 4 g fiber, 109 milligrams (mg) sodium

Eggs Beneficial Breakfast Sandwich
(number of Powerfoods: 5)

1 large whole egg

3 large egg whites

1 tsp ground flaxseed

2 slices whole-wheat bread, toasted

1 slice Canadian bacon

1 tomato, sliced, or 1 green bell pepper, sliced

Scramble the whole egg and egg whites in a bowl. Add the flaxseed to the mixture. Fry it in a nonstick skillet treated with nonstick cooking spray and dump it onto the toast. Add the bacon and tomato, pepper, or other vegetables of your choice. Wash it all down with 8 ounces of orange juice, and make it the high-pulp kind. More fiber that way. Makes 1 serving.

Per serving: 399 calories, 31 g protein, 46 g carbohydrates, 11 g fat (3 g saturated), 6 g fiber, 900 mg sodium

The I-Am-Not-Eating-Salad Lunch Salad
(number of Powerfoods: 4)

2 oz grilled chicken

1 c romaine lettuce

1 tomato, chopped

1   small green bell pepper, chopped

1   medium carrot, chopped

3   Tbsp 94 percent fat-free Italian dressing or 1 tsp olive oil

1   Tbsp grated Parmesan cheese

1   Tbsp ground flaxseed

Chop the chicken into small pieces. Mix all the ingredients together and store in the fridge. Eat on multigrain bread or by itself. Makes 1 serving.

Per serving: 248 calories, 16 g protein, 33 g carbohydrates, 8 g fat (2 g saturated), 10 g fiber, 875 mg sodium

Salmon Rushdie Dinner
(number of Powerfoods: 5)

2   Tbsp olive oil

1   Tbsp lemon juice

¼   tsp salt

¼   tsp ground black pepper

1   Tbsp ground flaxseed

1   clove garlic

4   6-oz salmon fillets

1   c cooked rice

    Green vegetable of choice

In a baking dish, combine the oil, lemon juice, salt, pepper, flaxseed, and garlic. Add the fish, coat it well, cover it, and refrigerate for 15 minutes. Preheat your oven to 450°F. Line a baking sheet with foil and coat it with nonstick cooking spray. Remove the fish from the marinade and place the fish skin-side down on the baking sheet. Bake for 9 to 12 minutes. Serve with the rice and a green vegetable. Makes 4 servings.

Per serving: 433 calories, 42 g protein, 19 g carbohydrates, 20 g fat (3 g saturated), 3 g fiber, 252 mg sodium

The Gobbler Snack
(number of Powerfoods: 2)

3   slices low-sodium deli turkey breast

1½ slices fat-free cheese

Roll the turkey breast with the cheese. (Low-fat string cheese makes a nice roller, too.) Stuff in pie hole. Makes 1 serving.

Per serving: 93 calories, 14 g protein, 7 g carbohydrates, 1 g fat (0.5 g saturated), 0 g fiber, 990 mg sodium

To cut down on saturated fats even more, concentrate on fish like tuna and salmon, because they contain a healthy dose of omega-3 fatty acids as well as protein. A bonus benefit: Researchers in Stockholm found that men who ate no fish had three times the risk of prostate cancer of those who ate it regularly. It's the omega-3s that inhibit prostate-cancer growth.

8. Peanut Butter

(all-natural, sugar-free)
Superpowers: Boosting testosterone, building muscle, burning fat
Secret weapons: Protein, monounsaturated fat, vitamin E, niacin, magnesium
Fights against: Obesity, muscle loss, wrinkles, cardiovascular disease
Sidekicks: Cashew and almond butters
Impostors: Mass-produced sugary and trans fatty peanut butters

Yes, PB has its disadvantages: It's high in calories, and it isn't served in four-star restaurants. But it's packed with heart-healthy monounsaturated fats that can increase your body's production of testosterone, which can help muscles grow and fat melt. Three tablespoons a day should guarantee the benefit without overloading on the fat.

9. Olive Oil

Superpowers: Lowering cholesterol, boosting the immune system
Secret weapons: Monounsaturated fat, vitamin E
Fights against: Obesity, cancer, heart disease, high blood pressure
Sidekicks: Canola oil, peanut oil, sesame oil
Impostors: Other vegetable and hydrogenated vegetable oils, trans fatty acids, margarine

No need for a long explanation here: Olive oil and its brethren will help control your food cravings; they'll also help you burn fat and keep your cholesterol in check. Do you need any more reason to pass the bottle?

10. Whole-Grain Breads and Cereals

Superpowers: Preventing your body from storing fat
Secret weapons: Fiber, protein, thiamin, riboflavin, niacin, vitamin E, calcium, magnesium, potassium, zinc

Fight against: Obesity, cancer, high blood pressure, heart disease
Sidekicks: Brown rice, whole-wheat pretzels, whole-wheat pastas
Impostors: Processed bakery products like white bread, bagels, and doughnuts; breads labeled wheat instead of whole wheat

There's only so long a person can survive on an all-protein diet or an all-salad diet or an all-anything diet. You crave carbohydrates because your body needs them. The key is to eat the ones that have all their heart-healthy, belly-melting fiber intact. Whole-grain carbohydrates can play an important role in a healthy lifestyle. Whole-grain bread keeps insulin levels low, which keeps you from storing fat.

11. Extra-Protein (Whey) Powder

Superpowers: Building muscle, burning fat
Secret weapons: Protein, cysteine, glutathione
Fights against: Obesity
Sidekick: Ricotta cheese
Impostor: Soy protein

Whey protein contains essential amino acids that build muscle and burn fat. But it's especially effective because it has the highest amount of protein for the fewest number of calories, making it fat's kryptonite. But that's not all. Whey protein can help protect your body from prostate cancer. It's a good source of cysteine, which your body uses to build a prostate cancer–fighting antioxidant called glutathione. Adding just a small amount of whey protein to your diet may increase glutathione levels in your body by as much as 60 percent.

12. Raspberries and Other Berries

Superpowers: Protecting your heart, enhancing eyesight, improving memory, preventing cravings
Secret weapons: Antioxidants, fiber, vitamin C, tannins (cranberries)
Fight against: Heart disease, cancer, obesity
Sidekicks: Most other fruits, especially apples and grapefruit
Impostors: Sugary jellies

Depending on your taste, any berry will do (except Crunch Berries). I like raspberries, as much for their power as for their flavor. One cup packs 6 grams of fiber and more than half of your daily requirement of vitamin C.

Blueberries are one of the most healthful foods you can eat. They beat out 39 other fruits and vegetables in the antioxidant-power ratings. And

ABS DIET SNACKS

Most diet plans portray snacking as a failure. I want you to think of snacking as exactly the opposite—as a key to success! But the secret to effective snacking is doing so at the optimum time—about 2 hours before you're scheduled to eat your next meal. That'll be enough time to head off hunger pangs and keep you full enough to avoid a meltdown at mealtime. Pick from any of the categories below, but make sure you toss in some protein.

Protein

2   tsp reduced-fat peanut butter

1   oz almonds

3   slices low-sodium deli turkey breast

3   slices deli roast beef

Dairy

8   oz low-fat yogurt

1   c 1 percent milk or chocolate milk

¾   c low-fat ice cream

1½ slices fat-free cheese

1   stick string cheese

Fruits or Vegetables

1   oz raisins

Unlimited raw vegetables (celery, baby carrots, broccoli)

1½ c berries

4   oz cantaloupe

1   large orange

1   can (11.5 oz) low-sodium V8 juice

Complex Carbohydrates

1 or 2 slices whole-grain bread

1 bowl oatmeal or high-fiber cereal

strawberries (along with grapefruit, peaches, apples, and oranges) contain another valuable form of fiber called pectin that can make you feel fuller for hours.

THE ABS DIET QUICK GUIDE *(continued)*

Guideline 5: Stop Counting

Though calorie burning is paramount to losing fat, calorie counting will make you lose focus and motivation. The great news is that when you zero in on the Abs Diet Powerfoods, you'll be healthy and won't feel hungry as often. Plus, the most energy-efficient foods are almost like doormen at a nightclub: They're not going to let in any of the riffraff without your approval.

Guideline 6: For One Meal a Week, Forget the Guidelines

I would never advocate cheating on your spouse or your taxes. But I want you to cheat on this diet. Take one meal during the week and forget everything about good carbohydrates and good fats. Have whatever it is—pizza, buffalo wings—that you miss the most. Think of this cheat meal as the carrot at the end of a good week of eating. Enjoy your meal of gluttony, but please, don't make the carrot literally a carrot.

Excerpted from *The Abs Diet*, copyright 2004 by Rodale Inc.

Eat Right Every Time

Life is an all-you-can-eat buffet. Pick the wrong foods and you expand your gut, harm your heart, and shave years off your life. Make the right choices and you look better, feel better, and feast longer. What'll it be, friend?

By David Zinczenko

Like sleep and daily Britney Spears gossip, most of us take eating for granted. Insert food into mouth, chew, and swallow. Game over. But when you consider that 65 percent of American adults are overweight or obese, the game's not even close; fat wins in a rout. Why? Because we've become a nation that considers drive-thrus fine dining, that saves money by ordering two pizzas instead of one, that's been snowed into thinking bacon is a diet food, and that builds its food pyramids on top of a "family-size" order of 50 wings.

When we eat—whether it's at home or on the road, on vacation or at the ballpark—we forget that we have choices. See, it's a fallacy that easy eating has to mean greasy eating. Truth is, you can learn how to make smart food choices without sacrificing taste or splitting your pants. I know most people don't have a lot of time to whip up elaborate meals. Part of the reason I wrote *The Abs Diet*, and why it has quickly helped so many people, is that we all need easy eating—but not in its current form: one fat bomb, hold the pickles. There's a better way. Just build your home meal plan around the Abs Diet Power 12 foods (as we showed you on page 6): almonds and other nuts, beans and other legumes, spinach and other green vegetables, dairy products, instant oatmeal, eggs, turkey and other lean meats, peanut butter, olive oil, whole-grain breads and cereals, extra-protein (whey) powder, and raspberries and other berries. When you're on the road, follow our directions to healthy eating (below). It's like an emergency diet kit from FEMA: When nutritional disaster is in the forecast, we'll help you dodge the heavy winds.

ON THE ROAD

If you're one of those guys who consume more meals behind the wheel of a car than they do at the head of the table, we can help you arrive safe and skinny. Here's the best stuff we found when we vetted the restaurant-chain gang and scouted around the generic eateries you'll find in any town.

At the Sandwich Shop

Strategy: Opt for whole-wheat bread. Go easy on the cheese, heavy on the vegetables and lean meats (turkey, ham, roast beef).

SCHLOTZSKY'S DELI

Eat This:

Dijon Chicken Sandwich (small)

329 calories, 4 grams (g) fat (saturated-fat content not available), 1,456 milligrams (mg) sodium

Fresh Fruit Salad (small)

86 calories, 1 g fat (saturated fat NA), 22 mg sodium

Not That:

The Original Sandwich (small)

525 calories, 24 g fat (saturated fat NA), 1,781 mg sodium

SUBWAY

Eat This:

6-Inch Roast Beef Sub

290 calories, 5 g fat (2 g saturated), 920 mg sodium

Oatmeal Raisin Cookie

200 calories, 8 g fat (2.5 g saturated), 170 mg sodium

Not That:

6-Inch Meatball Marinara Sub

560 calories, 24 g fat (11 g saturated), 1,610 mg sodium

At the Fast-Food Joint

Strategy: Beware special sauces and creamy dips. Likewise, inspect your salad; at some burger joints, they're worse than the burgers. And above all, don't fall for combo meals, which add cost, trans fats, and liquid obesity (high-fructose corn syrup).

CHICK-FIL-A

Eat This:

Chargrilled Chicken Sandwich

270 calories, 3.5 g fat (1 g saturated), 940 mg sodium

Carrot & Raisin Salad

170 calories, 6 g fat (1 g saturated), 110 mg sodium

GUILTY PLEASURE MEN FEEL GUILTIEST INDULGING IN:

Fast Food

Not That:
Chicken Deluxe Sandwich (fried)
> 420 calories, 16 g fat (3.5 g saturated), 1,300 mg sodium

Waffle Potato Fries (small)
> 270 calories, 13 g fat (3 g saturated), 115 mg sodium

MCDONALD'S

Eat This:
Chicken McGrill
> 400 calories, 16 g fat (3 g saturated), 1,010 mg sodium

Side Salad with Low-Fat Balsamic Vinaigrette
> 55 calories, 3 g fat (0 g saturated), 740 mg sodium

Not That:
Bacon Ranch Salad with Crispy Chicken (includes dressing)
> 520 calories, 31 g fat (8 g saturated), 1,560 mg sodium

WENDY'S

Eat This:
Chili (small)
> 220 calories, 6 g fat (2.5 g saturated), 780 mg sodium

Sour Cream and Chives Hot Stuffed Baked Potato
> 330 calories, 5 g fat (3.5 g saturated), 40 mg sodium

Not That :
Spicy Chicken Fillet Sandwich
> 510 calories, 19 g fat (3.5 g saturated), 1,480 mg sodium

At the Diner (7 a.m.)

Strategy: Eggs are a potent Powerfood. So regardless of which greasy spoon you're at, start your day with plain eggs, whole-wheat toast, and lean grilled meat.

Eat This:
2 poached eggs
> 148 calories, 10 g fat (3 g saturated), 295 mg sodium

1 slice plain wheat toast
> 128 calories, 2.5 g fat (0 g saturated), 160 mg sodium

1 slice Canadian bacon
> 44 calories, 2 g fat (1 g saturated), 365 mg sodium

Not That:
Western omelet
> 520 calories, 39 g fat (13 g saturated), 1,280 mg sodium

Plain biscuit

> 280 calories, 12 g fat (3 g saturated), 760 mg sodium

2 sausage links

> 250 calories, 22 g fat (6 g saturated), 370 mg sodium

At the Italian Restaurant

Strategy: Ask for fiber-filled whole-wheat pasta. Or look for entrées that feature lean protein or vegetables as their centerpiece, instead of cheese and carbs.

Eat This:

Minestrone (1 cup)

> 100 calories, 1 g fat (0 g saturated), 610 mg sodium

Chicken Marsala

> 460 calories, 25 g fat (7 g saturated), 790 mg sodium

Not That:

Antipasto (half order)

> 315 calories, 24 g fat (8 g saturated), 1,480 mg sodium

Lasagna

> 960 calories, 53 g fat (21 g saturated), 2,060 mg sodium

At the Sports Bar

Strategy: Order before alcohol impairs your judgment.
Eat This:

Salted nuts (1 ounce)

> 168 calories, 15 g fat (2 g saturated), 190 mg sodium

Or

Plain buffalo wings (half order)

> 350 calories, 24 g fat (8 g saturated), 510 mg sodium

Not That:

Cheese fries with ranch dressing (1 cup)

> 750 calories, 54 g fat (23 g saturated), 1,225 mg sodium

Nor

Stuffed potato skins with sour cream (4 skins)

> 630 calories, 48 g fat (24 g saturated), 650 mg sodium

At the Mexican Restaurant

Strategy: Mexican restaurants can be good places to get vegetables, like the pile of grilled onions and peppers that comes with an order of fajitas. Just be careful of extra cheeses and refried beans, which are packed with fat.

Eat This:

12 chips with salsa (2 ounces)

    340 calories, 17 g fat (3 g saturated), 410 mg sodium

Chicken fajitas with lettuce and pico de gallo

    850 calories, 30 g fat (6 g saturated), 2,100 mg sodium

Side of black, kidney, or pinto beans

    120 calories, 2 g fat (0 g saturated), 400 mg sodium

Not That:

12 chips with queso dip (2 ounces)

    440 calories, 25 g fat (7 g saturated), 920 mg sodium

Chicken chimichanga

    1,100 calories, 50 g fat (15 g saturated), 3,300 mg sodium

Side of refried beans

    200 calories, 6 g fat (2 g saturated), 550 mg sodium

At the Chinese Restaurant

Strategy: You're in for a big dose of salt, whatever you do, so factor that into your daily meal plan. And pack half your meal away in a to-go box; a single portion will feed you twice.

Eat This:

Egg-drop soup

    60 calories, 3 g fat (1 g saturated), 1,000 mg sodium

Stir-fried vegetables

    750 calories, 19 g fat (3 g saturated), 2,150 mg sodium

Not That:

Chicken or pork egg roll

    200 calories, 10 g fat (1 g saturated), 450 mg sodium

General Tso's chicken

    1,600 calories, 60 g fat (10 g saturated), 3,200 mg sodium

AT THE GROCERY STORE

Strategy: Make a list before you shop. Be specific: Instead of writing "snacks" and buying the entire Dolly Madison collection, write "yogurt" or "sliced almonds." This way, you'll buy only what you need, instead of the crap they're trying to palm off on you. (For more grocery-cart must-haves, go to www.menshealth.com/absdietchallenge.)

Produce

Work the greens: Green vegetables form a crucial part of the Abs Diet. Most produce is just as nutritious frozen as it is fresh, so be judicious. If you rarely use vegetables, buy frozen. If you burn through greens like Ernie Els, stick with fresh.

MIXED-GREENS SALAD BLEND

Best buy: The more colors, the more antioxidants. Look for one with red radicchio, pale green endive, and dark green spinach.

BROCCOLI

Best buy: Tight buds mean fresh broccoli.

NUTS

Best buy: Look for unroasted and unsalted loose nuts, to cut sodium.

Meat

Your muscle maker: The Abs Diet is partial to turkey, but that doesn't mean other meats are off-limits. The key is getting the most lean protein for the least amount of saturated fat. Turkey does the job exceptionally well—but only if you buy breast meat. Mixed ground turkey can contain as much saturated fat as beef.

FRESH TURKEY OR CHICKEN CUTLETS

Best buy: Check the label for sodium; some raw meats are plumped with a salt solution you don't need.

FRESH SALMON

Best buy: Fillet cuts (the oblong strips) cook quicker and more evenly than steaks (the U-shaped cuts).

LEAN GROUND BEEF

Best buy: Pick the 95 percent lean to dodge saturated fat. Mix in vegetables like chopped onions or spinach to add moisture and flavor.

Dairy products

The great white help: Think of the dairy section as fat-loss central—if you play the percentages.

1 PERCENT MILK AND REDUCED-FAT YOGURT

Best buy: Horizon and Stonyfield Farm organic varieties. Cow antibiotics are for sick cows, not healthy guys.

EGGS

Best buy: Eggland's Best. They're fortified with an extra shot of heart-healthy omega-3 fatty acids.

SHREDDED CHEESES

Best buy: Sargento Reduced Fat Shredded Cheese. Why grate your own? These melt evenly, unlike most other low-fat cheeses.

And when you're in the health food store or GNC, pick up this great muscle-boosting, fat-cutting by-product of the dairy industry . . .

WHEY PROTEIN

Best buy: Look for protein powder that also includes casein, another dairy-based muscle builder.

Canned Foods

What's in storage: Canned foods are guy foods—they last forever. Just watch out for sodium, the hypertensive preservative.

CANNED TOMATOES

Best buy: Del Monte Diced Tomatoes, No Salt Added—low sodium and no high-fructose corn syrup.

TUNA

Best buy: StarKist Premium Chunk White Albacore Tuna in Water. Water cuts the fat, but the no-draining-needed bag seals the deal.

PEANUT BUTTER

Best buy: Crazy Richard's Natural. Peanuts—and just a touch of salt—are its only ingredients.

OLIVE OIL

Best buy: Extra virgin, which means the goods haven't been damaged by mixing with other lesser oils.

Grains and baked goods

The incredible bulk: Fiber is crucial to weight loss, and the best place to find it is in whole-grain baked goods. If the first ingredient listed isn't "whole grain" or "whole wheat," keep looking.

WHOLE-WHEAT BREAD

Best buy: Pepperidge Farm or Milton's. Both offer a variety of high-fiber whole-wheat breads.

PASTA

Best buy: De Cecco Whole Wheat. Although it's high in fiber, this brand isn't too tough or chewy.

OATS

Best buy: Arrowhead Mills Steel Cut Oats will take 7 to 9 minutes in the microwave, but they pack a potent 16 grams of fiber per $1/2$ cup.

Frozen foods

Cold comfort: Shop here last, and you'll likely make it home with your ice cream intact. "Ice cream?" you say. Right. This plan is designed for human beings rather than robots.

BERRIES AND FRUIT

Best buy: Cascadian Farm Organic. Go organic. Berries and fruit often top the lists of high-pesticide produce.

WAFFLES

Best buy: Van's Gourmet Flax. Slightly sweet whole-wheat flavor, with 1.6 grams of omega-3 fatty acids.

ICE CREAM

Best buy: Edy's Slow Churned Light Ice Cream is sweet and creamy, and it has half the fat and one-third the calories of regular.

AT HOME

The Abs Diet recommends eating six meals a days to keep your belly full and your energy levels up. So your jaws have a lot of work to do. Start with these 15 meal makers, which incorporate as many of the Abs Diet Powerfoods as possible. So sharpen your cutlery. It's time to eat.

Breakfasts

The Super Bowl of Breakfast

1 egg; $3/4$ c oatmeal; 1 c 1 percent milk; 1 tsp vanilla whey-protein powder; 1 tsp ground flaxseed; 1 Tbsp chopped pecans or sliced almonds; $1/2$ c mixed berries; $1/2$ banana, sliced; 1 Tbsp plain yogurt

Makes 1 serving.

Powerfood count: 8

How to make it: Stir up the egg, then add the oatmeal, milk, whey-protein powder, flaxseed, nuts, and berries in a microwavable bowl and nuke

FOOD THE AVERAGE GUY IS MOST LIKELY TO BINGE ON IN THE MIDDLE OF THE NIGHT: Ice Cream

for 2 minutes. Remove and let cool for a minute or two. Top with the banana and yogurt.

> Per serving: 587 calories, 30 g protein, 76 g carbohydrates, 17 g fat (5 g saturated), 13 g fiber, 254 mg sodium

Jam Session

1 whole-wheat toaster waffle; 2 Tbsp peanut butter; $1/4$ c slightly crushed blueberries, blackberries, or raspberries

Makes 1 serving.

Powerfood count: 3

How to make it: Prepare the waffle according to the package directions. Spread the peanut butter on the waffle, cup the waffle in your hand, add the berries, then squeeze lightly. Think of it as a blueberry breakfast taco.

> Per serving: 308 calories, 12 g protein, 24 g carbohydrates, 21 g fat (3.5 g saturated), 5 g fiber, 212 mg sodium

Foxy Lox

1 toasted whole-wheat English muffin, 2 Tbsp part-skim ricotta, 1 slice tomato, 1 oz smoked salmon

Makes 1 serving.

Powerfood count: 3

How to make it: Spread each muffin half with the cheese and top with the tomato and salmon.

> Per serving: 214 calories, 15 g protein, 29 g carbohydrates, 5 g fat (2 g saturated), 5 g fiber, 1,027 mg sodium

Smoothies

Punk'd Pie

$1/2$ c canned pumpkin, $3/4$ c instant oatmeal nuked in water, $1/4$ c unsalted pecans, 2 Tbsp low-fat vanilla yogurt, 2 tsp vanilla whey-protein powder, 1 tsp ground flaxseed, 3 ice cubes

Makes 2 servings.

Powerfood count: 5

How to make it: Blend all of the ingredients together.

> Per serving: 270 calories, 9 g protein, 29 g carbohydrates, 12 g fat (1 g saturated), 6 g fiber, 19 mg sodium

Honey-Nut Cheery Oats

$3/4$ c instant oatmeal nuked in water, $1/4$ c 1 percent milk, 1 Tbsp peanut butter, 2 tsp whey-protein powder, 1 tsp ground flaxseed, 1 tsp honey, 6 ice cubes

Makes 2 servings.

Powerfood count: 5

How to make it: Blend all of the ingredients together.

> Per serving: 206 calories, 11 g protein, 26 g carbohydrates, 6 g fat (1 g saturated), 4 g fiber, 51 mg sodium

The Neapolitan
$^3/_4$ c 1 percent chocolate milk, $^1/_2$ c vanilla yogurt, $^3/_4$ c sliced strawberries, 1 tsp ground flaxseed, 2 tsp vanilla whey-protein powder, 3 ice cubes
Makes 2 servings.
Powerfood count: 5
How to make it: Blend all of the ingredients together.

Per serving: 154 calories, 9 g protein, 25 g carbohydrates, 2 g fat (1 g saturated), 2 g fiber, 114 mg sodium

Lunches

You're Fired! Wrap
1 Tbsp Dijon mustard, 1 whole-wheat tortilla, $^2/_3$ c chopped cooked chicken, desired amount of hot sauce, $^1/_4$ c diced tomato, $^3/_4$ c mixed greens, 2 Tbsp shredded reduced-fat Mexican-blend cheese
Makes 1 serving.
Powerfood count: 4
How to make it: Spread the mustard down the center of the tortilla. Add the remaining ingredients. Fold the outside edges in, then roll.

Per serving: 244 calories, 30 g protein, 28 g carbohydrates, 6 g fat (2 g saturated), 3 g fiber, 1,089 mg sodium

El Tequila Ensalada
$2^1/_2$ c mixed greens, $^1/_4$ c drained black beans, 1 chopped Roma tomato, 1 sliced green onion, 1 tsp diced cilantro, $^1/_2$ sliced avocado, 1 tsp olive oil, 1 Tbsp tequila or, for the less stout of heart, lime juice
Makes 1 serving.
Powerfood count: 5

Per serving: 325 calories, 8 g protein, 23 g carbohydrates, 21 g fat (3 g saturated), 13 g fiber, 250 mg sodium

Day-after-Thanksgiving Wrap
2 Tbsp cranberry relish, 1 whole-wheat tortilla, 3 slices turkey, 1 slice Muenster cheese, $^3/_4$ c mixed greens
Makes 1 serving.
Powerfood count: 4
How to make it: Spread the cranberry relish down the center of the tortilla. Add the remaining ingredients. Fold the outside edges in, then roll.

Per serving: 311 calories, 24 g protein, 40 g carbohydrates, 11 g fat (6 g saturated), 3 g fiber, 1,063 mg sodium

Snacks

Berry Easy Parfait
1 c plain yogurt, $^1/_2$ c mixed berries, 1 tsp ground flaxseed
Makes 1 serving.

GIVE ME ABS OR GIVE ME DEATH
How belly fat kills

Step 1: The Breakdown

After you eat a calorie- and fat-laden meal, your small intestine breaks fat molecules down into glycerol and fatty acids, which end up in your bloodstream.

Step 2: The Breakout

Fatty acids circulate through your entire body and are absorbed into fat cells, where they're reassembled into fat molecules and stored for the next famine. Excess glucose and amino acids are also absorbed by fat cells and converted to fat molecules. If the famine doesn't come, you grow.

Step 3: The Love-Handle Connection

Men are most likely to accumulate fat under the skin in the abdominal area, giving them a beer belly or love handles. Some unlucky guys store it as visceral fat, the kind that globs around your internal organs. If your gut is round and firm, your waist is bigger than your hips, or you wear a size 40 or larger, you're one of the latter. The theory: Your body is looking for someplace else to store excess fat—namely, your organs, or worse, within your muscles, heart, liver, or pancreas.

Step 4: Moving In for the Kill

There's a correlation between a guy's visceral fat and a host of ill-health markers, such as insulin resistance, high LDL cholesterol, low HDL cholesterol, elevated triglyceride levels, and even high blood pressure. The reason: Your liver taps into the pool of fat surrounding it for energy. Using it produces cholesterol, which in turn gunks up your arteries, leaving you at risk of strokes, heart disease, and diabetes. Back slowly away from the doughnut and nobody gets hurt.

Powerfood count: 3

Per serving: 204 calories, 14 g protein, 27 g carbohydrates, 5 g fat (2.5 g saturated), 4 g fiber, 173 mg sodium

94 Percent Fat-Free Microwave Popcorn (Pop Secret, 3 c)

120 calories, 4 g protein, 26 g carbohydrates, 2 g fat (0 g saturated), 4 g fiber, 380 mg sodium

Roasted Almond Granola Bar (Nature Valley)

190 calories, 4 g protein, 28 g carbohydrates, 7 g fat (1 g saturated), 2 g fiber, 170 mg sodium

Dinners

Sergeant Pepper Beef

6 oz flank steak (about half of one); $^1/_2$ green or red bell pepper, cut lengthwise into strips; 2 green onions, sliced; 3 Tbsp reduced-sodium soy sauce; desired amount of hot sauce; 1 tsp sugar; $^1/_3$ c cashew pieces

Makes 2 servings

Powerfood count: 4

How to make it: Cut the meat diagonally and across the grain into thin strips (freezing it for 20 minutes first helps). Place in a large ziplock bag with all the other ingredients except the cashews. Shake well to combine. Dump into a skillet that's preheated over medium-high. Cook, turning often, for 5 to 6 minutes or until the meat reaches desired doneness. Top with the nuts.

> Per serving: 363 calories, 29 g protein, 14 g carbohydrates, 22 g fat (7 g saturated), 2 g fiber, 870 mg sodium

The Aqua Man

$^1/_2$ c trimmed asparagus; $^1/_2$ c matchstick carrots; 1 clove garlic, crushed; 1 tsp olive oil; juice of 1 lemon; $^1/_2$ tsp lemon rind; salt and pepper to taste; 2 tilapia fillets

Makes 2 servings

Powerfood count: 3

How to make it: In a small bowl, mix the vegetables with the oil, lemon juice and rind, and salt and pepper. Arrange the fish in a small, shallow, microwavable baking dish. Pour the vegetable mixture over each fillet. Wrap tightly in plastic wrap, pricking a couple of times with a fork or toothpick. Microwave for 3 to 4 minutes, or until the fish flakes with a fork.

> Per serving: 137 calories, 29 g protein, 14 g carbohydrates, 3 g fat (1 g saturated), 2 g fiber, 215 mg sodium

Mighty Meat Muffins

1 egg, 1 lb lean ground beef, $1^1/_2$ Tbsp balsamic vinegar, $^1/_2$ c oats, $^1/_4$ c minced onion, salt and pepper to taste.

Makes 3 servings

Powerfood count: 3

How to make it: In a large bowl, whisk the egg. Add everything else and mix it with your hands until well blended. Divide the mixture evenly into a 6 c, nonstick muffin pan. Bake for 25 minutes in an oven that's preheated to 375°F. Serve with mustard.

> Per serving: 349 calories, 35 g protein, 13 g carbohydrates, 16 g fat (6 g saturated), 1.5 g fiber, 329 mg sodium

Contributors: Phillip Rhodes, Ted Spiker. Researcher: Erin Hobday

Excerpted from *The Abs Diet Eat Right Every Time Guide,* copyright 2005 by Rodale Inc.

Global Thinning

Boost your health and drop pounds with these powerful eating strategies from around the world

By Phillip Rhodes

Every nation has its weapons in the nutrition wars. For the Chinese, it's anti-oxidant-rich green tea. The French have their red wine. In Italy, it's olive oil—bottles and bottles of the stuff.

Americans? We tend toward fad diets and expensive shortcuts like gastric-bypass surgery. But we're also big on openness and acceptance. So, in the best melting-pot tradition, we asked international nutrition experts, cooks, and the editors of our overseas editions of *Men's Health* for healthy-eating tips from their homelands. It was like having a dozen ethnic-restaurant menus slipped under our door, but with the healthiest items circled.

Then we culled out our favorites, compiling the best and most useful information from around the globe for fighting disease and battling the bulge. Like that exchange student who broke your heart back in 11th grade, it could change your life.

ARGENTINA

Secret weapon: Great beef. An Argentine is likely to eat 30 pounds more beef each year than you do—without raising his risk of heart disease. How's that? "The beef in America is grain-fed, but in Argentina the cattle eat only grass, which is natural for a cow," says Alicia Rodriguez, chef and co-owner of Chimichurri, an Argentine steakhouse in New York City. "The beef has about half the calories and a lot less fat and cholesterol." In fact, one independent test found that a 4-ounce cut of American beef contained 10.8 grams of saturated fat and 328 calories, while the same cut of Argentine beef had 2.5 grams saturated fat and 140 calories.

American translation: Sizzle lean. As you peer through the shrink-wrap, look closely at the marbling—the fat inside the muscle, not the easy-to-remove rind on the outside. You want less. Better yet, go grass-fed. It's leaner, like the Argentine steaks. Buy it at www.grasslandbeef.com.

AUSTRALIA

Secret weapon: Smart fast food. "Most of our fast-food outlets offer healthier choices that aren't available in the United States," says Sharon Natoli, director of Food & Nutrition Australia. A typical Aussie breakfast: "a low-fat fruit smoothie along with raisin toast or a fruit salad, which are much healthier options than coffee and a doughnut." Their hamburgers "come covered with salad. It could be plain lettuce, tomato, and onion, with or without the addition of beetroot, pineapple, or cucumber," she says.

American translation: Toss the bun, low-carb style, and "ask for more salad on your burgers," says Natoli. Skip the cheese and mayo and pile on leafy greens, tomato, onion, and pickles. It could start a healthy habit: Did you know you can eat leafy greens without ground beef?

GERMANY

Secret weapon: Some kind of healthy wheat beer, right? Actually, no. "In 2003, for the first time, Germans drank more water than beer," says Kirsten Segler, nutrition editor of *Men's Health* Germany. "Germans on average drank 129 liters of water but only 117.5 liters of beer." The quality of tap water equals and sometimes exceeds that of bottled water, she says. Just like here!

American translation: If the Germans can cut back, so can you. And get creative with water. "A lot of German people prefer a mixture of apple juice and water if they want some flavor," says Segler. "We call it *Apfelschorle.*" We call it a smart idea.

GREECE

Secret weapons: Lemon and oregano. Lemon was originally used in Greece to kill bacteria, says Elena Paravantes, RD, a member of the Hellenic Dietetic Association. "Today, Greeks add it to anything. Not only is lemon an excellent source of vitamin C [a potent antioxidant], but it has fewer calories than other citrus fruit," she says.

American translation: Paravantes recommends whipping up a batch of the ultimate free-radical-fighting salad dressing or meat marinade. "Just mix lemon juice with olive oil, oregano, and garlic," says Paravantes. There's your dressing. You can toss that bottle of goopy ranch now.

INDIA

Secret weapon: The original smoothie, the lassi. "Smoothies in America have fruit syrups and unnecessary sugar," says Suvir Saran, author of *Indian Home Cooking.* "Our smoothies are made with yogurt and fresh fruit or spices." That's it. The wholesome combination delivers calcium, vitamin C, and protein, which helps keep you feeling satisfied so you'll eat less during the meal. The dairy also neutralizes chili peppers' burn—which will come in handy if your Indian-restaurant order includes the word "vindaloo."

American translation: "Put yogurt in a blender with a few slices of mango or orange," Saran says. It's that easy.

LATIN AMERICA

Secret weapon: Shopping socially. "In Central and South America, you do your shopping on a daily basis, and it becomes a social thing. You find friends; you talk to people. It's like going to happy hour," says Claudia Gonzalez, MS, RD, a spokeswoman for the American Dietetic Association. It's also an active pursuit that could prompt you to eat more fresh fruit and vegetables.

American translation: Instead of the monthly run to Sam's Club or Costco for frozen dinners in bulk, stop at the market—or better yet, a farm stand—once or twice a week for your meats, fruits, and vegetables. Get to know the farmer. Maybe he has a daughter.

OKINAWA

Secret weapons: Shiitake mushrooms and other low-calorie, nutrient-dense foods like soy, seafood, and sweet potatoes. Bradley Willcox, MD, who coauthored *The Okinawa Diet Plan* with his brother, Craig Willcox, PhD, says shiitakes are among the most nutritious of mushrooms. They're a good source of protein, their calorie content is negligible, and "compounds found in shiitake mushrooms have been shown to lower blood-cholesterol levels and high blood pressure," he says. Which helps explain why these islands off Japan are home to more centenarians per capita than anywhere else on Earth.

American translation: Buy shiitakes fresh or dried (rehydrate them with hot water for 15 minutes). Chop them into soups, salads, and pasta dishes, or just brush them with oil and slap them on the grill. "With its meatlike quality, this mushroom acts as a meat replacement," Craig Willcox promises. Beats raw fish, right?

NEED TO KNOW

Sleep It Off

Snooze and you'll lose—literally. A recent Columbia University study shows that people who sleep less weigh more. Men and women who grabbed only 6 hours of shut-eye each night were 23 percent more likely to be overweight than those who slept for 7 to 9 hours. Study author James Gangwisch, PhD, points to a growing body of research suggesting that a sleep deficit upsets the body's hormonal balance. "Ghrelin levels increase in sleep-deprived people, leading to increased appetite and food consumption," he says. If you have trouble falling asleep, another hormone may help. A recent study review, which was sponsored by the National Institutes of Health, showed that melatonin supplements can effectively decrease the time it takes to fall asleep after hitting the hay.

B Lighter on Your Feet

Vitamin B_{12} has gone A-list. In a decade-long study of nearly 15,000 people, scientists at Seattle's Fred Hutchinson Cancer Research Center discovered that vitamin B_{12} may help eliminate extra pounds. Test participants who consumed at least 35 micrograms (mcg) of B_{12} daily gained 5 fewer pounds than those who took in less B_{12}. "Vitamin B_{12} is involved in metabolism, and it may help dieters utilize energy rather than store it," says *Men's Health* nutrition advisor Mary Ellen Camire, PhD. Since most men's multivitamins contain only about 18 mcg, up your B_{12} intake; six oysters provides 16 mcg, while a trout fillet or salmon steak will net you about 5 mcg.

Dying to Be Thin

Losing weight shouldn't mean losing your life. But Georgetown University scientists have found that a popular weight-loss supplement may mimic ephedra's killer instinct. In a review of the efficacy of bitter-orange extract (aka *Citrus aurantium*), researchers discovered that not only does bitter orange fail to melt fat away, but it could also cause a heart attack. It contains synephrine, which is chemically similar to epinephrine, the stuff that redlines your heart's rpm and causes blood pressure to spike. In tests with intravenous doses of bitter orange, systolic blood pressure rose from 123 millimeters of mercury (mm Hg) to 150 mm Hg. A heart attack that may have been caused by Citrus aurantium has been reported in the *Annals of Pharmacotherapy*. Lead researcher Adriane Fugh-Berman, MD, recommends that you run, not walk, away from any supplement containing it.

Size Matters

Boston University researchers recently found that having a waist size of 40 inches or more can double your risk of colon cancer. Too much saturated fat and not nearly enough fiber are possible culprits, as is the insulin resistance that often develops with big weight gains. "Central obesity is associated with increased insulin problems that are thought to promote tumor growth," says study author Lynn Moore, DSc. Her prescription: exercise. It will reduce your waist size, trim fat stored around your middle, and improve your body's ability to use insulin, she says. And when you're not lifting weights, lift more calcium-rich food to your mouth. Previous research shows that consuming 700 milligrams of calcium per day (about two glasses of milk) may reduce the risk of colon cancer.

Appetite for Destruction

Turns out cutting calories is like icing down your arteries. That's because losing weight may reduce chronic inflammation, a possible risk factor for heart disease, according to a study from the Wake Forest University School of Medicine. Researchers divided 316 people into two groups: one that followed a workout routine and another that lowered their calorie intake. While the exercise group experienced some beneficial effects, the diet group had the most dramatic results, with their blood levels of C-reactive protein (CRP)—a key inflammation marker—decreasing by nearly 6 percent. Why did diet work better than exercise? "Nobody knows the real answer," says Barbara Nicklas, PhD, lead author of the study. "The diet group lost more fat tissue, and we speculate that losing fat, which produces the stimulus for CRP, reduces CRP itself. But more studies are needed."

PERCENTAGE OF MEN WHO EAT MORE THAN USUAL ON DAYS WHEN THEY DON'T GET ENOUGH SLEEP: 20

The Skinny on Liposuction

People who lost 28 to 44 percent of their belly fat through liposuction showed no change in risk factors for diabetes or heart disease, say Washington University researchers. Lipo only removes fat under the skin; exercise and a healthy diet help shed the dangerous fat around internal organs.

Diet and Exercise: The Perfect Pair

The calorie-burning benefits of exercise are well known. But now a study published in *Diabetes, Obesity, and Metabolism* reveals that a regimen combining aerobic and resistance exercise lowers levels of leptin, a hormone that programs the body to hang on to blubber in the event of a famine. The researchers suggest that exercise helps "reset" the body's leptin concentrations, so you produce less of it to begin with.

In related news, Japanese researchers found that cardiovascular exercise can curb your desire for calorie-laden junk foods. According to a preliminary study from Osaka University, exercise raises sensation-regulating endorphins, one of which, beta-endorphin, can cause sweet flavors to taste sickeningly strong.

Travel Lighter

With room-service temptations and expense-account justifications, it's easy to pack on pounds when you're on the road. That's what makes *The Athletic-Minded Traveler* (SoCal Publishing, $18.95, www.socalpress.com) so valuable. Frustrated business travelers Jim Kaese and Paul Huddle created this directory of 500 of the best hotels and fitness venues in 50 cities. Before you hit the road, get this book, then check with www.healthclubs.com to see whether your gym belongs to the International Health, Racquet and Sportsclub Association—you might get discounts at other member clubs.

You've Been Served

The more food on your plate, the more you'll eat, regardless of hunger. Penn State University researchers recently carried out a sneaky study, replacing a restaurant's standard serving of baked pasta with one nearly 50 percent larger. When customers were surveyed about both serving sizes, they rated each "appropriate." They also polished off the plus-size portion, netting an extra 172 calories. Short of pulling out a scale and weighing every entrée, your best defense is the salad bar, says lead researcher Barbara Rolls, PhD: "Water and fiber-rich foods fill people up without adding so many calories."

GALLONS OF FAT, ON AVERAGE, SUCKED OUT
OF PEOPLE BY PLASTIC SURGEONS EACH YEAR:

150,000

Have a Few Cold Ones

The bachelor diet is back: Eating frozen dinners can help you lose weight and burn fat, according to research from the University of Illinois. In the 8-week study, men who followed a diet of frozen dinners lost 31 percent more weight and 30 percent more fat than their free-eating counterparts. All the credit goes to the packaging. "Accurate portion control is an important factor in weight-loss success, and that control is easier to achieve with packaged entrées," says study author Sandra Hannum, MS, RD. Try Ethnic Gourmet's Pad Thai with Shrimp or the Lemongrass and Basil Chicken.

Combo Meal

Research in the *Journal of Nutrition* says a diet that combines low-carb and low-fat approaches may be better for your health than either diet alone. Reason number one: It works. In a study of 20 adults, those on a low-carb/low-fat diet and those on a traditional low-fat diet each lost 6 percent of their body weight in 6 weeks. Reason two: Several of the traditional low-fat dieters dropped out due to "unendurable hunger," while the low-carb/low-fat dieters were able to stick with their protein-heavy plan. "Protein is considered the most satiating nutrient," says lead researcher Carol Johnston, PhD. Reason three: Neither group saw a spike in cholesterol levels, a common side effect of many popular low-carb diets (which often come with a high price tag for saturated fat and cholesterol).

Fill Up on Fiber

In a Tufts University study of 459 people, those who reported eating the most fruit, reduced-fat dairy products, and high-fiber grains were found to have waists 2 inches smaller than those of people who said their diets were more meat- or sweets-based. Study author P.K. Newby, PhD, attributes the slimming effect (in part) to fiber's filling powers; the thin crowd ate 10 grams more fiber per day than the others. You can easily obtain a healthy dose of fiber from a cup of kidney beans (16 grams). Add them to soups, stews, or salads.

WHAT'S NEW

A Band-Aid for Obesity

In a University of Illinois at Chicago study, 925 obese adults shed 42 percent of their excess weight a year after their stomachs were fitted with a gastric band. The clamplike band reduces stomach size and limits food intake. The best part? Since your stomach isn't sliced in half, you don't have to live with a golf-ball-size gut forever. Some hospitals now offer banding as outpatient surgery.

Take an Extra-Long Lunch Break

Dental researchers have developed a new device that helps people painlessly shed pounds. Called the "DDS system," the plastic appliance fits flush against the roof of the mouth, forcing the wearer to take smaller bites and chew more slowly. (No, it isn't visible to others.) When Louisiana State University researchers tested the system on 16 overweight people, they found that the subjects immediately began consuming an average of 659 fewer calories a day. "Eating slower allows time for the satiety response in the brain to kick in," says D. Walter Cohen, DDS, of the University of Pennsylvania School of Dental Medicine. Find a dentist that sells the system ($500) at www.ddssystem.com.

Penalty Box

The University of Virginia Health System has installed specially modified vending machines that penalize unhealthy choices. Pick a snack in the "red" category—such as candy bars or chips that derive 10 percent or more of their calories from saturated fat—and you pay a 5-cent surcharge. "We're seeing an increased interest in the healthy items," says a hospital spokesman.

PERCENTAGE BY WHICH RISK OF OBESITY INCREASES FOR EACH HOUR SPENT IN THE CAR: 6

Batter Up

There may yet be hope for healthy fried chicken, now that USDA scientists have developed a better batter for fried foods. Made from long-grain-rice flour, the new batter absorbs 55 percent less oil than conventional flour batter, resulting in substantially fewer calories. The trick: Rice retains more water during deep-frying than does wheat flour, leaving less room for oil, says researcher Fred Shih, PhD. Look for commercial applications soon.

Don't Break a Sweat

Scientists around the world are approaching the Holy Grail of weight-loss research: exercise in pill form. A gene called IDPc has been found to control the metabolism of dietary fat. It's the first genetic discovery of its kind. (Most other gene research has focused on the mechanics of appetite and fullness.) Next up for the Korean research team: learning how to manipulate IDPc to produce a slimming effect.

Meanwhile, Australian researchers recently mapped the structure of an enzyme (called AMP-activated protein kinase) that regulates metabolism and controls how the body burns fat, bringing them one step closer to developing a drug that simulates exercise without the sweat. And scientists at the University of Pennsylvania found that mice injected with high levels of adiponectin, a hormone that is produced in small amounts by fat tissue, saw their body weight shrink by about 25 percent, apparently as a result of a dramatic boost in metabolism. Next, researchers plan to study the effects of the hormone in humans.

Toxic Waist

Scientists at Laval University in Quebec may have discovered why losing weight often seems to get harder as you go. In a small study, researchers found that when people lost weight, trace elements of toxins (such as pesticides and PCBs) that their bodies had absorbed from food or the environment were released from shrinking fat cells into the bloodstream. It's theorized that this influx of contaminants may interfere with calorie burning or throw off the balance of crucial hormones such as leptin, slowing weight loss. More research is needed to determine the prevalence of these toxins, as well as just how much impact their release may have on leptin levels.

FAST FIXES

There's a war on. No, not that one. This one hits even closer to home—in our kitchens, at our dining-room tables, down at the diner, in the drive-thru lanes—and it's a struggle for our very lives.

You've heard the statistics. Nearly two-thirds of adult Americans are overweight. A third of our children have followed that example. Complications from all this fat will soon overtake smoking as the leading cause of early death. "Most families live in a nutritional environment that can best be described as toxic," says David L. Katz, MD, a professor of medicine, epidemiology, and public health at the Yale University School of Medicine and the author of *The Way to Eat*. "It's not their fault; they're just following the path of least resistance."

And who can blame them? According to one survey, family leisure time has shrunk by 37 percent since the 1970s. Tired, stressed, and run ragged, families aren't ignoring the get-lean message; they just don't have the time and resources to figure out a way to make a healthy lifestyle work for them.

So that's exactly what we've set out to supply. Armed with the expertise of nutritionist Heidi Skolnik and strength coach Charles Staley, CSCS, we put together the following fast fixes to get you and your family off the fat track.

THE DIET FIXES

The problem: Hectic schedules undermine mealtimes. Without structured meals, you and your fellow family members are often left to your own dinnertime devices—or vices. You grab whatever's quickest and easiest in the fridge. Or worse, you hit a fast-food drive-thru and scarf down dinner in the car.

Fix #1: Take the coach approach. Devise a game plan—one that the entire family is invested in. "Spend half an hour together on Sunday putting together a food plan for the coming week," says Skolnik. Then develop a specific menu for each day. Shop accordingly so the food you need is always on

NUMBER OF DEATHS IN AMERICA EACH YEAR THAT ARE ATTRIBUTABLE SOLELY TO POOR DIET AND PHYSICAL INACTIVITY: 400,000

hand, and the junk you don't need is still taking up shelf space at the Piggly Wiggly. Having more meals at home will automatically improve kids' eating habits. A Harvard University study found that in families who eat meals together, children consume higher amounts of calcium, fiber, iron, and vitamins B_6, B_{12}, C, and E, as well as take in less overall fat, than children who frequently miss family mealtimes.

Fix #2: Be practical in your planning. Anticipate roadblocks that may cause plans to go astray. When circumstances zig, you can zag. "If you know Tuesdays are crazy, make it an order-in pizza night; that's okay," Skolnik says. "Go ahead and write that into your plan. Then, if you know that Thursday night is always a good night to cook, plan on making a meal that includes lots of healthier stuff and allow for that, too."

The problem: You skip breakfast. With a busy schedule, breakfast is often the first meal axed.

The fix: Wake up at 6:55, not 7:00. Five minutes is all you need to toast a waffle, heat instant oatmeal, microwave some sausage links, or fix any of the three complete breakfasts below. "Studies have shown that when you eat breakfast, you eat less later in the day," Skolnik says. "Taking your calories more evenly throughout the day helps you avoid big deficits and high peaks. It's the best way to control the body's fat distribution."

1. *The commuter breakfast:* Half an apple, cored, then spread with peanut butter and topped with raisins. *Drink:* Bottled yogurt smoothie. *Prep time:* 2 minutes.

2. *The energy-boosting breakfast:* Bowl of instant oatmeal, cup of berries topped with a big spoonful of yogurt. *Drink:* Orange juice. *Prep time:* 4 minutes.

3. *The muscle-building breakfast:* 2 scrambled eggs, 2 links of turkey sausage, $1/2$ bagel. *Drink:* 2 percent milk. *Prep time:* 5 minutes.

The problem: Restaurants are a meal ticket to overeating. When you're paying for food, you want your money's worth. Combine that with a pragmatic clean-your-plate mentality, and it adds up to a recipe for dietary disaster.

Fix #1: Skip the starters. A plate of those loaded cheese fries weighs in at nearly 3,000 calories. Avoiding this kind of appetizer will cut hundreds of calories out of the meal.

Fix #2: Always order a salad. "Front-load the meal with more nutritious stuff to take the edge off your appetite," Dr. Katz advises. You can still enjoy the entrée, just less of it. And when in doubt about dressing, always choose the vinaigrette. It's guaranteed to contain a balance of good fats and calorie-free vinegars.

Fix #3: Head off half of the dish. "Ask the server to split the portion before it arrives at the table, and then take half home," Dr. Katz says. "Congratulations—you just got two meals for the price of one."

Fix #4: Apply the brakes. As the stomach fills, it produces a hormone called ghrelin that tells your brain to make you stop eating when your stomach is full. Shovel the food in too fast, and the brain can't catch up. Here are six slow-down tactics.

1. *Cut food into smaller pieces.* Taking bites that are actually bite-size will help slow the rate at which your stomach fills.
2. *Set down the cutlery in between bites.* Picking it up and using it to cut the next bite adds time to the meal.
3. *Give your jaw a workout.* Completely chew and swallow each bite before taking the next one.
4. *Sip water frequently.* Liquid takes up stomach space, too.
5. *Chat more, chow less.* Use mealtime to exceed the national average of $14^1/_2$ minutes of daily family conversation.
6. *Check your hunger level.* As you eat, ask yourself if you're still hungry. When the answer is no, stop eating.

The problem: You're a binge snacker. *Animal Planet* is not the place to get your food cues. "When omnivorous animals have food available, they just keep eating until their bellies hit the ground," Dr. Katz says. "Binge eating is our normal behavior, but only if we have to fend off the threat of starvation." You're not starving, but your evolutionary impulses remain. It's up to you to fight them.

Fix #1: Go on a pantry raid. Trade the chips, cheese crackers, and cookies for filling foods—quality complex carbs such as whole-wheat crackers, oatmeal, fruit, and protein-packing string cheese, yogurt, and trail mixes. Because you digest fiber- and protein-filled foods at a slower rate, they stay in your stomach longer, leaving less room for junk. And because proteins and carbs have about half the calories of fats, they cause less caloric damage.

Fix #2: Develop a traveling snack strategy. All of the above smart snacks are portable. Bring them with you in the car, and keep some stashed at the office.

The problem: Sugar is like God; it's everywhere. Spend 10 minutes watching Saturday-morning television and you'll see why kids grow up craving sugary foods; advertisers know their demographic. According to a Food Institute estimate, food marketers spend $13 billion each year targeting children. They aren't hawking apples and bananas.

PERCENTAGE OF MEN WHO PLAN TO EAT LESS JUNK FOOD THIS YEAR: 39

Fix #1: Pass fizz ed. Measure out teaspoons of sugar equivalent to what a single 20-ounce bottle of soda contains (1 teaspoon holds 4 grams). You'll wind up with a 17-teaspoon mound. When we tried this trick with one family of four, they were stunned. "That's a lot of sugar," said their 11-year-old, as the pile grew. Try tea instead. Some bottled varieties, such as Tazo and Republic of Tea, contain less than half the sugar that colas do.

Fix #2: Foil a cereal killer. Some breakfast cereals start kids' days with half as much sugar as you'd find in a bottle of cola. "Mix in some Cheerios with the sweeter cereals to help cut down on sugar and provide fiber," Skolnik says. "The kids will still have the taste they love, but they'll get more long-lasting fuel and energy out of it.

THE EXERCISE FIXES

The problem: Workouts take up too much time. This is the single biggest obstacle busy families face. Between full-time work and hectic family schedules, parents often feel that they don't have time to exercise. After all, who wants to get up at 4:30 in the morning to exercise?

The fix: Learn one highly effective, time-saving exercise habit. Instead of exercising each body part with the traditional three-sets-of-10 approach, Staley advocates a condensed form of weight training he calls escalating-density training (EDT). Here's how it works.

Step 1: Make time seem more manageable by breaking each workout into 15-minute increments. "This way, when you start, you already know when you'll be finished," Staley says. If you have time, add another 15-minute session.

Step 2: Choose two opposing muscle groups to work during each 15 minutes. For example, work biceps and triceps or chest and back. This will improve recovery between sets and automatically help you avoid overtraining one area of the body.

Step 3: For each exercise, identify the maximum weight you can lift 10 times and begin with these amounts.

Step 4: Start the clock. Do 5 repetitions of the first exercise, followed immediately by 5 reps of the second exercise, resting for as long as you want in between and occasionally lowering the weight if needed. "Focus on the time and the reps—it takes your mind off the exercise," Staley says.

Step 5: At the end of the 15-minute session, add the total number of repetitions to establish a personal-record benchmark. "EDT automatically gives you a personal best—a measure of your progress and a goal to work toward," Staley says. When your personal record improves by 20 percent, increase the amount of weight you're lifting by 5 percent. (See www.edtsecrets.com for more information on this training method.)

The problem: The kids aren't all right with exercise. Many kids are held hostage by electronic media, substituting virtual activity for the movement of real activities. In fact, according to a study published in the journal *Applied Developmental Psychology*, the average American child spends more than 5 hours a day watching television, playing video games, or surfing the Internet.

Fix #1: Entice activity with creativity. "Younger kids respond really well to games," says Michael Mejia, CSCS, advisor to the Center for Sports Parenting. Try a 10-minute game of tag with the kids and see if you aren't panting a little bit, too. For teenagers, do the same thing your parents did: Harness the power of indentured servitude. "Chores can fall into the exercise category. Have your kids mow the lawn or shovel snow," he says. "Use enticements for a job well done—an extra dollar of allowance or 15 extra minutes before bedtime."

Fix #2: Find the right sport. Competitive sports may not appeal to children with weight problems. "They may not want to play because they're embarrassed," says Sylvia Rimm, PhD, a clinical professor of psychiatry and pediatrics at Case Western Reserve University and the author of *Rescuing the Emotional Lives of Overweight Children*. She advocates swimming. "Unlike with running, overweight kids aren't at a particular disadvantage in swimming," she says. And since swimming engages the entire body, it's an unbeatable weight-loss exercise. Other noncompetitive activities include biking, walking, and inline skating.

Fix #3: Kill your television. Every expert we spoke with agreed on this one. Dr. Rimm recommends limiting total screen time to 2 hours a day. Staley suggests moving TV sets out of rooms where everyone tends to gather. "Get the TV out of the living room," he says. If it's not there, the family won't be drawn to it.

OUR FINAL ANSWERS

Weighty Issue

How can I tell if I'm losing fat or muscle when I'm losing weight?

—T.B., Ithaca, New York

You're probably losing both, but strength training and weight lifting while you're cutting calories will help lessen muscle loss. To check your fat-to-muscle ratio, have your doctor or the trainer at your gym measure your body composition.

Don't Stuff Yourself

What if I'm not hungry enough to eat several small meals a day to keep my metabolism up?

—K.B., Nashville

Here are our rules of weight loss: Don't skip meals. Rely on healthy snacks to bridge the gaps between meals (which may mean eating five or six times a day). And—this is crucial—obey your body's signals of hunger and fullness. The key is to avoid overeating, not to log a certain number of meals.

No Need to Cut Caffeine

Caffeine is in diet supplements, so why do some diets forbid coffee?

—E.K., Raleigh, North Carolina

Caffeine stimulates the central nervous system, increasing your basal metabolic rate so you burn more calories. (Exercise is better at this, without the negative side effects of weight-loss supplements.) Some diet authors claim that excess caffeine can cause a drop in blood-sugar levels, leaving you craving sweets, but this has not been substantiated. If you're eating a well-balanced meal along with your caffeine, you shouldn't have a problem. Plus, chlorogenic acid, an antioxidant compound found in coffee, may improve glucose metabolism to further aid in keeping the pounds off.

Cutting Cheese

I hate cottage cheese. Is there anything else I can eat that offers the same weight-loss benefits?

—T.W., Woodsboro, Maryland

Sure. It's the calcium in dairy products that's been linked to weight loss, and you can pick that up from other dairy foods, like milk, yogurt, and cheese. Try string cheese—a single stick contains more calcium than $1/2$ cup of cottage cheese.

Go with the Grain

How can I eat enough fiber if I'm supposed to avoid carbohydrates?

—L.N., Vail, Colorado

Keep fruits, vegetables, and whole grains in your diet. When Harvard University researchers analyzed the diets of more than 27,000 men over 8 years, they discovered that the men who added one serving of whole-grain foods daily weighed 2.5 pounds less than the men who ate only refined-grain foods. Plus, men who eat at least one serving of whole-grain breakfast cereal per day have been found to have a 27 percent lower risk of death from heart disease, compared with those who rarely hit the bowl. Try oatmeal, brown rice, sweet potatoes, and whole-grain crackers—and limit processed starches.

Bowled Under

I feel like I never get full on one bowl of cereal. Why?

E.K., Huntsville, Alabama

One small bowl of cereal isn't enough to fill your stomach—or to satisfy your hunger. Use 1 percent or 2 percent milk instead of skim to fill up faster. Couple your cereal with a slice of whole-grain toast and peanut butter. Or toss some nuts in your cereal bowl—the protein and good fat will help top off the tank. Also, make sure your cereal is high in fiber and low in sugar, so you'll feel more satisfied.

Frozen, in Time

I don't have time to cook. Which frozen dinners are healthiest?

—R.G., Pueblo, Colorado

Many frozen meals are high in sodium and too low in calories for a full meal (250 to 350 calories is low for a guy). So you'll have to supplement your dinner with fruit, vegetables, salad, or yogurt to take in enough nutrients and calories. Or heat a sweet potato in the microwave, and you'll have a healthy meal. As for frozen-meal brands, try Amy's Organic, Healthy Choice, and Cedar Lanes.

Send Stress Packing

I've read so much about how cortisol makes my body store visceral fat. Should I take a cortisol blocker?

—D.N., Columbus, Ohio

Don't bother. While it's true that high levels of cortisol can make your body store visceral fat (the nasty kind that gathers around your waist), permanently lowering cortisol is a bigger health risk. Cortisol is essential for proper functioning of every organ in your body, even your brain. "If you have too little of it, you'll die," says Pamela Peeke, MD, a cortisol researcher and author of *Fight Fat After Forty*. "It's when cortisol goes up and stays up that it's a problem." The preferred remedy? Attack stress, not the stress hormone. Regular exercise, or relaxation techniques like yoga and massage, will keep cortisol naturally in check by releasing beta-endorphins. If you're still tempted, consider this: The main ingredient in many cortisol blockers is *Citrus aurantium*, or bitter-orange peel—another form of ephedra. (See "Dying to Be Thin" on page 33.) Other ingredients include magnolia bark and caffeine. "It's like speed," says Dr. Peeke. "You might experience some appetite suppression, but there's no evidence that any of this will reduce cortisol."

TWO

MUSCLE UP

READ UP ON IT

100 Ways to Build Big Muscles

Simple fitness and nutrition tricks to help accelerate your gains and elevate your goals

By Scott Quill

Watching those makeover shows on TV, you might think the only way to change your body is to recruit a pack of plastic surgeons and line up a camera crew to record it for prime time.

With all due respect to the geniuses who produce network TV, we heartily disagree. When it comes to building new muscle, a few tweaks to your diet and fitness routine may be all you need to unleash your potential. But, just to be safe, we'll spot you a hundred. Use them, and you may want to call that camera crew after all.

BIGGER ARMS

1. Pinch to grow an inch. To strengthen your grip, try this plate pinch from Strongman competitor C.J. Murphy, MFS, owner and head strength coach of Total Performance Sports in Everett, Massachusetts: Place a pair of 5- or 10-pound plates together, smooth sides out. Pinch the plates between your thumbs and forefingers. Try holding the weights for 30 seconds. Add plates as you gain strength. And watch your toes.

2. Change grips. It can help you do more reps. Try a set of barbell curls with a narrow grip. When you begin to fail, slide your hands out farther. "You'll get more out of your biceps," says celebrity trainer Gunnar Peterson, CSCS.

3. Do chinups at a dip station. Using the parallel bars of a dip station simulates a chinup without lifting all your body weight. Besides your back muscles, you also strengthen your forearms. Grab the bars from underneath and place your feet on the floor. Keeping your body straight, pull yourself up, pause, then lower yourself.

4. Use a mirror. "It promotes better technique and helps prevent injury," says Chris Jordan, CSCS, of LGE Performance Systems in Orlando.

5. Add extra tension to any move. At the end of your arm workout, wrap one end of a resistance band around the handle of a dumbbell and place the other end under your foot. Now do a set of biceps curls and overhead triceps extensions to fatigue your arms, says Tim Kuebler, CSCS.

6. Pick up drop sets. Doing 5 reps or fewer per set with a weight you can lift only five times trains your muscles to grow bigger and stronger, says Mark Peterson, an exercise and sport scientist at Arizona State University. Do three to five sets without rest, reducing the weight by 10 percent to 25 percent each set.

A HARDER CORE

7. Hit the upper abs first. By doing 20 to 30 crunches, you'll limit the upper abs' assistance when you move on to the lower portion, says Gunnar Peterson. This can help define the inguinal crease—the lines that run from hip to groin.

8. Tighten your belt. One-legged lifts contract your transverse abdominis—a belt of muscle surrounding your abdomen—says Jon Crosby, CSCS, of Velocity Sports Performance in Baltimore. Grab a pair of dumbbells and raise your left thigh until it's parallel to the floor and your left knee is bent at 90 degrees. Bend your right knee slightly and do a set of shoulder presses, biceps curls, or lateral raises.

9. Squeeze a tennis ball while you do crunches. "Squeezing your hands as hard as you can causes radiational tension, which allows you to contract other muscles harder," says Murphy.

10. After you bench-press, do 25 crunches on the bench. You'll be less likely to skip them than if you have to go find an exercise mat.

11. Make a bet. Pick a date 8 weeks away and set a goal: You and your buddies wager over squatting your body weight, for instance, or decreasing your body fat below 15 percent. Add a dollar to the pot whenever you work out. Winner takes all.

ATHLETIC SUPPORT

Seven tools to make training time improve game time

Tips 12 to 18

12. Problem: No hops when you play hoops
Solution: Weighted vest
NBA all-star center Dirk Nowitzki practices with one to add loft to his jumper.
13. Problem: Shin splints
Solution: Exercise band
Your pain may vanish if you work your glutes and hip flexors. Wrap a band around both ankles and take five to 12 steps to the left, then repeat to the right.
14. Problem: Sore joints
Solution: Indo board

It strengthens the smaller stabilizing muscles in your lower body, says John Davies, founder of Renegade Style Training. Try walking the board (www.indoboard.com) around by thrusting your hips and feet.

15. Problem: Weak grip
   Solution: Towels
   Place two towels over a pullup bar at shoulder width. Grab both halves of each hanging towel and pull yourself up.

16. Problem: Short breath
   Solution: A straw
   Build strong respiratory muscles by breathing through a straw for a few minutes, gradually building up to 30 minutes, says triathlete coach Matt Fitzgerald. Try this while watching TV or reading.

17. Problem: Sinking
   Solution: A mirror
   To swim like a fish, practice in front of a mirror. "Work on proper body roll," says Fitzgerald. As you extend one arm overhead, twist your body 60 degrees to the opposite side while keeping your head and neck neutral.

18. Problem: Sore shoulder
   Solution: Resistance tubing
   Try this move from Tyler Wallace, CPT, of the National Academy of Sports Medicine, to strengthen your rotator cuffs, a common site of shoulder pain: Attach a piece of tubing to a sturdy support at waist level. With your right hand, hold the tubing in front of your navel, with your elbow bent 90 degrees and your forearm parallel to the floor. Rotate your hand away from your body to a 2 o'clock position, then return to the starting position. Do two or three sets of 12 to 15 with each arm.

POWERFUL LEGS

19. Start with leg curls. Most guys' quads are overly dominant, says Dave DiFabio, CSCS. So practice the preexhaustion principle. Do a few sets of leg curls at the start of your leg workout to build your hamstrings before you squat. Then use the squats to push the hamstrings even further. This will help them keep up with your quads and also help prevent injury.

20. Move the weight to the front during squats. It's easier to keep your back upright—and avoid injury—if you hold the weight across your chest, not behind your neck. This position also generates more power.

21. Stagger your squat stance every third workout. "It will prevent your dominant leg from doing more than its share," says Gunnar Peterson. Simply move one foot a few inches ahead of the other.

22. Make like a one-legged Romanian. Single-leg Romanian deadlifts strengthen the hamstrings and create more flexibility, says Carter Hays,

CSCS. Stand holding a light dumbbell in your right hand. Lift your left leg off the floor and keep it close to your right leg. Bend forward at the hips to lower the weight to your right shin. Slowly stand up. Do two or three sets of 15 reps on each leg.

23. Squeeze your knees. This move works your hamstrings and glutes and will aid in preventing groin pulls, says Larry Brun, CSCS. Lie on your back with your knees bent 90 degrees and your feet flat on the floor. Place a squeeze ball between your knees. Lift your hips until only your heels, upper back, and head touch the floor. Pause, then lower your hips toward the floor without touching it, and repeat.

24. Finish with walking lunges. "They're a greater challenge at the end of your leg workouts," says Shawn Arent, PhD, CSCS, an exercise scientist at Rutgers University. Take large steps forward until the thigh of the front leg is parallel to the floor and the knee is over (not past) your toes.

25. Pedal your stationary bike with one leg. "This targets your hamstrings. You have to pull the pedal up to complete each rotation," says German mountain biker Lado Fumic. Pedal with one leg for 60 seconds, then

ADDITION BY SUBTRACTION
15 ways to replace the top overrated muscle-building strategies

Tips 29 to 43

29 to 30. Standard crunches. Abs are all about body fat. Once you get your percentage into single digits, try doing planks (work up to holding the position for 2 to 3 minutes) and Swiss-ball crunches (start with 10 reps and work up to 30 to 40). "Both are better than the standard crunch for bringing out your abs," says Tom Seabourne, PhD, CSCS, an exercise physiologist and sports psychologist at Northeast Texas Community College in Mount Pleasant.

31. Protein. Too much of a good thing can be, well, a bad thing. "Your body can use only so much protein, and then some of it is just converted into fat instead of going to your muscles," says Mike Bracko, PhD, CSCS, an exercise physiologist at the Institute of Hockey Research in Calgary, Alberta. He recommends consuming no more than 0.5 to 1 gram of protein per pound of your body weight each day.

32. Calf raises. "Squats work all those tiny muscles in and around the calves, so you don't need to use calf-raise machines," says Seabourne. He recommends doing three sets of 8 to 12 squats with heel raises. Lower your body into a squat. Pause, then stand back up and rise onto the balls of your feet.

33. Jogging. If you're devoting too much time to cardiovascular workouts, it could be compromising your muscle development. When you jog, you use mostly slow-twitch muscle fibers, and the constant pounding seems to have a shrinking effect on your upper-body muscles. It's best to do sprints for your cardio at a track or football field. On a treadmill, after a light 3-minute warmup jog, sprint for 30 seconds, then rest for a minute, and repeat this sequence for 10 minutes.

switch. Then spin easily using both legs for 30 seconds. Repeat this six to eight times.

26. Warm up actively. Take your joints through a full range of motion to prepare for challenging workouts, says Crosby. Place your right hand on a doorjamb, and swing your right leg forward (through the open door), then backward (bring your heel to your butt). This loosens your quads and hamstrings. Then swing your leg from side to side with your toes pointed down to stretch your thighs. Repeat with your left leg.

27. Change your center of gravity. Make balancing during a single-leg squat even harder by using your arms. Stand with your right foot slightly off the floor (don't move it behind you) and your right arm straight above you. Bend both knees to lower your body, then bend forward and reach for your left foot with your right hand. Return to the starting position, finish a set, and repeat on the other side.

28. Split your cardio in thirds. Do three 10-minute bouts on three different machines. "You'll work more muscle mass and burn more calories," says Jordan.

34. Curls. "Curls are a waste of time because they isolate a muscle group that's the size of an orange," says Juan Carlos Santana, MEd, CSCS, director of the Institute of Human Performance in Boca Raton, Florida. Instead, work larger muscle groups with pulling exercises such as lat pulldowns and rows. Then do two or three sets of 12 to 15 repetitions of either barbell curls or standing dumbbell curls.

35. Workout streaks. "I've observed that when people finally take a day off in their weekly strength programs, they start to get stronger and bigger," says Seabourne. That's because muscles grow during rest. Two days a week of strength training per muscle group is all you need.

36. Rest between sets. "Less rest time can sometimes increase the amount of testosterone your body is producing," says Dr. Bracko. Try supersets—performing two exercises back-to-back without rest. For instance, do a set of bench presses immediately followed by a set of seated cable rows. Then rest for 90 to 180 seconds.

37. Leg extensions. Switch to body-weight lunges instead. Leg extensions isolate only your quads, while lunges work your quadriceps and butt and force you to stabilize your abs, lower back, and hips.

38 to 42. Bench presses. Do more pushups, which build core musculature and upper-body strength. Santana recommends limiting your bench presses to three to five sets per week (38) and incorporating six to 12 sets of pushups, including three-point pushups (39) and those in which you wear a weighted body vest (40), elevate your feet (41), or hold a medicine ball between your hands (42).

43. Chest stretches between sets of bench presses. For up to 15 minutes following a static stretch, your muscles and tendons stay stretched and are temporarily weakened. "A doorway stretch done between sets of bench presses actually makes your muscles weaker, so you won't be able to lift as much," says Dr. Bracko. Save it for afterward, during your cooldown.

BUILD A BROADER BACK

44. Embrace depression. Before a set of lat pulldowns, grab the bar with an overhand grip and your hands slightly wider than shoulder width apart. Squeeze your lats to pull your shoulder blades down (it's called scapular depression), lowering the bar just a bit. Hold for a second, then let the bar rise back up. "This helps focus the move on your lats," says Murphy. Do 10 to 12 depressions, then begin your lat-pulldown routine using the same technique to begin each repetition.

45. Issue a retraction. After you depress your shoulder blades to begin a lat pulldown, focus on retracting, or pulling your shoulder blades together.

46. Stand at the seated row. This on-your-feet row will train your back muscles and rear deltoids in a more functional, athletic-stance position, says Brun. Attach a parallel-grip bar to the low pulley and pull it toward your midsection. (Keep your abs drawn in.) Pause, then slowly let your arms extend back out in front of you.

47. Row with one hand. Working your middle trapezius—a tough muscle to target—can add bulk to the region between your shoulder blades and improve your posture, says Brun. Attach a single handle to the low pulley on the seated row and grab it with your right hand, palm facing down. As you pull the handle, twist your upper body so the handle moves toward your right hip. When your elbow is behind you, squeeze your shoulder blade in toward the midline of your back. Pause when the handle reaches your hip, then return to the starting position. Repeat the move with your left arm.

48. Roll away back pain. Using a foam roll can help your core muscles recover faster and with less pain. Lie on the floor, place a roll under your lower back, and move back and forth over it. Buy two and use the second one for the next tip.

49. Roll in strength gains. Build your core and back stabilizers with this move from Scott Rankin, a strength coach in Toronto. Get down on all fours and place one foam roll under your left hand and one under your right knee. Lift your right arm and left leg at the same time (straighten your leg). Maintain a flat back and a tight core. Pause, then return to the starting position. Move the rolls under the opposite hand and knee, and repeat the movement.

BOLDER SHOULDERS

50. Change your front raises. Use a weight plate instead of dumbbells—it takes a great deal of stress off the rotator cuffs, says Murphy. Also, raise the plate to eye level, instead of stopping when your arms are parallel to the floor.

51. Add a shrug. Instead of lowering the weight at the top of a standing shoulder press, lock your elbows, pause, and shrug as if you were trying to touch your shoulders to your ears. Your trapezius and deltoids will benefit.

52. Switch gears. Varying the tempo of your lifts can jump-start muscle growth, says Jim Liston, CSCS. Use a tempo of 4 seconds up, 4 down for eight weight-lifting sessions, then adopt a 2-seconds-up, 2-seconds-down tempo for your next eight.

53. Shrug at the calf-raise machine. Doing a move for your lower body immediately followed by one for your upper body (or vice versa) forces your circulatory system to work harder. "You'll be more challenged and burn more calories," says Gunnar Peterson.

54. Work your weaknesses. "Strengthening what's already strong doesn't lead to tremendous gains," says DiFabio. "You can produce more results by working a weakness." Rear deltoids and hamstrings are often underdeveloped in comparison to biceps, pecs, and abs.

55. Use your legs for shoulder presses. Just a slight dip of the knees as you start each shoulder press will help you push more weight over your head, says Kuebler. Your legs won't help you lower the load, so your shoulders reap the rewards.

56. Swim out of water. Isolate your rear deltoids with this move from Kuebler. Lie chest down on a bench. Hold a 5-pound plate in each hand, arms straight in front of you. Keep one arm still and swing the other arm as if you were swimming freestyle. Alternate sets of 6 to 10 reps with each arm.

HAVE A BALL

Add a Swiss ball or medicine ball, and these 10 common exercises become uncommonly better

Tips 57 to 66

57. Bench press. Lie on a Swiss ball and have your workout partner hand you a barbell loaded with a 5-pound plate on one side and a 10-pound plate on the other. (You can use dumbbells if you train alone.) As you press the weight up and lower it, focus on keeping the bar from dipping to the heavier side, says *Men's Health* exercise advisor Mike Mejia, CSCS. This will work the small, stabilizing muscles in your shoulders. Do five or six slow, controlled repetitions.

58. V-up. Grab a medicine ball and lie faceup on the floor. Raise your legs and back until only your butt is touching the floor and your body forms a V. Holding the medicine ball in front of your chest, twist your torso to the left and touch the ball to the floor, then twist to the right and touch the ball to the floor. That's one rep. Do two sets of 15.

59. Hamstring curl. Improve your core stability with this move from Jon Crosby, CSCS, of Velocity Sports Performance in Baltimore. Lie on the floor with your calves on top of a Swiss ball, your back on the floor, and your arms out to the sides. Squeeze your glutes and raise your hips off the floor so your body forms a straight line.

Maintaining this bridge position, pull the ball toward your butt by digging your heels into the ball. Pause when your butt is high in the air, then push the ball away until your legs are straight.

60. Situp. Lie with your back on a Swiss ball and your feet flat on the floor, holding a medicine ball with your arms straight above your head. Have your workout partner sit on a Swiss ball about 10 feet in front of you. As you sit up, throw the ball to your partner—aim over his head—and remain in an upright position. He should catch the ball and immediately lower his upper body on his Swiss ball, then toss the medicine ball to you as he returns to an upright position. Do 12 repetitions. Jim Liston, CSCS, says this is better than any ab move you can do on the floor.

61. Incline chest press. Grab a pair of light dumbbells and lie on a Swiss ball, with your hips and thighs in a straight line and parallel to the floor. Holding the weights in front of your shoulders, crunch forward so that your upper body is in an inclined position. (Your hips and legs should stay still.) Now press the weights straight up from this crunch position, lower them to your shoulders, and repeat.

62. Decline chest press Position yourself so your shins are resting on a Swiss ball and your hands are on the floor directly under your shoulders. Keeping your abs tight, do a pushup. Then bring your knees to your chest to roll the ball forward. Pause, then straighten your legs to roll the ball back out. This really fatigues your shoulders and builds your hip flexors, says Crosby.

63. Leg raise. Start in the same position as for the decline chest press, above, but with your toes on the ball. After you do a pushup, roll the ball toward you by raising your hips, bending your knees, and pulling the ball with your feet. Pause, then lower your hips to roll the ball back to the starting position. You'll feel this in your abs, chest, and shoulders, says Scott Rankin.

64. Lateral lunge. Stand with your feet about 6 inches wider than hip width apart and hold a medicine ball in front of your belly. Lower your body by bending your right knee as you twist your torso and reach your arms to the left. Repeat on the other side. This works your obliques, quads, hamstrings, and glutes, says Liston.

65. Squat. After your squat routine, grab a medicine ball and hold it with arms straight so it's in front of your belly button. Lower your body until your thighs are parallel to the floor. Pause, then jump up as you toss the ball into the air. (Not in the basement, dude.) Move to catch the ball, then get back into position and repeat.

66. Chest pass. This medicine-ball drill can boost your power in sports that require a lot of stopping and starting, says Rankin. Place a medicine ball on the floor and crouch behind it with your hands on the ball. Now quickly explode up and forward, pass the ball to a training partner, and continue sprinting for 10 yards. Repeat this eight times, then recover while he tosses the ball to you. Do three sets.

A STRONGER CHEST

67. Pull the bar apart. When you lower the bar as you bench-press, imagine you're spreading your hands as if you were trying to pull the bar apart. As you push it overhead, imagine pushing the bar back together. "This helps stabilize your shoulders, which helps you lift more weight," says Hays.

68. Bench with your back. It's not just about heaving weight up into the heavens with your chest and arms. You'll find that you are able to lift more weight if you press your back and butt into the bench and drive your feet into the floor as you raise the bar, according to Hays.

69. Beat the clock. Perform as many reps as you can in a minute. "Your type 2 muscle fibers are required to move a heavy weight, but as they fatigue, your type 1 fibers will kick in to keep you going," says Murphy.

70. Never wait for a piece of exercise equipment. Your body is the best fitness tool you have, says Jordan. Next time a bench is bustling, add a set of pushups to your chest routine.

71. Stretch after your last set. "While your heart rate is up, blood is pumped through the working muscles," says Crosby. By stretching those areas at the end of a workout, you keep your muscles long and strong—instead of short and injury-prone.

72. Twist your torso for power. Rotational exercises can strengthen your core and help you build a powerful chest, says Tyler Wallace, a certified physical therapist, of the National Academy of Sports Medicine. Try this move: Hold a medicine ball in front of your chest. Rotate your upper body and right foot to the left as you toss the ball against a wall 10 feet from you at your right side. After a set, switch sides and repeat for a total of three to five sets of 8 to 10 reps.

MUSCLE MEALS

73. Shrimp. Three ounces—about 12 large shrimp—has almost 18 grams of protein.

74–76. Oysters, clams, mussels. Three ounces of oysters will net you 11 grams of protein, while the same amount of clams or mussels has nearly double that.

77. Quinoa. That's "keen-wah." Think of this South American grain as rice with a turbocharger. It has more protein than any other grain (22 grams per cup). You can find it at health food stores and many upscale grocery stores.

78. Couscous. Pasta is not the only energy food. Couscous is easy to cook. All you need is water, a microwave, and about 2 minutes.

79. Sloppy joes. Beef has a higher creatine content than any other food. Try making it with Manwich Original Sauce. Dodging fatty toppings will save you nearly 20 grams of fat, says Cynthia Sass, MPH, RD, a spokeswoman for the American Dietetic Association.

80. Baked beans. "A half cup serves up 6 grams each of protein and filling dietary fiber," says Sass. Avoid extra saturated fat by choosing vegetarian baked beans.

81. Portobello mushrooms. "They're a great way to serve stuff. Just fill the cap with some diced chicken, pour in tomato sauce, and bake it for 10 minutes," says Vinny Steinman, a chef in San Diego. "It's a plate you can eat." And one with 1.5 grams of fiber and 2 grams of protein.

82. Prunes. Okay. Laugh. But they have high levels of antioxidants, and damaging oxidative stress is often a result of heavy exercise, says Janet Walberg Rankin, PhD, a professor of human nutrition at Virginia Tech. So eat up and help your body recover faster.

83. "Fried" chicken. Chicken breasts are expert protein-delivery systems. You're also sick of them. So try this fake-out tactic. "Dip the breast in a beaten egg and roll it in a mixture of crushed cornflakes, salt, pepper, and poultry seasoning. Bake at 350°F for 20 minutes, or until golden brown," advises Katherine Tallmadge, RD, author of *Diet Simple*.

MUSCLE MIXOLOGY
Seven supplements to accelerate your growth
Tips 84 to 90

84. Multivitamins
Why: Antioxidants protect against muscle damage and help you recover faster from workouts.
How much: One pill a day
When: Mealtime

85. Creatine
Why: Creatine helps muscles grow up to twice as fast, according to a study from Pennsylvania State University.
How much: Take small, consistent doses. Shoot for 0.03 gram of powdered creatine monohydrate per pound of body weight.
When: After your workout, in a protein shake.

86. Caffeine
Why: Consuming it before exercise reduces the perception of pain. Less pain, more gain.
How much: Begin with a low-dose pill (50 to 100 milligrams) to assess your tolerance. Then increase the dose gradually until you reach 200 to 300 milligrams. And yes, the pill form is better than the varieties you drink.
When: About an hour before exercise. Skip it if you work out in the evening. You need sleep to grow muscle.

87. Whey protein
Why: Whey is rich in glutamine, which can help your muscles repair themselves, and in other amino acids that trigger growth.
How much: Mix 30 to 40 grams of whey with 17 ounces of water. Don't take more than 8 grams of powder for every 3.4 ounces of water.

When: 10 minutes before your workout. There's no need to guzzle it before you lift—just keep sipping until it's gone.

88. Fish oil
Why: Fish oil slows the loss of protein from muscle.
How much: About 1 to 2 grams per day
When: Anytime, with meals or in between

89. L-carnitine
Why: It can reduce muscle damage by up to 45 percent.
How much: 2 grams a day
When: 1 gram with breakfast and 1 gram with lunch. Your body absorbs L-carnitine better in smaller doses.

90. HMB
Why: Beta-hydroxy betamethylbutyrate is thought to prevent the breakdown of muscle tissue during exercise.
How much: 3 grams a day
When: If you eat six small meals a day, take two 250-milligram capsules with every meal. Like L-carnitine, HMB is better absorbed when you take it in small, frequent doses.

SMART SNACKS

91. Dried figs. They take top fiber honors for dehydrated fruit. "Figs will give you slow-burning energy to see you through a workout," says Sass. They're also loaded with potassium, the muscle-repair mineral.

92. Sunflower seeds. Buy them unhulled, and you'll get a mini tongue-and-lip workout trying to pop them open. The tiny seeds also flex some surprisingly large protein muscle—5 grams per half cup.

93. Soft-serve ice cream. "The chief ingredient in hard ice cream is saturated fat. In soft serve, it's milk, which has more whey protein and fewer fat solids," says Sass.

94. Frozen waffles. "Whole-grain toaster waffles have a near-perfect balance of complex carbohydrates, fiber, protein, and unsaturated fats," says Sass. The blend will boost your energy without causing crash-and-burn blips in your blood-sugar levels—a useful quality in any snack.

95. Chocolate milk. A University of Washington study found that drinks that blend carbohydrates and protein, such as chocolate milk, are nearly 40 percent more effective than protein alone at helping your muscles repair themselves and grow after a workout.

SMOOTHIE MOVES

Try these easy upgrades for your protein shakes.

96. Condensed milk. A half cup of condensed milk adds nearly 400 milligrams of calcium. Stronger bones mean a stronger frame to hang muscle tissue on.

97. Vanilla extract. It's the secret ingredient that made nearly everything your mom baked taste better. A couple of drops will do the same for your smoothie.

98. Pumpkin. Canned pumpkin is already cooked to a smooth consistency, so it slips easily into a protein shake. And a cup of it delivers 7 grams of fiber, the crucial nutrient that most muscle-building, high-protein diets lack.

99. Flaxseed. Dropping 1 tablespoon of flaxseed (available at any health-food store) into the blender adds nearly 1.5 grams of omega-3 fatty acids, which lock protein into your muscle fibers. The seeds' nutty flavor goes particularly well with chocolate and peanut-butter smoothies.

100. Peaches. A cup of frozen peaches ups your shake's vitamin C count by 235 milligrams. That'll boost blood levels of cytokines—compounds that keep colds and flu at bay. You can't work out when you're sick.

Seven Days to a Six-Pack

You give us a week of lunch hours, we'll make you strong
up the middle

By David Zinczenko

When I was in college, I had a friend who argued that he knew the key to a six-pack: "All you have to do is 1,000 crunches a day for a month." He was wrong. For one, crunching won't burn fat. And 1,000 repetitions? Come on. There's only one thing most of us would do 1,000 times a day if it were physically possible, and it wouldn't be a crunch. But if you want abs that will make you stronger, healthier, and better looking, you do have to work them. And that takes discipline—but not as much as you'd think. That's why I've devised the Abs Diet: a nutrition and exercise plan that can turn your belly bulge into speed bumps.

Here's what you need to know. Though your midsection works as a unit, it actually has five regions: the upper abs, the lower abs, the obliques, the transverse abdominis, and the lower back. (See "Reacquaint Yourself with Your Abs," on page 64.) The good news is that you already have all of these muscles; you just need to break them out so they can be seen. To help you manage that, we've put together a perfect program: our exclusive fat-burning, ab-building workout, paired with a nutrition and weight-loss program. It's a one-two combination, helping you reach the ultimate goal: the lean, hard stomach you want.

STEP 1: THE ABS DIET WORKOUT

Because you're a man of action, you probably want to start with the exercises first. My instincts exactly. Starting on page 63, you'll find a rock-solid weeklong workout plan that can get you up to speed fast. After that, you'll probably want something to eat. The Abs Diet delivers that, as well, but with an added bonus—the foods I prescribe will help you strip away the fat that's swaddling your midsection.

But first, the exercises. When you build your workout schedule, be sure to follow these principles.

- Leave at least 48 hours between weight workouts of the same body parts. Your muscles need time to repair themselves and grow.
- Take 1 day each week to rest, with no formal exercise.
- Warm up for 5 minutes before starting to exercise, by either doing a light jog, riding a stationary bike, jumping rope, or performing some slow jumping jacks.

HOW TO GET STARTED

You know this one already: Don't start any diet or exercise program without checking with your doctor. He doesn't want you keeling over from some undiagnosed condition, and neither do we.

If you don't already exercise: For 2 weeks, concentrate on settling into the Abs Diet nutrition plan that appears on page 4 (or go to www.menshealth.com/abs dietchallenge for more information). If you want to exercise during this time, try this light strength-training program three times a week: Alternate between three sets of eight to 10 pushups and three sets of 15 to 20 squats with no weight. Rest for a minute between sets. When that routine becomes too easy, increase the number of pushups and hold some kind of weight—dumbbells are best—while doing the squats. This light workout, combined with 30 minutes of brisk walking, will really fire up your fat burners.

If you're already in the exercise habit: Experts agree that mixing up your workouts every month or so is the best way to maximize your results. That's because your gains in strength and overall fitness come from challenging your body to perform in ways it's not used to. So consider switching from your current routine to the Abs Diet workout, at least for a few weeks. You're probably going to build more muscle and burn more fat if you throw your body a curve.

Here are the three components of your plan.

1. Strength training: Three times a week. These are total-body workouts, with one workout that puts extra emphasis on your legs.

2. Cardiovascular exercise: Optional, on non-strength-training days. Examples are cycling, running, swimming, walking, and stairclimbing. I recommend an interval workout (for suggestions, see "Abs Interval Workout," on page 69) 1 day a week, and light cardiovascular exercise like walking for 2 of your non-strength-training days.

3. Ab exercises: Two or three times a week. Do these before your strength-training or interval workouts. (There are 15 great exercises to work your abs on these pages. For even more ab trainers, plus home-gym exercises, go to www.menshealth.com/absdietchallenge.)

STEP 2: THE ABS DIET ABDOMINAL EXERCISES

Abs are like any other muscle in your body. They grow when they're at rest, not while you're working them. So working them every day—or 1,000 times a day, as my misguided buddy advised—doesn't give them a chance to get strong and grow. You will develop abs by working them two or three times a week, mixing and matching from the menu of moves that follows. Try adding the abs circuit to the beginning of your workout. Saving abs until the end of the workout means there's more possibility that you'll skimp and take shortcuts.

Hit the whole region. You have five regions of your abdominals to work.

For each workout, pick one exercise per region to ensure that you're hitting every area.

Change ab exercises every workout. Working your muscles in slightly different ways each time you work out is the best way to keep them stimulated and growing.

Do a circuit. In the first 2 weeks of workouts, do two sets of each of the core exercises (10 to 15 repetitions, depending on the exercise). In the third and fourth weeks, do three sets. Perform them in a circuit so that you've done every exercise once before repeating an exercise. Rest for up to 2 minutes between circuits.

Go slowly. Each repetition of an ab exercise should last slightly longer than you lasted on prom night—4 to 6 seconds. Any faster and you run the risk of letting momentum do the work. The slower you go, the higher the intensity. The higher the intensity, the stronger the abdomen.

Invite your wife or girlfriend to join in. Men have guts; women have tummies. Both can stand to shrink them—maybe even together. It's a front-porch renovation you finally can agree on. Show her the photos (note helpful inclusion of female model) and let her know your plans. She just might sign on.

THE BASIC WORKOUT

Monday, Wednesday

Total-body strength-training workout with emphasis on abs

Choose an ab exercise from each of the categories that follow and complete one set of each. Then run through the core exercises—in order—twice.

Ab Exercises	Repetitions	Sets
Upper-ab exercise (see page 65)	12–15	1
Lower-ab exercise (see page 65–66)	6–12	1
Transverse abdominis exercise (see page 66–67)	5–10	1
Oblique exercise (see page 67–68)	10 each side	1
Lower-back exercise (see page 68–69)	12–15	1
Core Exercises		
Squat	10–12	2
Bench press	10	2
Pulldown	10	2
Military press	10	2
Upright row	10	2
Triceps pushdown	10–12	2
Leg extension	10–12	2
Biceps curl	10	2
Leg curl	10–12	2

For videos of the exercises, go to www.menshealth.com/absdietchallenge.

REACQUAINT YOURSELF WITH YOUR ABS

You use your abs in virtually every movement that matters. Lifting. Running. Jumping. Reproducing. (It takes a lot of midsection stability to stand over that copy machine.) So the stronger they are, the harder and longer you'll be able to play. Here's a quick course in the anatomy of your abs.

Rectus abdominis: The six-pack muscle. Helps you maintain good posture.

External and internal obliques: Extend diagonally down the sides of your waist. They rotate the torso.

Transverse abdominis: Known as "the girdle." Compresses the abdomen.

Lower back: Anchors all of the above.

Tuesday, Thursday (optional)

Light cardiovascular exercise such as walking

Try to do 30 minutes at a brisk pace.

Friday

Total-body strength training, with emphasis on legs

Same workout as Monday and Wednesday, but replace the ab exercises with traveling lunges and stepups (10 to 12 with each leg). Complete two circuits.

Saturday (optional)

Ab workout plus interval workout

Complete one set of five ab exercises from the menu below, then do an interval workout (see "Abs Interval Workout" on page 69).

Ab Exercises	Repetitions	Sets
Upper-ab exercise (see page 65)	12–15	1
Lower-ab exercise (see page 65–66)	12–15	1
Transverse abdominis exercise (see page 66–67)	5–10	1
Oblique exercise (see page 67–68)	10 each side	1
Lower-back exercise (see page 68–69)	12–15	1

Sunday: Rest

THE EXERCISES
UPPER ABS

Traditional Crunch

Lie on your back with your knees bent and your hands lightly behind your ears. Slowly curl your upper body up, bringing your shoulder blades off the ground. Return to the starting position. 12 to 15 repetitions

Modified Raised-Feet Crunch

Same as traditional crunch, but raise your feet just a few inches off the floor and hold them there throughout the movement. 12 to 15 repetitions

LOWER ABS

Figure-8 Crunch

Lie on your back with your feet flat on the floor and your knees bent at a 90-degree angle, with a light medicine ball squeezed tightly between them. Place your hands behind your ears and slowly raise your head, shoulders, and feet off the floor. Now move your knees in a wide figure-8 motion. Do three repetitions in one direction, then reverse the motion for three repetitions. 6 repetitions

Bent-Leg Knee Raise

Lie on your back with your feet flat on the floor and your hands near your hips. Raise your knees up toward your rib cage, then slowly lower your legs back to the starting position. As soon as your feet lightly touch the floor, repeat. 12 repetitions

TRANSVERSE ABDOMINIS

Two-Point Bridge

Get into the standard pushup position. Lift your right arm and your left leg off the floor at the same time and hold for 3 to 5 seconds. That's one repetition. Return to the starting position, then repeat, lifting your left arm and right leg. 6 to 10 repetitions each side

Swiss-Ball Pull-In

Get into the pushup position, resting your shins on a Swiss ball. Your body should form a straight line from your shoulders to your ankles. Roll the Swiss ball toward you by pulling your knees toward your chest. Pause, then return your legs and the ball to the starting position. 5 to 10 repetitions

OBLIQUES

Medicine-Ball Torso Rotation

Sit with your knees bent and your feet on the floor, and hold a medicine ball in front of you. Twist to your left and set the ball behind your back, then twist to the right to pick it up again. Bring the ball to your left and set it down again. Repeat to finish the set, then do a set in the opposite direction. 10 repetitions each side

CITY WHERE THE MOST MEN LIFT WEIGHTS:

San Jose, California

Two-Handed Wood Chop

Hold a dumbbell with both hands next to your right ear. Flex your abs and rotate your torso to the left as you extend your arms and lower the dumbbell to the outside of your left knee. Return to the starting position, finish your set, and repeat, moving the weight from your left ear to your right knee. 10 repetitions each side

LOWER BACK

Twisting Back Extension

Position yourself in a back-extension station and hook your feet under the leg anchor. Place your fingers lightly behind your ears. Lower your upper body, allowing your lower back to round, until your torso is almost perpendicular to your legs. Now raise and twist your upper body until it forms a straight line with your legs and is facing left. Pause, then lower your torso and repeat, this time twisting to the right. 12 to 15 repetitions total

ABS INTERVAL WORKOUT

Slow and steady does win the race—if you're content to finish as a fat guy. But men who want to cut a dashing figure on the winner's stand do interval workouts, which alternate high-intensity levels with lower-intensity efforts. This formula keeps your body burning calories long after you've stopped working out. Interval workouts mimic sports—start-and-stop motions with periods of sprinting or close-to-sprinting speeds, followed by light jogging or rest. If you use exercise machines, don't choose the interval workout; choose the manual one and create your own intensities by adjusting them yourself. It'll give you greater control over the speeds and will help you burn fat faster. You'll derive benefits in as little as a 20-minute interval workout. As you build up endurance and strength, you can add time to your sessions.

Standard Interval Plan

The following is a typical interval workout. You alternate periods of low intensity with equal-length periods of higher intensity.

- 3- to 5-minute warmup (light jog at low intensity, gradually increasing effort by the end of the warmup period)
- 1 minute at moderate or high intensity, followed by 1 minute at low intensity (repeat six to eight times)
- 3- to 5-minute cooldown (light jog at low intensity, gradually decreasing effort by the end of the cooldown period)

Swiss-Ball Superman

Lie facedown on a Swiss ball so that your hips are pressed against the ball and your torso is rounded over it. Bend your elbows 90 degrees, so your hands are pointing forward and your elbows are pointing back. Slowly extend your back until your chest is as far off the ball as possible, extend your arms forward, and hold that position for a few moments. Draw your arms back into the starting position as you return your torso to the ball. 12 to 15 repetitions

FIVE ABOVE-THE-BELT TIME-SAVERS

Looking to shave even more time off your workout while shaving fat from your waistline? These exercises work several areas of your midsection simultaneously. Use any one of the following substitutions to cover two areas with one exercise, and you can reduce your workout plan to just a few exercises instead of five.

ABS AND OBLIQUES

Crunch/Side-Bend Combination
Targets upper abs and obliques

Lie on your back with your knees bent and hold a dumbbell against your chest. Curl up so that your shoulder blades are off the floor. Bend your right armpit toward your left hip. Straighten, then repeat to your left. 8 repetitions each side

Corkscrew
Targets lower abs and obliques

Lie on your back with your legs raised directly over your hips and your knees slightly bent. Place your hands with the palms down at your sides.

Use your lower abs to raise your hips off the floor and toward your rib cage, while simultaneously twisting your hips to the right in a corkscrew motion. Hold, then return to the starting position. Repeat, twisting to the left. 10 repetitions

UPPER ABS AND LOWER ABS

Bicycle
Targets upper and lower abs

Lie on your back with your knees bent 90 degrees and your hands behind your ears. Pump your legs bicycle-style as you rotate your torso. 20 pumps

Hanging Single Knee Raise
Targets lower abs and obliques

Hang from a chinup bar and raise your right knee toward your left shoulder. Hold, then lower the leg. Repeat with your left leg. 8 to 12 repetitions

Stick Crunch
Targets upper and lower abs

Lie on your back, holding a broomstick out past your head. Crunch up so the stick extends past your knees. 12 repetitions

PERCENTAGE OF MUSCLE MASS A MAN LOSES BETWEEN AGES 25 AND 50: 10

PERCENTAGE HE LOSES BETWEEN AGES 50 AND 80: 35

STEP 3: THE ABS DIET NUTRITION PLAN

Everybody paints a big weight-loss bull's-eye on belly fat. That's because losing it will make any body look better. But a better reason to target it is that eliminating it will help you feel better and live longer. Study after study has shown that people with the largest waist sizes have the greatest risk of life-threatening diseases. And the most dangerous kind of fat—called visceral fat—is a type that rubs up against your internal organs, literally placing the threat right in the position where it can do you the most harm.

We've got the tools you need to defuse the fat bomb. Just turn to "The Abs Diet" on page 3 for nutrition basics that can shrink the flab layer off your abdomen.

Excerpted from *The Abs Diet*, copyright 2004 by Rodale Inc. For more information or to order, go to www.menshealth.com/absdietchallenge.

Mind over Muscle

Five psych-out secrets to trick your body into working out harder, faster, and longer

By Michael Tennesen

What surrenders first, the brain or the body?

Feels like the body, doesn't it? When your stride gets choppy on the running trail or your form goes wobbly in the gym, you tell yourself to go a bit more, but your body won't let you. So your mind drifts to a hot shower and a cold beer. It's quittin' time.

There it is: Your mind drifts. Your body's got plenty more, and scientists have proved it. Researchers at the University of Cape Town in South Africa have pinpointed where the stop order comes from. It has to do with receptors in the brain called interleukin-6.

"Our brains turn on the pain before we actually run out of fuel," says Timothy Noakes, MD, a professor of exercise and sports science at the University of Cape Town. It's a safety measure. The brain tells the body to shut down to protect it from injury.

In short, our brains screw with us. They stop us from getting the most out of our workouts and from losing that last 10 pounds. Guys like Lance Armstrong and Michael Phelps have figured out how to fool the brain and body into giving more. It's a bit more than "I think I can." But not much. Here's what the experts say.

RUN ANOTHER MILE

Why you stop: You're running low on glycogen, the primary fuel source for your muscles. But it's not the only one. Any body fat you have is available. Your brain knows this, but it's not telling you.

Keep going: Try this trick from Jane Hahn, a senior editor at *Runner's World* magazine. If a runner is in sight, slowly reel him in. "Imagine there's a magnet attached to him," says Hahn, "and it's pulling you toward him." (Or her. Imagining it's Scarlett Johansson works well.)

Some practical preparation: Include long runs in your training, no matter how short your races are. "Long runs teach the body to run more efficiently and to use energy stores more effectively," says Hahn.

BENCH-PRESS YOUR LAST REP

Why you quit: You need an absolute goal. If you think that anywhere from six to 12 repetitions will suffice, then 12 is unlikely. Pick eight or 10, and nail it. Good form is essential. Your body uses 32 muscles to lower and lift the weight. As you tire, your form can falter.

Lift more: Start with eight to 10 reps with an empty bar to reinforce your form, says C.J. Murphy, MFS, owner and head strength coach of Total Performance Sports in Everett, Massachusetts. Then pull your shoulder blades together and hold your elbows slightly in, not out at 90 degrees. Squeeze your lats and push the bar as fast as you can without losing control. Then lower it under control.

PEDAL FASTER

Why you slow down: You've run out of gas.

Speed up: Get off the bike. Bill Foran, strength and conditioning coach for the Miami Heat, suggests simple intervals.

- **Fours:** Run four lengths of a basketball court "as hard as you can, with the goal of finishing in under 24 seconds," says Foran. Rest 40 seconds and repeat eight to 12 times.
- **17s:** Run sideline to sideline 17 times. The challenge is changing direction. Try to finish in about a minute. Rest 2 minutes; repeat for a total of four or five runs.
- **Suicides:** These haven't changed since high school. They're still hard, still effective. Starting at one baseline of a basketball court, run to the near free-throw line and back, then continue back and forth to the midcourt line, the opposite free-throw line, and the opposite baseline. Try to run the whole thing in 30 to 33 seconds, then rest for a minute. Complete six to eight suicides.

SWIM ANOTHER LAP

Why you sink: The burning sensation in your muscles is partly a result of an accumulation of lactic acid, says Shawn Arent, PhD, CSCS, an exercise scientist at Rutgers University. You reach a point called your lactate threshold, when your body can't flush it out fast enough and you need to slow down. Any kind of interval training can push your threshold higher, but there's another trick.

Swim farther: "You'll send less lactic acid into your muscles if you're relaxed," says Joel Kirsch, PhD, a sports psychologist and director of the American Sports Institute. Removing the tension in your muscles lets your limbs fully extend and your stride—or stroke—lengthen, says Kirsch. "Check your muscles as you move and ask yourself, 'Are my legs moving freely, or am I pushing them?'" If you're pushing, focus on easing the muscles. At your desk, practice tensing the muscles in your arms and legs, then slowly relaxing them. You'll get the hang of controlling your muscles, says Kirsch.

CITY WHERE THE FEWEST MEN SLING IRON:

Pittsburgh

DO THAT LAST CRUNCH

Or skip it: "I'd rather see you do 20 good reps than 30 crappy ones," says Dr. Arent. Your abs, like any other muscle, grow in response to increased stress, not continual stress.

Do them well: Here are three keys to the proper crunch: Focus on lifting your shoulder blades off the floor, not pulling your head up with your hands. Pause at the top of the move and lower your body slowly. Keep your abs tight throughout the exercise.

NEED TO KNOW

Think Yourself Thin

Next time you plan to skip a workout, think hard about it. That's right—all you have to do is really think about how bad you know you'll feel later. This isn't psycho–mumbo jumbo, it's backed by science. According to a study at the University of Sussex in England, simply imagining the feelings of regret for bailing on a sweat session makes an individual more likely to head to the gym. When you think you can't work any exercise into your day, give some thought to how guilty you'll feel about it and how disappointed you'll be in yourself. You'll be more likely to make sure those feelings never materialize— and end up feeling better.

Find Your Balance

Are your ankles worth 5 minutes? A recent study in the *American Journal of Sports Medicine* found that spending 5 minutes on a balance board as part of a warmup for your workout can reduce ankle injuries by 60 percent. The men in the study performed basic moves such as standing on one leg, squatting, and tossing a ball while standing on the board. The authors suggest that balance-board training is particularly beneficial for men with a history of ankle injuries.

Great Squat

Auburn University researchers have found a leg exercise that could spare your wheels from stress. They studied 19 swimmers who did either four sets of 10 squat jumps (bending the knees 90 degrees) or half-squat jumps (bending them 45 degrees) three times a week. Both groups had gained equal power by the end of the 9-week period. "We wanted to see if you could do something that's a little less strenuous on the joints and still enhance your lower-body power," says Peter Grandjean, PhD, the lead study author.

First Thing's First

If your workout regimen includes strength training and cardio—as it should— it's best to lift weights *before* your cardio workout. You'll have more energy to lift and have the proper hormonal release, which stimulates growth in the body, so you'll get better results, says Mark Verstegen, owner of Athletes' Performance in Tempe, Arizona, and Los Angeles and author of *Core Performance*. Just do less cardio. Thirty minutes five times a week is counterproductive, burning calories that could be used for building lean mass. If you want to add size, do 15- to 60-second sprints on whatever contraption you choose, following each with a rest period one to two times as long. (A 30-second sprint earns you 30 to 60 seconds of rest.) Make the whole thing last for 12 minutes twice a week, and you're done. If you want to get lean, do the same 12-minute torture twice a week, but add 2 days of 30 minutes at an easier pace.

Fit for a Genius

Want to boost your brainpower? Then listen to music while you exercise. Researchers at Ohio State University found that people did twice as well on cognitive tests after exercising with a soundtrack than after sweating in silence. Exercise fights off decay in the area of the brain responsible for "executive function" tasks, such as reasoning and sequencing. Music may "enhance organization of cognitive material, which is also an executive-function task," says lead author Charles Emery, PhD. The study used Vivaldi, but other types of music (yes, even Ozzy) may have a similar effect.

Stretch Your Limits

Research supporting this isn't plentiful, but a study of 93 people shows that holding a stretch for 30 seconds improves range of motion, while holding it for 15 seconds does zilch, says study author Bill Bandy, PhD, a professor of physical therapy at the University of Central Arkansas in Conway. Simple rule of stretching: If you're not feeling it, you're not doing it.

Rubbed the Wrong Way

You may love a postworkout massage, but it isn't necessarily helping muscle recovery. In a British study, physiotherapists massaged the quadriceps of 13 men following a leg workout. Bloodflow to their quadriceps wasn't increased enough to accelerate recovery. Study authors say a massage may still offer psychological benefits.

Similarly, ice on a sore muscle isn't as useful as you might think, according to a study in the *Journal of Sports Medicine and Physical Fitness*. Researchers studied nine men performing biceps curls and found that applying ice to sore muscles immediately after exercise (then 24 hours and 48 hours after) didn't help with soreness or performance any more than giving no treatment.

Take a Break

If you enjoy the stress relief exercise gives you, make sure you don't overdo it. Overtraining can actually cause stress. According to a report in the *Journal of Strength and Conditioning Research,* excessive training elevates cytokine levels in the blood, which tells the brain to raise levels of the stress hormone cortisol.

WHAT'S NEW

Keep the Cardio

Recent research published in *Circulation* found that men on a vigorous lifting program had a 21 percent increase in arterial stiffness after 4 months. That may be a good thing; the body might be strengthening the arterial walls to prevent rupture. Or it could be "a maladaptation that increases the risk of heart disease, or both," says Motohiko Miyachi, PhD, the study author. Combine aerobic exercise with lifting, Dr. Miyachi says, to "restrain arterial stiffening while increasing strength and power."

Are Muscles in Your Genes?

German physicians have found that a 4-year-old boy with muscles twice the size of those of other kids his age has a genetic mutation that blocks myostatin, a protein known to decrease muscle mass in animals. Lou Kunkel, MD, a professor of pediatrics and genetics at Harvard Medical School, says reducing myostatin could increase muscle mass. With this in mind . . .

- The pharmaceutical company Wyeth has begun human trials to see whether antibodies that block myostatin are safe and effective. This could be especially useful in rehabilitation—"bulking up after injury," says Dr. Kunkel.
- The National Institutes of Health is funding a study in which 1,000 people will do a 12-week program of biceps curls. Scientists will see who gained the most and least muscle, check their genetic makeup, and figure out which genes influence the body's response to exercise. This could lead to more-personalized workout programs.

Bionic Legs

Researchers at the University of California at Berkeley have developed real bionic legs. The system features robotic leg braces that provide the power and strength to walk longer distances. It also comes with a power unit, as well as a backpacklike structure that makes it easier to carry heavy loads.

THE COST OF . . .

. . . Skipping Your Workouts

Missed a workout or two? Here's what falling off your fitness routine could cost you over the next 9 months.

You get . . .	Research shows . . .	You pay . . .
Viagra	Men who don't work out have an increased risk of developing erectile dysfunction.	$135
A good tailor (to adjust your suits to your expanding waistline)	Weight loss achieved through exercise can reduce abdominal fat more successfully than diet alone.	$40
SmartSet CD/clock radio (you'll need extra help waking up)	Men who don't exercise have more trouble nodding off and staying asleep.	$80
2 sick days	Those who exercise less are more likely to contract upper respiratory tract infections.	$296
Wednesdays on the couch with Dr. Headshrink	A workout is a good way to fight stress and anxiety.	$3,240 ($90/week)
Swopper ergonomic chair	Sitting in this chair will help you deal with back pain; aerobic exercise relieves pain all over your body, including your back.	$500
ER visit	Skip your daily workout and your bones won't get the protective benefit of exercise, putting you at risk for bone breaks.	$159
Gym dues	If you're not using the gym, it's wasted money.	$296
TOTAL		$4,746

FAST FIXES

You've put in the time. The sweat. Maybe the tears when you don't see results. Quit blubbering. It'll be fine.

Entering the weight room is the first step toward building muscle, but it's not the last. What you do before, during, and after a workout can either negate your hard work or elevate your growth to a new level.

"Your personal habits, your social life, even which exercises you choose to do can take away from what you're trying to build," says Jeff Bell, CSCS, an exercise physiologist and the owner of Spectrum Wellness in New York City. Bell and other experts helped us pinpoint seven factors that sabotage results. "Add them up, and they could be why your muscles have nothing to show for all your time served," Bell says.

Our surefire fixes will help you eliminate these seven saboteurs—so you can get out of your own way and watch your muscles grow.

1. Skipping basics. Plenty of lifters believe that doing isolation exercises like chest flies and leg extensions is the only way to make their muscles grow. But basic moves such as bench presses and squats force several muscle groups to work together, imposing more stress on your body for bigger gains.

"Your body reacts to all that stress by having the anterior pituitary gland issue more growth hormone to compensate for the extra effort," says Allen Hedrick, CSCS, head strength-and-conditioning coach at the Air Force Academy in Colorado Springs. Of course you need variation, but don't abandon basic moves in favor of intermediate isolation exercises.

Fix it: Write down the exercises in your routine to see what percentage of them are compound moves. "If it's not in the range of at least 40 to 50 percent, then you're doing too many isolation exercises," says Bell.

2. Lunchtime hoops. Playing sports too often can sidetrack your muscle-growth goals. Muscles typically need 48 hours of rest to adapt to the stresses placed on them during exercise. "Engaging in extra activity also makes your body more likely to use any excess calories it has for fuel, and not for rebuilding itself," says Bell.

Fix it: "Pull your cardiovascular activity back to the bare minimum—20 minutes, three times a week—to see what effect it has on your body," Bell says. If cardio is indeed stealing your muscle, you should begin to notice strength improvements—being able to lift more weight or complete more repetitions—within 2 to 3 weeks. If your primary goal is to increase muscle size and strength, and not necessarily to build your overall health, try pulling back further. Can't miss a game? During your workout, ease up on the muscles you use most in your extra activity so they have more time to recover.

3. Smoking and drinking. You know smoking is stupid. You know you're gambling with cancer, stroke, and other health issues. But did you know you're also sabotaging your strength training? "Smoking places carbon monoxide in your system, which prevents your muscles from getting as much oxygen to use for energy," says Scott Swartzwelder, PhD, a clinical professor of medical psychology at Duke University. "The less oxygen your muscles have to draw from, the less efficient they are at contracting, which can limit their capacity for work." As for alcohol, it can cover your abs with a layer of lard and interfere with hormones that help build them. "Drinking alcohol on a regular basis can also keep your testosterone levels lower than usual and decrease muscle mass," says Dr. Swartzwelder.

Fix it: Quit smoking, and don't worry about becoming a cold-turkey butterball. "Getting in at least 30 minutes of exercise three or four times a week, not only helps control body weight, but can also produce positive psychological effects that might diminish the need to smoke," says Dr. Swartzwelder. Drinking moderately (two drinks or less per day) won't harm testosterone levels and can actually improve your cardiovascular health, he says.

4. Starvation. You need to eat after your workout. Right after a session, your body is hustling to convert glucose into glycogen so your muscles can repair themselves and grow. "If you don't eat after exercise, your body breaks down muscle into amino acids to convert into glucose," says John Ivy, PhD, chairman of kinesiology at the University of Texas.

Fix it: After you work out, eat a high-carbohydrate meal—and don't forget the protein. A study in the *Journal of Strength and Conditioning Research* found that a 4:1 carbohydrate-to-protein ratio can provide 128 percent greater muscle-glycogen storage than a high-carbohydrate drink alone. (They used Endurox R^4 Recovery Drink in the study.) For even greater results, have a sports drink before and during exercise.

5. Craig Kilborn. If you don't get enough deep sleep, your muscles can't recover. Moreover, says Catherine Jackson, PhD, chairwoman of the department of kinesiology at California State University at Fresno, when you work out on insufficient sleep, you exercise at a lower intensity than you realize—but you feel as if it's high. So your muscles are less likely to receive enough stress to grow.

Fix it: Go to bed and wake up at set times every day, even on weekends, to keep your sleep cycles regular. Avoid caffeine—and perhaps exercise—for 4 to 6 hours before bedtime. Elevating your heart rate before bed can interfere with sleep, Dr. Jackson says.

6. Sugar. Sugary drinks like soda can fool your body with a blood-sugar spike, making you prone to skip "other, nutrient-dense foods you could be eating," says Bell. If your sugar habit limits your intake of muscle-building amino acids, it will sap the fuel you need for your workouts, says New York City-based celebrity trainer Steve Lischin, MS, CPT.

Fix it: Water and low-sugar sports drinks are your best bets. But sugar hides elsewhere. "Watch out for dried fruits, certain nutrition bars, and even ketchup," Lischin says.

7. Thirst. For the active man, eating about a gram of protein for every 2.2 pounds of body weight helps build muscle—if the protein is processed correctly. "A high-protein meal has a slight diuretic effect," says Lischin. When the body uses protein for energy, it has to remove the nitrogen component of the molecule to turn it into glucose. "This requires plenty of water," he says.

Fix it: Drink eight to 10 glasses of water a day and divide your protein among five or six small meals throughout the day. "Eating an average of 25 to 30 grams each meal is ideal," says Lischin. "Not only will you put less stress on your kidneys, but you'll also utilize more of the protein you're ingesting by giving your body only as much as it can use each time."

OUR FINAL ANSWERS

Buying Bulk

I want to bulk up. I can afford a machine for about $250 that I saw on the Body by Jake Web site. Should I get it?

—D.J., Huntsville, Alabama

No. For $250 you can get a 300-pound Olympic barbell set and probably a used bench, if you hunt around. If you buy a used bench and weights, you might be able to afford some adjustable dumbbells, too. No gimmicky machine is going to help you significantly. For that, you need iron. Fortunately for you, it's plentiful and cheap.

Do Some Heavy Lifting

I don't want to gain any more weight, although I wouldn't mind getting stronger. How many sets and reps should I do?

—L.D., Kirksville, Missouri

There's no such thing as a system of sets and reps that prevents weight gain. If you don't want to gain more weight, don't eat more. If you want to get stronger, do fewer reps and more sets with heavier weights, with more recovery between workouts. Also, when you're lifting heavy, make sure you strike a balance between pushing and pulling exercises. In other words, don't do 12 sets of bench presses without doing a comparable number of rows.

Muscle Menu

What should I eat after I lift?

—J.P., Barstow, California

Research shows that a combination of protein and carbohydrates is best. The ratio depends on your goals. If you're trying to pack on muscle, have a 1:2 ratio of protein to carbs within 10 minutes after you work out. (For example, have some low-fat milk on cereal.) If you're trying to increase lean body mass while losing body fat, go with a 1:1 or 2:1 protein-to-carb ratio, like EAS Myoplex Shake. And if you're just trying to lose weight, have a preworkout protein shooter, such as a bottle of Amino Vital Pro, then eat a light meal within an hour after your workout.

'Rhoid Rage

My doc says I have a hemorrhoid from straining during weight lifting. I'm only 25, so how can I make sure this doesn't happen again?

—K.P., Gary, Indiana

Lifting weights, constipation, and sitting on the throne too long while thumbing through a magazine are common causes of hemorrhoids, which are dilated veins in swollen tissue. Preventing them isn't always possible. Try wearing a belt when you lift, and make sure you're not holding your breath. Also, use lighter weights while increasing the number of repetitions. To tackle the problem at the source, stay hydrated and eat plenty of fiber.

Sore Subject

Will running when my legs are still sore from a workout hurt my strength gains?

—T.H., Jackson, Tennessee

If you're beginning a workout program, your legs may be sore from new stress. If running is part of your first week's plan, it's fine to work through the soreness; but if you're still hurting after a week, stop running. Instead, rest more between workouts. That said, long, slow distance runs hurt your strength gains, whether you're sore or not. Sprints and intervals complement strength training while improving your cardiovascular system.

Sick Question

If you have a cold, should you still work out?

—A.T., Jamestown, North Dakota

Not if you go to our gym. The biggest problem with working out while you have a cold is spreading your germs. If the symptoms are above the neck (stuffy nose, itchy eyes, mild sore throat), hit the gym. Anything below the neck (fever, coughing, aches), wait it out. And try not to sneeze on the weights.

MAKE YOUR SEX LIFE SIZZLE

THREE

READ UP ON IT

Instant Heat

You're ready now. She needs to preheat. Here are 40 simple ways
to stoke her furnace—and a few ideas for what to do once she's hot

By Ted Spiker and Siski Green

Most bedroom problems boil down to this: Men are microwaves and women are slow cookers.

With men, all you have to do is push a few buttons, and we're hotter than an habanero. But with women, it's an all-day process. You have to buy the ingredients, mix them together, and then put everything in the pot and let it simmer . . . and simmer . . . and simmer.

That's why we're offering a microwave mentality for the Crock-Pot reality: quick, easy things you can do to make her heating speeds better match yours. Our suggestions take anywhere from a few seconds to a few minutes. The payoff? They'll quickly adjust her thermostat to high heat.

WARM UP

Buy her a silk thong. A gift of lingerie is clichéd, right? So twist it. Give it to her when you (seemingly) don't expect sex right then and there. Pass it under the table at a restaurant and ask her to go to the ladies' room and change into it. "It's a little naughty, but she has a chance to play back," says Joy Davidson, PhD, a relationship therapist in Seattle. Not recommended for a first date.

Embrace her until she makes the move to leave. Good kissing tops most women's lists of turn-ons, but don't underestimate the heating power of a great hug, especially when she initiates it. "Let her know how much you savor it," says Lou Paget, author of *365 Days of Sensational Sex*. Make it clear you don't want the hug to end.

Wear her name. Women love to hear men use their names. The more unexpected the place—like in the middle of a sentence—the better. Better still, write her name on your shoulder, your hand, or anyplace she'll have a chance of spotting it. It's a tattoo without pain—one that gives only pleasure. "It will make her laugh and think you're so adorable," says Dr. Davidson. "It says, 'You matter.'"

Whisper into her ear. In public, at a party, tell her what you want to do to her later: "Tonight, I'm going to make you have as many orgasms as possible." For women, anticipating it can be as exciting as the actual event.

Skip the flowers. Blooms at the office are overdone. If you want to stand out, send a card instead. "It's really the thoughtful things you do at nonsexual times that make a woman want you," says Paul Joannides, author of *Guide to Getting It On!* Go with a thank-you. Write out a few things you've never thanked her for—making breakfast on Sunday, cleaning your stubble out of the sink. An appreciated woman during the day is an appreciative woman at night.

Plant a picture. Stash a photo of her in your wallet. She'll deny it, but all women rummage at some point. You might as well turn it to your advantage.

Say why. Anyone can say "I love you," so explain why. Maybe it's the way she nibbles at a KitKat, or how her nose scrunches when she drinks tequila. The more unique your reasons, the more special she'll feel.

Get your story straight. For a happy ending (tonight and every night), remember the beginning: the details of your first meeting—where you were, what she was wearing, what you said, and how you felt. Recount them. Often.

Make yourself sick. Leave love notes around the house—in the fridge, on the bathroom mirror, under her pillow. That much sweetness might make you nauseous, but it'll make her feel like a lovesick teenager.

Apply her lipstick. "Grooming a woman is kind of a role reversal," says Linda De Villers, PhD, a California sex therapist and author of *Love Skills: A Fun, Upbeat Guide to Sex-cessful Relationships*. "She's being doted on and served, and it shows that you think a certain part of her body is attractive." Other ideas: Shave her legs, paint her toenails, or brush or wash her hair. According to a MensHealth.com poll of 3,200 men, 76 percent said they have shampooed their woman's hair. And *Men's Health* readers don't waste their time on things that don't work.

SIMMER

Kiss and lick her hinges. You've got the obvious kiss spots covered. Now concentrate your efforts elsewhere—on her elbows, knees, shoulders, ankles, neck, and hip joints. "They're rarely attended to with long caresses," says Dr. Davidson. "It's a super sensation." See if you can make her come unhinged.

Bear fruit . . . Chocolate syrup and whipped cream get all the kinky play in movies. Instead, turn her body into a juicer. "The best foods for sex are fruits that you can rub onto the body, such as soft mango or papaya," says Ava Cadell, PhD, EdD, a sex therapist in California and author of *12 Steps to Everlasting Love*. "Then devour both her and the fruit." Get sticky, shower, repeat. If you're Mickey Rourke, skip the shower.

. . . and berries. Forget coffee and toast—bring hot chocolate (a sexual stimulant for her) and raspberries and strawberries to bed. The berries

PERCENTAGE DECREASE IN A MAN'S LEVEL OF SEXUAL INTEREST WHEN HE'S STRESSED:

28

replenish the zinc you lose when you ejaculate—5 milligrams, or a third of your daily requirement.

Try the no-move move. When you start foreplay, tell her you're not going to move on to another action until she tells you what to do next. This works physically and mentally: It's a way to encourage her to open up and direct you to what she really wants. Now, your turn.

Give her a massage. But make it interesting:

- In hot weather, roll a chilled can of soda along the backs of her thighs.
- In cool weather, warm a towel in the microwave for 10 seconds and massage her with it.
- Season her belly with a little salt, and then slowly lick it off. Add tequila to taste.
- Turn winter gloves inside out, put them on, and massage her with the soft side.

Give her chills. "Cold is sensed by more nerve endings than mere touch can reach, so you're expanding her range of response," says Phillip Hodson, a British sex therapist. Do this: Chill a bunch of grapes for at least 20 minutes. Then trail a small sprig of them along her neck, nipples, and inner thighs. Nibble away. Now put a grape in your mouth and gently press it against her clitoris by holding it in your teeth or between your lips.

Come clean. Here's a master class in the notoriously tricky art of bath sex. Start by slinging in a generous quantity of bath gel, advises Anne Hooper, a sex therapist and author of *Ultimate Sex*. Fill the tub with 5 inches of hot water, then pour more foaming bath gel onto your bellies, chests, and legs. Have her lie on top of you and use her body as a scrub brush. To add to the fun, throw in a set of Rub-a-Dub Dice ($10)—floating foam cubes that, when "rolled," reveal sexy commands like "sponge belly" or "kiss back"—or a Rubba Ducky ($25), a vibrating bath massager you'll both enjoy. Both are available at www.mypleasure.com.

Rub her down. For extra shower power, pour a couple of drops of shower gel into a spray bottle and mix it with water. Spray her, then rub. She'll feel three different types of stimulation—the steady pelting of the shower, the soft spray of the soapy gel, and the firm caresses of your hands. That's the kind of threesome that turns her on.

BOIL

Make a bedroom burrito. Bondage is appealing for a good reason: It heightens the anticipation for the one who's receiving the pleasure. But anything with locks, Velcro, or ties can freak her out (us, too), so try this: While you're rolling around in bed, wrap her up in the sheet so she can't do anything with her arms (think burrito or straitjacket). Leave her head, shoulders, and lower legs uncovered. Now kiss every inch of exposed skin. It's simple, spontaneous, and soft-core.

Blindfold yourself. Many women who are insecure about their bodies stick to the missionary position because you can't see their bodies that way. If you really can't see her because your eyes are covered, she'll do a lot more with you, to you, and for you.

Ask permission. Before you enter her, ask if it's okay. "Some women find it incredibly endearing," says Barnaby Barratt, PhD, president of the American Association of Sex Educators, Counselors, and Therapists. "It gives them a sense of respect. It gives them the security to become more sexually relaxed." And when you're first entering her, kiss her lips or caress her face. "Give her stimulation in addition to penetration," Dr. De Villers says.

Practice reentry. After you first enter her, do it again—slowly. Repeat it over and over. "One of the huge turn-ons is anticipation," Dr. De Villers says. "Don't pull out all the way, but when you pull almost all the way out, she gets the anticipation of the stroke that comes back in."

Do it in public. Or just pretend. Exhibitionism is a secret thrill for many women, but the threat of arrest deters them. So have sex standing up, with her near the bedroom window. It's easy to duck out of the way. If she's semi-clothed, your neighbors will be none the wiser.

SEVEN HOT THINGS TO SAY TO A WOMAN

1. *"I love your eyelashes."*
2. *"Sex with you just gets better and better."*
3. *"You look beautiful when you're sleeping."*
4. *"The way you dance is really sexy."*
5. *"You have a wonderful laugh."*
6. *"You're so clever."*
7. *"Your skin smells fantastic."*

AMOUNT OF TIME BEFORE THE AVERAGE GUY WILL TELL THE WOMAN HE'S DATING HE LOVES HER:

3 months

Blow bubbles. Take a swig of champagne before going down, then use your tongue to swirl the bubbles around her clitoris. Nerve endings react to bubbles. In a very good way.

Use the cottons cycle. "The washing machine is the biggest vibrator in the house," says Hodson. Sit on it and have her sit on top of you—the vibrations carry through your penis. Cottons get the longest, fastest spin.

Go into the closet. Novelty is an aphrodisiac. Any unusual setting, with strange sensations, smells, and muffled sounds, will make sex feel new. Confined spaces add urgency. "They're great for a quickie," says sex therapist Louanne Cole Weston. Watch that shoe tree!

Work the angle. Liberator Shapes (www.liberator.com) velvet cushions create an "orgasm-optimum" 26-degree pelvic tilt, which means maximum contact between your body and her clitoris, and minimum demands for foreplay. Feel free to adjust the angle slightly; there's evidence that 27 degrees works as well.

Or call a squeeze play. With her facedown and you on top, have her cross her legs, and position yours outside of hers. Her vagina will feel tighter, and the added friction means more pleasure.

Get bigger. When you're on top, place her legs over your shoulders. This shortens her vaginal canal, so your penis feels bigger inside her.

Stand by your woman. For better from-behind sex, have her kneel on the edge of the bed with her upper chest touching the mattress. This elongates the vaginal barrel, making it feel tighter. You get a fantastic view, and she'll enjoy the nipple stimulation from rubbing the mattress.

Make it easy. For oral sex, stand while your partner kneels or sits on the bed. This angle lets her take more of you, gives her better control, and is less tiring.

Let her give you a pearl necklace. But not a real one. Lightly lubricate the pearls and your penis. Have your partner wrap the pearls around the shaft and slowly stroke up and down with a gentle rotation. The beads feel warm and smooth, creating a new level of sensation.

Direct a fan at her. Then pour peppermint schnapps into her belly button, dip your fingers and tongue, and trace her body.

Sex on the Brain

What are these soft, sultry creatures called women? Why do they tempt us so? Take a tour of the human libido—its blinding intensity, its darkest corners—and you'll soon be having the most incredible sex of your life

By Daniel Amen, MD

You're sitting behind the wheel of your van at an everlasting traffic light. The only thing slower than the traffic is your perception of time's passage.

Then you notice her.

She appears at the curb, waiting to cross. No, she's not the love of your life. She's more like the heat of the moment.

It's fortunate that your wife isn't there, otherwise you'd be in deep trouble as you take in the stranger's hips and breasts, and the way her waist scoops in to accentuate both. Time is enhanced; there's a pleasing buzz connecting your temples.

Your reaction is automatic, reflexive, and quite possibly the most powerful one you'll have this day. It temporarily blots out your long-range commitments—that 10-year marriage, that kid in second grade, that responsibility to keep eyes forward at traffic lights. You've surrendered control; you're captivated by the pleasure in the vision.

"You dog!" you may whisper under your breath, embarrassed by what you're envisioning as you sit there in your family van. But it might be more correct to say, "You dopamine fiend!" As a neuroscientist of 25 years, I know that your brain is command central for everything sexual.

When you spot the object of your desire, the neurotransmitter dopamine lights up areas deep within the brain, triggering feelings of pleasure, motivation, and reward. (Cocaine acts the same way.) You feel a rush, and your heartbeat quickens. Attraction, too, is a powerful drug. The brain stem also gets into the act, releasing phenylethylamine (PEA), which speeds up the flow of information between nerve cells. It's no wonder your neck and eyeballs track her every movement.

But she's not gawking back at you, and it's not just because you're driving a family bus with a paint scrape on the fender. Her brain acts very differently from yours. You're keyed in to beauty, shape, fantasy, and obsession; on some biological level that she may be unaware of, she's trolling for a mate who will sire healthy children and protect and provide for her and them. And yes, maybe even buy them a family van.

Her goals are programmed for the long range; yours are often shockingly short term, right up to and including thoughts of pedestrianophilia. And she knows it, which is why she presses those short-term buttons shotgun-style: She never knows when a suitable mate might be looking.

The whole encounter can leave you quivering with pleasure, hoping for more.

It can also hijack and ruin your life.

And between the "walk" and "don't walk" signals of delight and disaster, your brain is sorting information, making choices, spurring actions. But you don't want to passively accept all that, especially because your whole life is riding on the choices you make.

That's where I come in. I know the brain processes behind the temptations, and I can help you steer clear of trouble. After all, that woman in the crosswalk could help you realize your destiny—or derail it entirely. All the more reason to get to know that big sex organ between your ears so you can control the smaller, less important one between your legs.

WHY YOU'VE BEEN HORNY SINCE CONCEPTION (YOUR OWN)

You've been lit up on testosterone right from the start, even when you were just a multicelled notion in your mother's womb. The inherited Y chromosome that makes you male (thanks, Dad) triggers two bursts of testosterone that change your brain and body. The first produces a male brain: one that's more interested in objects, actions, and competition. The left (parietal) lobe flourishes in the testosterone bath and helps you visualize objects in three dimensions (good for catching a football or watching a woman cross the street), and it boosts your aptitude in mathematics (that's how you estimate that she's about a 34DD). In addition, testosterone beefs up your hypothalamus, the area of the brain that's interested in sex. The hypothalamus is twice as large in men as it is in women.

WHY YOU BECAME EVEN HORNIER IN JUNIOR HIGH

That's when the second big burst of testosterone hits, causing your hair to sprout everywhere, your voice to flip from Norah Jones to James Earl Jones,

AM I NORMAL?

I think about sex while I'm in meetings, the dentist's office, and, worst of all, church. Is this sick?
Peter W., Bridgeport, Connecticut

No, we are men. Men think about sex a lot, wherever we are, and that includes church. It can be highly irritating—singing the hymn and looking at the cute woman's rear end in the pew in front of us. But that's what our frontal lobes are for: to put a lid on the thoughts that threaten to take over our better judgment.

AM I NORMAL?

I prefer solo sex to the partner kind. Sick, or sane?
Dennis B., San Francisco

Neither. Solo sex is about fantasy and release; sex with a committed partner is about bonding and connection. Which do you want?

and your interest in third base to go from literal to metaphorical. (Touch 'em all!) Your body now harbors 20 times the level of testosterone found in girls your age, which accounts for your sexual obsessions. Unfortunately, your brain is maladapted for sociability, so she can overwhelm you with words, and all you have to counter them is silent (thank goodness) adolescent lust. It's an advantage she has that you'll never make up. On your side of the ledger: Your left brain—the planning center—is massive, which helps in planning the Panama Canal, a rocket launch, or a lifetime of wedded bliss.

WHY SHE'S STARING AT YOUR RING FINGER

Because it knows and tells all. University of Liverpool researcher John Manning has determined that the size of a man's ring finger is related to how much testosterone he received in the womb. That's true of your penis, as well. The more T, the longer they grow. It's interesting to note that your digital symbol of virility is also the finger on which she slips the golden shackle during the wedding ceremony.

WHY A GUY HAS TO WATCH HIS TESTOSTERONE LEVEL THROUGHOUT HIS LIFE

Women are more predisposed (in brain structure and hormone secretions) to settle down and start a family than you are. But committing to family life is easier for men who have lower testosterone levels. A study of more than 4,000 men found that men with high testosterone levels were 43 percent more likely to get divorced and 38 percent more likely to have extramarital affairs than men with less of the hormone. Guys with high levels were also 50 percent less likely to marry in the first place. Men with the least testosterone were more likely to get and stay married, maybe because lower testosterone levels make men more cooperative. If you're too cooperative for your own good, build some muscle: It will increase testosterone levels over time. You can even coordinate dating with workouts. A study at Baylor University determined that testosterone levels were highest 48 hours after weight lifting.

WHY NO MAN SHOULD MARRY BEFORE AGE 25

Quite simply, a man's brain is incomplete before then. Sure, his sexual organs are all present and accounted for, but his prefrontal cortex (PFC) is still developing. Which is too bad, because that's the part of his brain that's involved in judgment, impulse control, organization, planning, forethought, and learning from mistakes. And it won't be fully developed until he's 25.

WHY BEAUTIFUL WOMEN MAKE YOU STUPID

You act like a goof with the Hooters waitress, leaving a tip that doubles the bar bill. But why? Beautiful women cause a man's limbic system (the amygdala and other brain-stem structures that are in charge of emotion) to fire up at the same time that his PFC checks out, leaving the judgment area vacant. Las Vegas casinos hire beautiful cocktail waitresses, dress them in low-cut tops and miniskirts, and have them pass out free alcohol—all of which encourages men's self-control to take the day trip to Hoover Dam. No wonder the house has the edge.

HOW YOU CAN GET THE EDGE BACK

When faced with the dilemma of a bad bet on a beautiful woman, remember that her beauty is fleeting, but a bad decision can last a lifetime. It's a very PFC sentiment, in fact.

WHY YOU'RE CAPTIVATED BY PORN, BUT SHE CAN TAKE IT OR LEAVE IT

Guys aren't shallow; it's just that the visual parts of their brains are strong and tend to twang their emotions. Using sophisticated imaging equipment, researchers at Emory University in Atlanta found that the amygdala, which controls emotions and motivation, is much more activated in men than in women when they view sexual material for 30 minutes, even though both sexes report similar levels of interest. This may be one of the reasons men are

AM I NORMAL?

Is it bad that I seem to be attracted only to married women?
Tony T., Arlington, Virginia

Not bad, but weird. You may be commitment phobic—wanting something you can't have. Married women may appear safer. They're usually not looking for long-term commitments, just a deviation from routine—unless, of course, her husband finds you in bed with her and shoots your naked bottom.

much more captivated by pornography than women: For men, it's not just porn, it's personal. Back in the real world, women hijack men's brains by appealing to their strong visual sense. But women can take in a guy's visuals and think, Yeah, but how much does he have in his 401(k)? To avoid the tyranny of the visual, you need to kick-start your responsible prefrontal cortex by asking yourself, What's my goal in a relationship? That can divert you from those short-term, erotic visions.

HOW YOUR NOSE TRIGGERS AN ERECTION

There's a direct connection between the olfactory bulb, at the top of your nose, and the septal area, the arousal center of your brain. When cells in your

SEX MYTHS

You've heard the loose talk. Here's how it stacks up with reality

Men reach their sexual peak at 18, and women reach theirs at 28.

True. With regard to their supply of sexual hormones, at least. Testosterone peaks at age 18 in men; women's estrogen hits its high point in their mid-20s. "But peak hormones don't mean peak sexual performance," says Marc Goldstein, MD, a professor of reproductive medicine and urology at Cornell University's Weill Medical College. So feel free to try for a personal best—at any age.

Semen is low-carb.

False. "Semen is mostly fruit sugar [fructose] and enzymes—not low-carb," says Dr. Goldstein. Which finally explains why there's no Oral Sex Diet.

Masturbation yields the strongest orgasm.

True. But it's not a hard-and-fast rule, as it were. "It depends on the individual," says Jon L. Pryor, MD, a professor of urologic surgery at the University of Minnesota. "For some it does, but for others, there's nothing that beats good ol' intercourse."

The average erection measures 8 inches.

False. Relax, Shorty. It's closer to 6.

No penis is too large or too small for any vagina.

True. But perception still wins the game in the end. "I was once at a dinner meeting with seven other sex doctors—six men and one woman," says Dr. Pryor. "The men all agreed that size doesn't matter. The woman looked at us and said, 'Think what you want. Size matters.' We all left dejected."

Oysters make you horny.

False. *You* make you horny. "There is no scientific evidence that oysters increase libido," says Dr. Pryor. "But there may be a placebo effect, so if it works, great!"

nose are stimulated, they send signals to your libido (and hers) to stand up and pay attention. You know what smells turn you on; the evidence is obvious. As for her, a study at the University of California at Berkeley found that women become aroused when exposed to a chemical called 4.16-androstadien-3-one (AND). The good news? AND occurs naturally in men's sweat, hair, and skin. Take her someplace cold on your date—the favorite jacket or sweater you'll conveniently have on hand to lend her should be loaded with the stuff.

WHY YOU (SOMETIMES) LOSE YOUR ERECTION DURING SEX

Maybe little Willie is nervous during his big moment onstage. Performance anxiety is about the fear of being judged or not living up to expectations. The

Green M&M's make you horny.

False. Unless they do. Then it's true. Isn't the mind wonderful?

Men think about sex every 7 seconds.

False. That number is tossed around a lot, but the truth is that only 23 percent of men claim to fantasize frequently. But maybe the rest are just too distracted to check the clock.

Cutting out broccoli will make your semen taste better.

True. Semen is naturally bitter, and eating broccoli and drinking coffee can make it worse. A ray of hope for the Oral Sex Diet!

Having sex before an important event—the big game, the critical presentation—can ruin your performance in the event.

False. Swiss researchers performed stress tests on people 2 and 10 hours after the subjects had had sex and found that by 10 hours, the participants were fully recovered. There was only a small dip in performance 2 hours after sex.

Having sex in water (swimming pool, hot tub, shower) will kill sperm.

True. Some of your swimmers may die, but it isn't an effective method of birth control, according to Dr. Pryor. Though a hot tub can overheat your testicles and kill sperm, there should be plenty left for the egg hunt.

You can become addicted to Web porn.

True. But the risk is low. Only 1 percent of all people who check out Internet porn will become addicted. If you're sporting a ring, be careful: Thirty-eight percent of addicts are married.

body is programmed to see anxiety as a threat, and the nervous system sets up the fight-or-flight response, sending out chemicals to protect us: Your heart races, muscles tense, and blood is shunted from your hands, feet, and penis to the large muscles of the shoulders and hips so you can fight or run away. That's not such a good strategy in bed, however.

WHY ROBERT PALMER WAS RIGHT, YOU REALLY CAN BE ADDICTED TO LOVE

As with obsessive-compulsive disorder, love decreases brain levels of serotonin, the neurotransmitter responsible for mood and flexibility. Low serotonin means you can get stuck on ideas; you become obsessed. Which is just fine, unless she suddenly dumps you. That's when the short supply of serotonin makes you vulnerable to depression. In extreme cases, the serotonin shortage can trigger obsessive behaviors, such as exhibiting extreme jealousy or even stalking. To get those serotonin levels back up before the police come, try exercising more, eating more carbs, and generally distracting your lonesome thoughts. (Road trip!) All of them will boost your serotonin levels.

WHY TOUCHING HER STRENGTHENS YOUR BOND

Oxytocin is your brain's love juice—the bonding and attachment hormone. When you feel connected, empathic, in love, the oxytocin jets are spurting. Women have naturally higher levels of this chemical: It boosts nonsexual bonding between a mother and newborn, and it's responsible for putting babies to sleep after they nurse. Though both men and women secrete an extra jolt of oxytocin during orgasm, we men go through a 500 percent surge—which explains our special talent for falling asleep immediately after sex. If she complains that she doesn't feel close enough, ask for her help readjusting your oxytocin levels.

AM I NORMAL?

When I hear about a flasher or groper or peeping Tom, I'm almost sympathetic. If I had just a few more loose wires in my brain, that could be me. How warped is that?
Sebastian K., Venice, California

Actually, it's pretty normal. Most of us have twisted thoughts from time to time: flashing, sex with animals, voyeurism. But we don't act on these ideas because that brain wiring is properly connected. When some men go through the early stages of dementia, they start acting badly. As their brains deteriorate, the lid comes off of the twisted thoughts. Avoid damaging your brain with drugs, alcohol, and headbanging, and the lid stays on.

AM I NORMAL?

I got turned on when my teenage daughter's friends were running around in their pajamas during a sleepover. Should I have myself locked away?
Mike C., Upper Darby, Pennsylvania

Young, fertile teenage girls can be very appealing. It's innate . . . and dangerous. When those feelings are aroused, go for a walk, do the dishes, get out of the house. One of the worst things your daughter can experience is your sexual interest in one of her friends. Think about the look on her face when she catches you staring at her friend's developing chest. She'll feel dirty every time she talks to you for the next 6 months.

WHY WOMEN ARE MOST OFTEN THE DUMPERS, AND MEN THE DUMPEES

Women have greater access to the more negative right side of the brain, one of the reasons they suffer from depression twice as much as men. The right hemisphere also allows women to see the gestalt, or big picture, of relationships, so they tend to know before men do when a relationship is not working out.

WHEN THE THRILL IS GONE, WHERE IT WENT

Dopamine and PEA—your powerful attraction chemicals—are strong stuff. But, as with any high, it can't last. Intense feelings of euphoria and obsession start to wane. You again wonder what's been going on in the NFL or whether you should get together with your buddies. As you come down off the hard stuff, you may actually go through withdrawal, missing the high of the attraction stage.

HOW TO GET THE LOVE BUZZ BACK

You have a choice to make. Either you go right out and chase that high (and some comely tail) again, or you settle into the longer-term buzz of a committed relationship. Oxytocin and serotonin are your two best chemical friends for the drive toward your 25th wedding anniversary. They're not as exciting to the brain as the attraction chemicals, but they have longer-lasting effects. So you can trade the dizzying high for a sustainable one. Of course, if you're really smart, you can inject the hot stuff back into any love relationship. Take her away on a trip, spoil her rotten with La Perla lingerie, send her flowers with a dirty note attached, and the little dopamine chemicals come back out and play. Just like the night you met her.

WHAT MAKES THAT WANDERING EYE WANDER

Blame vasopressin. This hormone is involved in regulating sexual persistence, assertiveness, dominance, and territorial marking. And men have lots of it, naturally. In male voles (night-loving rodents, which probably describes you perfectly), the levels of vasopressin seem to make the difference between stay-at-home dads and one-night-stand artists. Your hormone levels are probably set at the genetics factory, but the more you give in to vasopressin, the more of it you produce. It's your choice.

SHOULD YOU STAY OR SHOULD YOU GO?

Only your prefrontal cortex knows for sure. Men who have healthy activity in their PFCs have greater empathy, can focus for longer periods of time, and tend to make better husbands. Men who have overactive PFCs tend to be obsessive, oppositional, and argumentative. This can turn them into major chick repellents. Likewise, men who have low activity in the PFC tend to be impulsive (more vulnerable to affairs), easily distracted (lousier at listening), easily bored (more "business" trips to Vegas), and constantly scamming for that attraction high (more given to looking for love in all the wrong places). To keep your PFC firing on all cylinders, protect it from injury, which can come from using too much alcohol, nicotine, or caffeine. Better still, exercise your PFC by setting goals and following through on them.

WHY THE GUYS IN THE BAND GET LUCKY

In a study in Finland, eight male volunteers underwent brain scans while they were having orgasms. (Must have been a fun study.) Overall bloodflow in the brain decreased during orgasm, but it skyrocketed in the right prefrontal cortex—as it does in creative people (like musicians) when they do their creative thing. Now, exactly why did you give up those guitar lessons?

WHY SHE CRIES OUT "OH GOD!" WHEN SHE'S HAVING AN ORGASM

It almost certainly doesn't have anything to do with you. In addition to its duties as an orgasm assistant, the right hemisphere has also been called the

AM I NORMAL?

I have measured my penis. Sick, or sane?
Steve F., Brooklyn, New York

So who hasn't? We all want to know how we measure up. In fact, men practically come out of the womb competing for our place in the world. Just don't waste much time on it. There are other, more important measures of your manhood.

AM I NORMAL?

I think about having sex with my boss. On her desk. But I don't even really like her. What gives?
Martin S., Birmingham, Alabama

You may be having an issue with a woman in power. Your fantasy suggests that you want to show her who's boss. And if you use sex to dominate, you have other problems. Big ones, in fact. Time for the shrink.

"God" area of the brain. When scientists stimulate the right hemisphere, their subjects have more religious or spiritual experiences. So it's not too much of a leap to guess that when she moans "Oh, God" in the throes of sexual ecstasy, she may be connecting pleasure to a deeper spiritual place in her brain. Music and dancing can jump-start the right hemisphere, which means the nuns at your high school were right to discourage it.

WHY HER ORGASMS ARE LIKE PAXIL, ONLY MUCH MORE FUN

Sexual climax has an antidepressant effect. Orgasms cause intense activity in the deep emotional parts of the brain, which then settle down when the sex is over. Antidepressants calm the same part of the brain. This calming effect may be why people who regularly have sex experience less depression.

WHY ORAL SEX IS ALSO LIKE PAXIL: IT WORKS BETTER IF SHE SWALLOWS

Prostaglandins, fatty acids found in semen, are absorbed by the vagina and may have a role in modulating female hormones and moods. I also feel duty-bound to report that women who perform oral sex on their mates are less likely to suffer from preeclampsia, a condition that causes a dangerous spike in women's blood pressure during pregnancy. Plus, sperm carries TGFbeta, a molecule that can boost the activities of her natural killer cells, which attack the rogue cells that give rise to tumors. Don't make her beg. Offer.

WHY FOOT MASSAGE IS FOREPLAY

When you rub the arch of her right foot, you affect her about 30 inches higher, and a little to the left. The foot-sensation area of the brain is next door to the clitoral (and penile) region, which may be a big reason that women are so focused on shoes—yours and hers. Carrie Bradshaw was on again, off again with any number of men, but her Manolos endured. And perhaps now we

AM I NORMAL?

I just got engaged . . . and I just had a one-night fling with a girl I work with. Is my marriage doomed?
Lester J., Portsmouth, New Hampshire

It's a bad sign. Being faithful doesn't get easier once you're married. So decide: Is your fiancée the one, or not? If not, cut it off. A bad marriage can cost half your net worth and much of your time with your future kids. Maybe your workmate was doing you a favor.

know why Imelda sought solace in 1,060 pairs of shoes. But even if you're not a Filipino dictator, you can make this work for you. "There are 36,000 nerve endings in the foot," says Kathleen Miller-Read, a massage therapist and spokeswoman for the American Massage Therapy Association. "By exploring these, you can find sore spots all over the body." If your girlfriend has her feet crammed in high heels all day, she's bound to have aching toes and a sore back. Use your thumb and forefinger to gently pull, twist, and rub below her toes.

For her back, focus on the heel of her foot, moving your knuckles in a circular motion all over the heel. She'll let you know when it's working.

WHERE YOUR SEXUAL KINKS COME FROM

Weird sexual fetishes or fantasies are brain symptoms. They fall into the category of impulsive-compulsive disorders: impulsive when you can't control the behavior and compulsive when, even though you may want to, you can't stop. A person who's prone to voyeurism, exhibitionism, bestiality, transvestism, S and M, or infantilism (deriving sexual pleasure from being treated like a baby) often has too much activity in the emotional parts of the brain, as we see in people who have obsessive-compulsive disorders, and too little

AM I NORMAL?

When I was in Vegas, I visited a cathouse. Does this make me a terrible husband?
Vincent F., Phoenix

It may be a sign that trouble is brewing. Once you step outside of your marital bounds, it's easier to do it again. And again. What's your goal, ultimately? A little fun, or a lasting marriage? If you're looking for long-term bliss, get better control over your impulses.

activity in the PFC, or judgment center. A study of 26 men with unusual sexual fantasies found that using medications to balance these two areas of the brain gave the men significant relief. But then, so did wearing an adult diaper and being handed a rattle. You can't tell with some people.

HOW TO STOP SEXUAL HANG-UPS FROM TAKING OVER YOUR LIFE
Even though men are programmed to look at beautiful women and populate the earth, the human brain, especially the prefrontal cortex, has evolved to the point where, with proper training, we can be thoughtful, goal oriented, and focused on our families. You are not a rodent, doomed to follow the pattern of hormone receptors in your brain. Ask yourself, What are my goals for my relationships? Stay focused on loving and protecting the people in your life, and it's mind over what really matters.

The *Men's Health* "Head Check" and "Am I Normal?" columnist, Daniel G. Amen, MD, is a psychiatrist and the author of *Healing Anxiety and Depression.*

Trigger Happy

Premature ejaculation doesn't have to mean a premature end
to your sex life. Use these strategies and ye shall, ahem, overcome

By Ian Kerner, PhD

Ultimately, it was the "stop-start" method that pushed my fiancée, Tara, over the edge. What with so much stopping and so little starting, not to mention all my various instructions—"Slow down, easy, easy, okay, go ahead, stop, I said stop!"—she finally blurted out, "Jesus, are we having sex or parking a car?"

As she jumped out of bed and reached for her clothes, I pleaded, "Wait. . . . You can't just get up and go—"

"Why not? That's what you do every time we have sex."

I stammered and said something about lasting 10 seconds—2 more than last month. She said something about menopause and how maybe we'd be able to have sex for a whole minute by then.

"I'm so sick and tired of saying, 'It's okay, really,' every time we have sex," she yelled. "It's not okay! This is your problem, not mine. And if you don't get it figured out by the time I get back from Hong Kong, the engagement is off!"

THE SEX LIFE OF A "PREEMIE"

Premature ejaculation (PE) has been, without a doubt, the single greatest factor in the formation of my character. Whenever someone asks me why I pursued a PhD in clinical sexology and became a sex therapist, I always say it's because of my struggles with PE and the years of quiet desperation I endured.

I still remember when my college girlfriend first went on the Pill. I was terrified. Until then, a condom lined with lidocaine (a numbing agent that rendered me barely able to feel my penis) had been my first line of defense. The sex wasn't pleasurable, but at least it wasn't totally humiliating. Now, however—could I go it alone? The first time we made ungloved love, I was overwhelmed by the sensations: the slippery warmth, the wetness of being inside her. It felt so amazing; I wanted desperately to savor the experience. But it was out of my control. On my very first thrust, I went in, but I didn't make it out. And as I lay on top of her—defeated, depleted—I cried. I wanted to make love like a man, but I was a little boy, incapable of controlling my bodily functions.

I considered PE my tragic downfall and believed myself cursed with an Achilles penis. Today, at least I know I'm not alone. Indeed, whenever I see a commercial for Viagra or one of its new competitors, I get ticked off: *Why isn't the media talking about PE?* According to urologists Andrew McCullough, MD, of the New York University School of Medicine, and James Barada, MD, of the Albany Medical College, PE is the number one sexual-health problem afflicting men, and it's *three times* more common than erectile dysfunction (ED). Estimates vary, but 20 percent to 30 percent of men suffer from PE, and those figures are based on self-reported studies.

What do women say? Nearly two-thirds of them have had sex with a man who experienced premature ejaculation, according to a recent survey of 900 women conducted by MensHealth.com and *Cosmopolitan* magazine. PE strikes men of all ages, and the condition affects virtually all men at some time in their lives. Dr. McCullough and Dr. Barada surveyed more than 1,100 men with PE and found that those men report less satisfaction and more anxiety about their sexual relationships. It can wreck their confidence and cause them to avoid new relationships.

A NEW LEVEL OF MATURITY

But what if premature ejaculation isn't a curse after all, but simply "survival of the fastest"? According to Mark Jeffrey Noble, MD, a consultant to the Cleveland Clinic Glickman Urological Institute, "One might find some logical sense, from an evolutionary point of view, to the idea that males who can ejaculate rapidly would be more likely to succeed in fertilizing a female than those males who require prolonged stimulation to reach climax." So in

WHERE'S THE LITTLE BLUE PE PILL?

When Viagra hit the scene, I was an early adherent. I hoped it would help my premature ejaculation, but while the little blue pill did promote a rush of blood to my genitals, it didn't prevent the rush back out. So, for all you "preemies" out there thinking that Viagra may be your golden ticket, think again: It may give you a bonus second erection, but it won't cure your problem. Even the medical and scientific communities freely admit that Viagra is not effective for treating PE, which is why the race is on for a viable PE drug.

The answer may be SSRIs—antidepressants like Paxil, Prozac, and Zoloft—which have a potential side effect: delayed ejaculation. Many doctors prescribe them in low doses to treat PE, but the reason the dosage is low is that SSRIs have another side effect: loss of desire, and sometimes even erectile disorder. How ironic is that? A man struggles with PE all his life, goes on a drug to deal with it, and now can't even get it up.

Still, any future PE pill will likely be based on some form of SSRI. In fact, Johnson & Johnson and Alza Corporation are hoping that dapoxetine, a drug similar to antidepressants, will be the first PE drug to market. The drug—which modulates serotonin levels in the brain and nervous system and has been shown to help with PE—has been submitted for FDA approval and soon may be available with a prescription.

that sense, maybe PE isn't a sexual dysfunction at all; it's a completely normal way of functioning, based on male physiology. That's why we should stop calling it "premature" ejaculation and come up with a new, more accurate

SIX STEPS TO BEAT PE

No torture. Just lots of sex

Men, you *can* last longer. For years, I silently battled premature ejaculation and test-drove every bizarre remedy I stumbled upon. Follow these exercises that finally worked for me.

Master masturbation. Masturbate with a woman's orgasm in mind, not your own. In other words, take your time: Work up to 15 minutes. Bring yourself close to the point of no return, but don't let yourself ejaculate until time is up.

Squeeze. If you're overheating during masturbation or sex, stop and squeeze right below the head of your penis. Apply firm pressure with your thumb and forefinger and focus your pressure on the urethra—the tube running along the underside of the penis. The squeeze technique, developed by those icons of sex therapy, Masters and Johnson, pushes blood out of the penis and momentarily decreases sexual tension and represses the ejaculatory response.

Pinpoint ejaculatory inevitability. Masters and Johnson broke the process of sexual response into four phases: excitement, plateau, orgasm, and resolution. It's the plateau and orgasm phases we're most concerned with, as most men crash through the former, straight into the latter. The trick is to slow down and recognize that there's a spectrum of feelings throughout the process of sexual response and to recognize your own point of ejaculatory inevitability. Rate your sexual excitement on a scale of 1 to 10. Try keeping yourself at 7.

Sexercise. Do your Kegels. A Kegel is an exercise that helps tighten the pubococcygeal (PC) muscles of the pelvic floor. Both men and women have them, and you can become familiar with the muscle group by cutting off the flow of urine and then starting and stopping repeatedly. (Begin with a full bladder.) Once you have the exercise down, practice your Kegels anywhere: at your desk, behind the wheel. Tighten your PC muscles and hold for a count of 10. Stronger PC muscles will help you exercise ejaculatory control when you approach the point of inevitability.

Press, don't thrust. Tease her, taunt her: Press the head of your penis into her clitoral head. Linger in her vaginal entrance, where the most sensitive nerve endings are. When you do have intercourse, focus on small, shallow movements that penetrate the first 2 to 3 inches of her vaginal canal. Press your penis against her G-spot. You'll last longer if you're not thrusting vigorously.

Show a little courtesy. Ladies first, gentlemen—and I'm talking about more than just holding the door open. Keep your woman happy. Women have an innate capacity to experience multiple orgasms. When you help her to her first one, it relieves you of some of the pressure to please and the psychological anxiety that feeds into PE. Use your fingers; use your mouth.

term: "immature ejaculation." Because, frankly, that's what it is: an immature way of doing things that largely stems from the way we're taught, or rather, not taught, to masturbate in childhood.

Most young men, fearing discovery, masturbate furtively and quickly, unwittingly exploiting, and simultaneously hard-coding, their natural propensity to rapidly achieve gratification. Weight lifters talk about "muscle memory." I believe that premature ejaculators experience "penis memory." No wonder the pioneering sex researcher Alfred Kinsey observed in his book *Sexual Behavior in the Human Male* that the average man can maintain penetrative thrusting for only about 2 minutes. (However, *Cosmo* readers said the average guy lasts 10 to 15 minutes.) We've trained ourselves to ejaculate quickly, and we need to relearn the process of sexual response in order to last longer.

THE TRIED AND UNTRUE

At first, like any overexcited teenager, I dealt with PE in the usual ways: masturbating before going out on dates (which helps but becomes less effective as you get older and require more downtime between erections); downing beers; and donning double, even triple, condoms. I even tried to delay orgasm in the heat of the moment by distracting myself with baseball statistics or images of dead people, and let me tell you, thinking about corpses during sex: definite mood killer.

Later, I graduated to herbal remedies, topical ointments, and miracle creams advertised in the backs of porn magazines. On one occasion, my little experiments led to an acid burn of my penis in the men's room of a Japanese restaurant.

In yet another doomed effort, I put the Errol Flynn method to the test: a dab of cocaine on the tip of the penis. The matinee idol once explained that it could be helpful "if you're quick on the trigger." But it didn't work for me, and I doubt it really worked for Flynn. He claimed to have slept with more than 13,000 women in his lifetime. Now, how the hell are you going to do that without being a premature ejaculator?

TOO LITTLE, TOO SOON

The day Tara left for Hong Kong—giving me 3 weeks to shape up or clear out—I spiraled to an all-time low. In a desperate attempt to keep that ring on her finger, I tried every type of radical therapy. There was biofeedback treatment, in which an electrode was inserted where I least wanted it, and I was encouraged to engage in an activity once thought to cause blindness in teenagers; self-hypnosis tapes that lulled me into such a deep trance with its sounds of water being stopped and started that I woke up soaked in my own urine; and a session with a German "masturbation specialist" who sternly observed and critiqued my methods of self-pleasure, all the while keeping

WHAT SHE THINKS:
WHEN A MAN COMES TOO SOON

By Nicole Beland, *MH* Girl Next Door

Whenever I hear a friend complain that a man lost it long before her clitoris registered so much as a tingle, I think it must be payback for all those nights back in high school. Back then, a boy would practically wear a hole through the crotch of his Levi's dry-humping our hips—and still we wouldn't lay a finger on his goods. We'd just send the poor soul off into the night with an aching penis. Do we mind now that the tables are turned? Did you mind walking away from a date with balls that felt ready to explode?

Of course we mind. It's frustrating. It's uncomfortable. It's disappointing. And, contrary to popular belief, women are *not* into sex just for the freakin' intimacy. But, as you did then, we tolerate orgasmless sex because, well, there's always a next time. We just take a deep breath and put it out of our minds—which, as it happens, adult women are much more capable of than teenage boys.

As long as you don't come too soon too much of the time, it's not such a big deal. We might complain about it to our friends once in a while, but we won't hold a grudge or start daydreaming about screwing Sting for days on end. Wait—we will daydream about screwing Sting—but it won't have anything to do with your sexual longevity.

What I don't understand is why, after enjoying the last waves of his orgasm, every man doesn't then offer a woman his still-firm fingers to finish the job. It would be proper etiquette in that situation, no? Maybe your partner will gently push your hand away and say she just wants to cuddle, but it's more likely that she'll writhe against your fingers in ecstasy. And she won't be the only one who benefits. Putting in that extra effort for the sake of fully satisfying your woman is the kind of thing that inspires future oral sex for you. You scratch our itch, we'll scratch yours.

---

time with a metronome and commanding me to "stop, start, squeeze; stop, start, squeeze!"

By the time Tara returned, I was a complete mess. I didn't know if I was coming or going. Or, for that matter, if I'd be coming and then going after having sex with her.

And as she emerged from the shower and came to bed, naked and glistening, I was so nervous, I didn't just prematurely ejaculate, I spontaneously ejaculated.

True to her word, she left me. Don't feel bad. I don't. (Anymore.) And don't worry, either. According to the MensHealth.com and *Cosmopolitan* survey, less than 10 percent of women say they've dumped a guy because he was quick on the draw.

Shortly after we broke up, I began working with a really terrific sex therapist. I overcame PE within a few months, using six techniques. (See "Six Steps to Beat PE," on page 108.) I was so transformed, and inspired, that I decided to change careers and go down that path myself. Today, I continue to learn about PE, which is exactly what the late sex therapist Helen Singer Kaplan, MD, PhD, advised in what is still considered the definitive guide to conquering PE, titled *How to Overcome Premature Ejaculation.* My struggles led me not only to my passion in life—writing about sex and helping others through sex therapy—but to the love of my life, as well: my wife, Lisa. My short story finally found a happy ending.

Ian Kerner, PhD, is a certified clinical sexologist and the author of *She Comes First: The Thinking Man's Guide to Pleasuring a Woman.*

NEED TO KNOW

Voice Your Opinion

How'd she sound on the phone? It matters. A voice holds clues to a person's body shape and sexual behavior, reports a study of 149 college students, published in *Evolution and Human Behavior*. Researchers recorded the voices of participants counting from one to 10 (that's hot!) and had members of the opposite sex rate each voice. Voices rated attractive belonged to people who were attractive physically (measured by waist-to-hip and shoulder-to-hip ratios) and who had the most sexual experience. So don't turn a deaf ear to a blind date. "At least have a phone conversation before you commit to a date with someone," says study author Susan Hughes, PhD, an assistant professor of psychology at Vassar College. Researchers couldn't pinpoint what makes a voice attractive, but the raters tended to agree on who sounded sexy.

First Date Food

Eat a small bowl of whole-wheat pasta 1 to 2 hours before a first date. A study in *Alcoholism: Clinical & Experimental Research* shows that taking in complex carbohydrates can help boost the brain's levels of the hormone serotonin. Impaired serotonin levels can lead to depression, anxiety, and aggression—none of which is attractive on a date. Just don't skip the meat sauce: Red meat might be the best thing that's happened to sex since the Internet. Inside that rib eye lies a treasure trove of the amino acid arginine, which helps the body form nitric oxides—compounds that relax the blood vessels in a manner similar to that of erectile-augmentation pills on the market today. "Arginine is a potent natural Viagra. It will get your gear up and running," says Eric Braverman, PhD, author of *Male Sexual Fitness*. "And beef is the best place to find it. It has the highest levels of naturally occurring arginine around."

Don't Be Cross

Hoping to attract a woman? Don't cross your arms. Open body language will help her think of you as attractive, potent, and active.

Make an Impression

Want to get the girl? Ace your opener. A new study shows that first impressions form faster and last longer than previously thought. University of Minnesota at Duluth students were paired off on the first day of school and talked for 3, 6, or 10 minutes. Evidence at 9 weeks showed that initial judgments guided how intimate relationships became, no matter how short the conversation. Study author Michael Sunnafrank, PhD, says a negative first impression is tough to shake because the person may avoid you. To have her at hello, note her eye color. "That forces you to focus on her eyes," says Tom Jaffee, founder of www.8minutedating.com, "and eye contact is the way people really connect."

Hold Your Liquor

Feeling frisky after two beers? Your date might not be. Men tend to become three times as uninhibited as women with the same blood alcohol levels, according to a University of Kentucky study. Men in the study reported more stimulation and arousal after three quick drinks, while women reported more sedation, says author Mark Fillmore, PhD, a professor of psychology. It might be a gender difference in how the body processes alcohol. Regardless, Fillmore says, "If you're drinking more than one drink an hour, you're going to run into behavioral problems. That's how long it takes for the body to metabolize one drink."

Pillow Talk

Don't skip the are-you-on-the-Pill chat with a new lover. The number of sexually active women who did not use contraception rose to 7.4 percent in 2002, from 5.2 percent in 1995, according to recently released data from a National

NUMBER OF MEN WHO SAY THEY WERE DRUNK WHEN THEY LOST THEIR VIRGINITY: 1 in 6

NUMBER OF MEN WHO SAY A FEW DRINKS MAKE SEX BETTER: 1 in 2

Center for Health Statistics survey of 7,600 women. This means at least 4.6 million sexually active women out there are at risk of unplanned pregnancy. Declining insurance coverage and the cost of the Pill are possible explanations for the increase.

Good Morning, Gorgeous

You've got a woman in your bed. Good work, lad. But is she there in the morning? "Chances are, if a woman hasn't tiptoed out in the middle of the night, she's looking for more than a one-night stand," says Yvonne K. Fulbright, author of *The Hot Guide to Safer Sex.* If you want to ensure repeat visits, treat her well at this point. She's vulnerable and doesn't want to seem trampy, Fulbright says. Know what to expect and what to do (and not do).

Don't stiff her. "A guy who wakes up with an erection is having a physical reaction that I had nothing to do with," says Jane, 34. Your bedmate may not be as ready as you are. "Women usually don't wake up aroused," says Ian Kerner, PhD, a certified clinical sexologist and the author of *She Comes First: The Thinking Man's Guide to Pleasuring a Woman.* "Cuddle, or whisper in her ear about a sexy dream you had." She can be convinced.

Clean up. She'll want to freshen up. Offer her a spare toothbrush. Or arrive bedside with bagels and coffee, Fulbright suggests. Your friend won't forget the sweet gesture, and it'll ease bad-breath concerns.

Compliment her. She'll be thinking about her smeared mascara and tangled hair. You're going to tell her she looks great. "When I woke up with my boyfriend after we first slept together," says Elaine, 30, "he told me how amazing my skin looked in the sunlight. He scored points for making me feel less self-conscious."

Think ahead. "The most impressive thing a guy can do after we've slept together the first time is ask me out for another date before I leave," says Jenny, 26. That will erase any worries that you think she's easy, Fulbright says, and it'll up the odds you'll share sheets again.

PERCENTAGE OF MEN WHO WOULD RATHER FIND THE LOVE OF THEIR LIFE THAN HAVE 6 MONTHS OF AMAZING SEX: 92

NUMBER OF MEN WHO SECRETLY LOVE THEIR PLATONIC GIRLFRIEND: 1 in 3

Slow down. Keep things relaxed. "Give her a pair of boxers and a T-shirt to lounge around in," Fulbright advises. Bene, 28, appreciates a guy who shares the newspaper: "Reading the paper over breakfast signals comfort and casualness, not to mention intellect." Remember, you are still technically on a date, so let her know you enjoy her company by not rushing her out the door.

Meet the Mrs.

How's this for defeating a purpose: Dating lots of women can hurt your search for The One. When prospects are plentiful, "at the first sign of a problem, men often move on to the next woman, instead of dealing with it," says Susan Campbell, PhD, author of *Truth in Dating*. Do these scenarios sound familiar?

You're setting a budget. "If you go into a date thinking, 'How much money am I going to spend?' you're sabotaging yourself," says Bill Horst, of the William Ashley agency, a matchmaking service.

The fix: It's fine to go on free or cheap dates. Taking money out of the equation will put the emphasis back on getting to know someone new.

You have no female friends. According to Dr. Campbell, people often meet through mutual friends. So you need platonic girlfriends for dating PR.

The fix: If you're not into her, kindly say you just want to be friends. If you impress her with your charm, you might meet her hot roommate.

You screen her calls. "If you stop communicating with someone for no clear reason, there's a problem," Dr. Campbell says. This is often a prelude to eternal bachelorhood.

The fix: Practice dealing with difficult situations, advises Dr. Campbell. If a woman says something that turns you off, tell her why it bothered you.

Fertile Ground

Scientists have conclusive evidence that women tend to have more sex when they're most fertile. A study in the journal *Human Reproduction* shows that frequency of intercourse goes up 26 percent during the 6 most fertile days of her cycle—the day of ovulation and the 5 days beforehand. Women in the study submitted daily urine samples and kept a sex diary, giving scientific proof to a long-suspected theory. Fair warning: "A woman is more likely to take a chance during the times when she can conceive," says study author Allen Wilcox, MD, PhD, a senior investigator at the National Institute of Environmental Health Science. The spike occurs either because a woman's libido increases during fertility or because the man is reacting to her pheromones—hormonally controlled odors. It's also thought that sex itself may stimulate ovulation.

WHAT'S NEW

Hard and Fast

Researchers are trying to develop an erection drug that targets your brain. Abbott Laboratories in Illinois says the investigational drug—probably 6 years from market—induces erections by stimulating the D4 dopamine receptor, an area of the brain responsible for arousal. Viagra and Cialis, by comparison, increase bloodflow to the penis by relaxing certain smooth muscles. The new drug could be an option for men who take nitrates for heart conditions but can't risk the potential blood-pressure drops associated with other erection drugs.

No Baby on Board

New research into an enzyme that affects sperm movement might be the key to someday developing a male contraceptive. Sperm in mice bred without the enzyme, GAPDS, can't swim toward the egg. Men have a similar enzyme, and researchers say a drug to disable it may work as a contraceptive. It'd be "sort of like making a smart bomb—it's only going to affect the sperm," says Louis De Paolo, PhD, associate chief of the reproductive-sciences branch at the National Institutes of Health. But it'll take at least a decade to get such a drug to market.

Another potential contraceptive being researched is a combination of injections and implants. The treatment uses the hormone progestin to stop sperm production. But this reduces testosterone levels and may cause lethargy and sexual dysfunction, so testosterone implants are required. When the treatment was studied with 55 couples, none of the women got pregnant, and the only side effect the men reported was increased sexual desire. Sounds like a win-win, but you'll have to wait several more years.

PERCENTAGE OF YOUNG ADULTS WHO ALWAYS ASK THEIR POTENTIAL PARTNERS ABOUT STDS BEFORE HAVING SEX: 51

Invisible Protection

British researchers are entering a phase 3 clinical trial of two gels that act like invisible condoms, blocking attachment of HIV to the surface of human cells. If effective, the gels could be available in 2008. Meanwhile, at the University of Massachusetts Medical School, scientists are beginning trials of a new HIV vaccine that incorporates DNA and viral proteins to stimulate the body's immune response. It could be available within 5 years.

STD Cures

Someday there may be a topical cream that cures genital warts. At least 50 percent of sexually active men and women will acquire genital human papillomavirus (HPV) at some point in their lives, the CDC says. Penn State University College of Medicine researchers have discovered a molecular therapy that shuts down HPV-induced warts, according to the journal *Gene Therapy*. A commercial product—which could also work on other kinds of HPV infections—is at least 4 years away, researchers say.

In related news, a Harvard Medical School researcher has developed a genital-herpes vaccine that is moving toward clinical testing in humans. In tests on mice and guinea pigs, the vaccine, d15-29, outperformed two other vaccines, one of which has already been tested in humans. Unlike other vaccines, d15-29 is a live, mutant strain of the herpes virus but is missing genes needed to replicate in the body.

THE COST OF . . .

. . . Not Having Enough Sex

If you're not getting some action at least twice a week, it can cost you in some surprising ways. Show this to your wife or girlfriend so she knows that it's in the interest of your health—and your wallet. Otherwise, going without for 3 months could cost you both.

You need . . .	Research shows . . .	You pay . . .
A gym membership to compensate for lack of physical activity	Having sex increases testosterone levels, which helps you gain muscle mass and lose fat.	$232
A couple of sick days	Men who have intercourse twice a week have 30 percent higher levels of immunoglobulin A, which boosts the immune system.	$284
Pay-per-view porn and a subscription to *Playboy*	Beggars can't be choosers.	$54
A daily aspirin, glass of wine, and fish-oil tablet, for heart health	Sex two or more times a week cuts a man's risk of heart attack or stroke in half. You'll need to take care of your ticker.	$321.86
A massage a couple of times a month for back pain	Sex causes the hormone oxytocin to surge to five times the normal level; this releases endorphins, which alleviate pain.	$739
To surprise your wife with a romantic weekend	Desperate times call for desperate measures. Hotel sex is a given.	$1,695.68
Couples therapy	Lack of intimacy can lead to marital problems and even divorce.	$1,500
TOTAL		**$4,826.54**

FAST FIXES

No penis is an island.

Or so J. Stephen Jones, MD, FACS, a urologist with the Cleveland Clinic, likes to tell his patients. If your penis were an island, it would be tempting to think of it as a hot spot in the Caribbean—calm and tranquil during the day, throbbing with activity at night, and the destination of a constant rotation of half-naked coeds.

As much as that sounds like paradise, Dr. Jones says a more precise urological/geographical parallel would be your penis as peninsula—a bodily extension that shares a supply of blood, oxygen, and nutrients with all your other organs. Unfortunately, that means if a natural disaster strikes the mainland, it's likely to affect any protruding landmasses, too.

"ED stands not only for erectile dysfunction but also for 'early diagnosis,' because you can use ED to predict a heart attack, potentially by years. Arterial damage from cardiovascular disease affects the small arteries in the penis first," says Christopher Steidle, MD, a clinical associate professor of urology at the Indiana University medical center at Fort Wayne. That's one reason it's a mistake to let Levitra, Viagra, and Cialis lull you into an I'll-fix-it-when-it-breaks mindset.

Here's another: Take steps to safeguard your sex life now and you may never need to pop the little blue pill. Or any other shade of erection aid. In other words, follow these hard-and-fast fixes, and every woman who visits your peninsula will leave with a smile.

PREVENTION

1. Spread blackberry jam on your toast. Dark fruits like blackberries, bilberries, and elderberries contain high levels of anthocyanins, ultrapowerful antioxidants that could act as erection insurance. Quick science lesson: Your penis's ability to rise and shine depends, in part, on the availability of nitric oxide, a blood-vessel-dilating chemical. When too many free radicals are present in your bloodstream, nitric oxide goes down—and so does your penis. Enter anthocyanins. These potent antioxidants attack free radicals before they have the chance to lower nitric oxide levels.

Here's proof of their power: Indiana University researchers found that arteries treated with anthocyanins retained high levels of nitric oxide even after being flooded with free radicals. "Antioxidants help keep free radicals under control so nitric oxide can do its thing," says David Bell, PhD, the lead study author. And that "thing" is giving your penis the blood it needs to turn excitement into an erection.

2. Shut down the smokestack. If you still light up, you've probably accepted your increased risk of heart disease, stroke, lung cancer, and bladder cancer. But how about dying young and impotent? A study published in the *Journal of Urology* found that smoking causes arterial damage that doubles a man's risk of total erectile dysfunction. The good news: "If men quit in their 50s or earlier, we can usually reverse the damage," says Andre Guay, MD, director of the Lahey Clinic for Sexual Function, in Massachusetts.

When Dr. Guay measured nighttime erections in 10 impotent smokers (average age 49), he noted a 40 percent improvement after just 1 smoke-free day. Swap the cancer sticks for fish sticks: Researchers at the Royal College of Surgeons in Ireland discovered that taurine, an amino acid found in fish, helps heal smoke-damaged arteries.

3. Become a more sensitive guy. Everyone knows stress is a psychological cold shower. But untamed tension also works in a more insidious way— by releasing epinephrine, a type of adrenaline that goes straight to your arteries and slowly wreaks havoc there. "Stress in the long term can contribute to hardening of the arteries," says Dr. Jones, who is author of *Overcoming Impotence: A Leading Urologist Tells You Everything You Need to Know.* In a great medical irony, being hard in the arteries can leave you soft in the shorts. The fix: Force yourself to concentrate on each of your five senses for a few minutes every day—focus on the feel of the steering wheel in your hands, the sound of the engine revving to redline, the sight of the hot brunette in the next car . . . "Obsessing on stressful thoughts will increase your epinephrine," says Jay Winner, MD, author of *Stress Management Made Simple.* "On the other hand, if you focus on current sensations, it decreases the epinephrine and ultimately improves your ability to have an erection."

4. Stop sawing wood. Snoring can sabotage a night of sex, and not just because it's difficult to engage in foreplay when you've been banished to the couch. "All of your tissue needs oxygen to be healthy, and the penile tissue is especially sensitive," says Dr. Jones. "When you snore, you're depriving your tissue of that oxygen."

That said, don't waste your money on OTC snore stoppers; research by the US Air Force shows that these products aren't effective. Instead, try placing bricks under the bedposts at the head of the bed. "Snoring has a lot to do with gravity," says Phillip Westerbrook, MD, founder of the sleep-disorders center at the Mayo Clinic. "If you elevate the torso without bending the neck, it changes the effect of gravity on the soft tissues of the throat."

5. Eat a dark-chocolate Dove Bar. It's erection medicine. Dark chocolate contains epicatechins, flavonoids that trigger the release of dilating chemicals in the inner, or endothelial, layer of the arteries. How much should you munch? A University of California at San Francisco study shows that those who ate a 1.6-ounce dark-chocolate bar each day increased their blood-vessel dilation by more than 10 percent. While the study wasn't done specifically on erectile tissues, anything that benefits your body's endothelial system will likely benefit your erections, since the penis is made up largely of endothelial surfaces. "Keeping those surfaces healthy is crucial to good arterial flow," says Kevin McVary, MD, a professor of urology at Northwestern University. Look for dark chocolate that bears the CocoaPro logo on the label. This symbol is a visible sign that the candy bar you're buying is chock-full of flavonoids.

TREATMENT

6. Lower your estrogen levels. Go to MensHealth.com and search on "BMI" to find our body-mass index (BMI) calculator. Now enter your vital stats. If your BMI comes in close to or over 25, you may be carrying just enough lard to drag down your erections. "We know that heavier men convert testosterone to estrogen and that a lower level of testosterone and a higher level of estrogen are not good for erectile function," says Larry Lipshultz, MD, a *Men's Health* advisor and chief of male reproductive medicine and surgery at Baylor College of Medicine.

Fortunately, even moderate weight loss can rid you of excess estrogen and put your sex life back on track. A study published in the *Journal of the American Medical Association* found that one-third of clinically obese men—BMI 30 or higher—with erectile dysfunction showed improvement after losing 10 percent of their body weight.

7. Get pricked. If you think the problem is that you, well, think too much, see an acupuncturist. The results of a study published in the *International Journal of Impotence Research* suggest that acupuncture can help treat psychologically induced erectile dysfunction. (Relax—the prick points are all in your back.) "In psychogenic erectile dysfunction, the patient has trouble with the balance of his sympathetic and parasympathetic nervous systems," says Paul Engelhardt, MD, the study author. "Traditional Chinese medicine tries to restore that balance."

AMONG 5,000 SINGLES POLLED, PERCENTAGE WHO SAID THEY WOULD NOT DATE SOMEONE WHO SMOKED: 45

Sure, it sounds like using feng shui for your underwear drawer, but it works—64 percent of the men who underwent 6 weeks of acupuncture regained sexual function and needed no further treatment.

8. Build a stronger floor. Go figure—one of the best ways to treat erectile dysfunction is to pretend that you suffer from premature ejaculation. British researchers discovered that the traditional treatment for a hair trigger—strengthening the pelvic-floor muscles—is also a remedy for men who can't point their pistols. In the study of 55 impotent men, 40 percent of those who practiced pelvic-floor exercises, aka Kegels, every day for 6 months regained normal sexual function. Apparently, the same muscle contraction that's used to stop peeing midstream can also prevent blood from escaping during an erection. "Unless they have severe back pain, all men with ED can perform pelvic-floor exercises," says Grace Dorey, PhD, the study author.

Here's the workout plan: Contract and relax your pelvic muscles anytime you're sitting, although you can also do them lying down. Work up to doing 18 contractions daily, holding each one for 10 seconds.

9. Open your medicine cabinet. And make a list of all the prescription pills you're popping. "A lot of prescription drugs may be associated with sexual dysfunction," says R. Taylor Segraves, MD, PhD, coauthor of *Sexual Pharmacology*. One possible culprit is the cholesterol-lowering drug simvastatin, brand name Zocor. If you think a drug you're taking could be causing a problem, talk to your doctor. Often a similar pill, sans side effects, is on the market.

Still not able to defy gravity? At this point, it makes sense to consider taking Viagra, Cialis, or Levitra to stimulate bloodflow to the penis, says Dr. Steidle. And who knows what miracles might happen once you prime the pump a few times? "What a lot of men find is that once they restart these medications, they may not need them for every episode of sexual activity— they may need them only now and then," he says. Similarly, if you suffer from performance anxiety, a drug-fueled romp or two may be just what the urologist ordered to restore confidence. And while all three erection medications have the power to prevent you from psyching yourself out in the sack, Cialis's ability to work for up to 36 hours may provide an advantage, says Julian Slowinski, PsyD, an assistant professor of psychiatry at the University of Pennsylvania School of Medicine. "This gives a man and his partner a lot of time over the weekend to be more spontaneous."

PERCENTAGE OF AMERICAN ADULTS WHO SLEEP IN THE NUDE: 10

OUR FINAL ANSWERS

Social Calls

How do you meet people—friends and dates—when you're new in town?

—T.H., Deland, Florida

Our mantra: Initiate—and then deliver. Invite your neighbors over for a few burgers. Organize the company softball team. Start a football pool. Be a leader. New friends—and potential dates—will follow.

Single Questions

What's the least obvious way to find out if a girl is in a relationship?

—J.H., Erie, Pennsylvania

If you don't like asking her straight up, try some recon. The best questions to ask are ones about traveling. It's simple, nonthreatening, and easy to talk about. If you ask where she's been, why she likes it, where she wants to go, and when she's going, you can certainly sneak in a question that starts with "who."

Moving On

Since my divorce, I can't stay in a relationship for more than 3 or 4 months before I start to feel smothered. Can you explain this?

—P.N., Mobile, Alabama

It sounds as though you're still mourning the loss of your marriage. Even if you were the one who initiated the breakup, divorce can, in some ways, be worse than dealing with death because your ex is around to remind you of the loss. Men often feel unbalanced for years because their limbic system, or the emotional part of the brain, is kicked into overdrive. If your relationships still feel unnatural after 2 years or so, you may need some counseling.

Checks and Balance

How can I politely insist on paying when a woman offers to pick up the tab during a date?

—C.L., Bend, Oregon

If you're not smooth enough to tell the waiter beforehand, then do this: When she puts her hand on the check, you put your hand on hers and say, "No, I'll get this." If she protests, then thank her and tell her she can get the coffee—or that you'll take her up on dinner next week. That way, you'll be buying yourself three things: a good meal, her respect . . . and another date.

Be Complimentary

What's the best thing to compliment a woman on?

—T.J., Burlington, Vermont

Her character. Sure, every woman wants to know that she looks terrific, says Hara Estroff Marano, editor-at-large of *Psychology Today* magazine and author of *Why Doesn't Anybody Like Me?* "But letting her know she has a positive impact on the world around her shows you value more than her looks." Which means if you tell her, "You're the most generous person I know," chances are tonight you'll find out just how generous she really can be.

See into the Future

How can you tell what a woman will look like in 10, 20, or 30 years?

—G.P., Hollywood, Florida

First, the obligatory tirade against shallowness: "Marry a girl because you love her, not based on how she looks," says Seth Matarasso, MD, a San Francisco dermatologist. "Because I'm telling you right now—looks fade." Okay, moving on. Ask yourself the following:

- **Who's her daddy?** Check out Mom and Dad. "Look at the hair, the skin, the wrinkles," says Dr. Matarasso. "Do they have that turkey-wattle neck? Do their earlobes sag?" Genetic tags are the biggest indicators of future aging.

- **Where's she from?** If she grew up in beautiful Seattle, Washington, she'll be less leathery than if she was raised in Death Valley. Most sun damage happens in our childhood years, when we didn't have jobs to keep us indoors.
- **Where is she now?** "Is she living where the air is clear and there are no pollutants? Those have a direct effect on your skin," says Dr. Matarasso.
- **What does she do?** High-stress jobs can add just as many years to a woman's face as to any man's. And if she works in a bar or another environment where she's exposed to secondhand smoke? It'll have the same drying, damaging effect as if she were a smoker herself.

The Gift of Love

How can I buy my girlfriend lingerie without making it look as if it's for my benefit?

—C.O., Atlanta

Think about what she wants to wear, not what you want her to wear, says Tracey Cox, author of *Supersex* and *Superflirt*. Black or red lace looks "tarty," she says, so stick with soft pink or white, or your girlfriend's favorite color. Cox also recommends Calvin Klein's boy shorts and tank tops—clingy and revealing, but not trashy. Second rule: With lingerie, always go high-end. "You can't go wrong with anything from Myla or Agent Provocateur," says Cox. "And package it beautifully. Even the most expensive lingerie looks cheap if it's not put in a box with a ribbon."

Be a Kiss Up

What's the best place to kiss a woman—besides her lips—to turn her on?

—S.G., Daytona Beach, Florida

On her earlobes. It's sensual, surprisingly intimate, and aimed at one of her body's main erogenous zones, says Linda De Villers, PhD, a California sex therapist and author of *Love Skills: A Fun, Upbeat Guide to Sex-cessful Relationships*. "There are men and women who can actually climax just from stimulation of the earlobes." Wow. Eargasms!

Rules of Engagement

My girlfriend constantly brings up marriage. Even though I want to marry her, I feel like I'm part of an agenda. And when I do propose, there will be no surprise. Can I fix this?

—A.F., Elmhurst, Illinois

The issue here isn't about getting married; it's about who has the power. If you do want to marry her, then tell her you'll ask when you're ready. But if she doesn't leave you alone now, she'll nag you about the bills, about watching too much sports, you name it. And once you're hitched, it's not like you can just switch the channel whenever you feel like it, if you know what we mean.

The Quicker, the Better

I love quickies. How can I get my wife to feel the same?

—J.K., Taos, New Mexico

Anticipation, friend. Bring up the topic when you're clothed, during the day, maybe in a phone call or e-mail. Reassure her that the quickie "won't become a replacement for romance or those long nights of passionate sex," says Tara Roth Madden, author of *Romance on the Run: Five Minutes of Quality Sex for Busy Couples*. Then let her simmer. When you finally do get your moment alone? Use a few of those precious minutes stimulating her manually to help her reach orgasm as fast as you will. Most important, says Madden: "Keep it hot, quick, and naughty."

FOUR

SAVE YOUR SICK DAYS

READ UP ON IT

The Truth Hurts

What your doctor isn't telling you could hurt you

By Kate Dailey

Before the feds brought him down in 1996, Edwin Kokes had a pretty good racket. Mr. Kokes convinced people that he was, in fact, Dr. Kokes and had cured thousands of AIDS and cancer patients. He encouraged folks to stop their medications and buy his potions instead, including one called M-Bone. Its special ingredient? Sulfuric acid.

Even if your doctor isn't intentionally out to mislead you, we'll bet a box of tongue depressors that he is keeping you in the dark about certain things. These are secrets that can save you money, time, perhaps even your life. Here's what you'll never hear—unless you know what to ask.

"YOU DON'T NEED THIS TEST."

To cover their own butts, doctors sometimes take a needless trip up yours. A nationwide sample of "surveillance" colonoscopies—follow-up procedures that are done after polyps are removed—found that up to 50 percent of doctors recommended these tests unnecessarily. This better-safe-than-sorry mindset helps protect docs against lawsuits, and it isn't limited to colonoscopies.

Get the truth: Watch out for the most overused procedures: MRIs and CT scans, echocardiograms, and stress tests all scored high in a survey of health insurers. "When your doctor does make a recommendation that seems aggressive, ask why and where you fit in the assigned guidelines," says Pauline Mysliwiec, MD, author of the colonoscopy study.

"THIS WILL COST YOU."

From deductibles to drugs, chances are your doctor visit will run more than insurance will pay. But while a *Journal of the American Medical Association* study showed that 79 percent of doctors think it's important to tell patients about these costs, only 35 percent actually do inform them. Their excuse? Many physicians say they're under time pressure and don't know how much patients are spending on out-of-pocket costs, says G. Caleb Alexander, MD, the study author.

Get the truth: Tell 'em where it hurts—in your wallet. If you mention medical expenses, most doctors will work with you to lower them, says Dr. Alexander. For instance, they can prescribe a 3-month instead of a 1-month supply of a drug to help you save on the co-pay. Or they can look at the prescriptions you take and services you receive, such as physical therapy, and reevaluate which can be used on an as-needed basis.

"THIS PILL IS BASICALLY A PLACEBO."

Not the sugar-filled kind, but equally ineffective. "Forty percent of patients with colds who go to a doctor get an antibiotic," says Howard Brody, MD, PhD, director of the Center for Ethics and Humanities in the Life Sciences at Michigan State University. "Doctors can spend 15 minutes explaining why the patient doesn't need medicine or take 1 minute to write a prescription."

Get the truth: Tell your doctor you hope your problem isn't so serious that it calls for medication. This lets him know you're not looking for a bottle of pills, and it may make him more likely to discuss other treatments, says Dr. Brody. And watch out if your diagnosis is sinusitis. Because it can be either bacterial or viral in nature, sinusitis is one of the top conditions for which antibiotics are unnecessarily prescribed. Ask for a C-reactive protein rapid test—a raised CRP level signals a bacterial infection. Danish researchers recently showed that doctors who gave the test to sinusitis patients prescribed 20 percent fewer antibiotics than their peers who skipped the test.

"I'M TRAINED TO FIX PROBLEMS, NOT PREVENT THEM."

Whoever first said "An apple a day keeps the doctor away" probably wasn't an MD. A study published in the *American Journal of Clinical Nutrition* found that only one in six doctors preaches to patients about nutrition's role in preventing disease, while Colorado researchers found that just 28 percent of doctors mention exercise. "We tend to be more pharmacologically oriented because of our MD training," says Mark Houston, MD, author of *What Your Doctor May Not Tell You about Hypertension*.

Get the truth: If your doctor doesn't have answers about nutrition or exercise, he knows someone who does. Many general practitioners collaborate with nutritionists and trainers who help treat patients with lifestyle-influenced health problems, such as type-2 diabetes. Ask for a referral to discuss basic preventive health strategies.

"DON'T JOIN THIS CLINICAL TRIAL."

Doctors can make $5,000 for each patient they recruit to a clinical trial, so you might receive advice colored by the promise of a kickback. That's scary, especially since clinical trials are crapshoots. "The drug is being tested precisely because we don't know how it will work," says Steven Joffe, MD, a researcher at the Dana Farber Cancer Institute. Plus, you could end up with a placebo and not see any benefits.

Get the truth: Start by asking your doctor to explain the proven benefits of existing medications versus the potential advantages of the trial drug. Next, find out more about the study in question at www.clinicaltrials.gov, a clearinghouse for information on trials. Go ahead and e-mail the organizer of the trial and ask if the organization is offering physicians any recruiting "incentives." If so, mention this to your doctor and ask if he still stands by his recommendation.

"THERE'S A CHEAPER PILL."

If a brand-name pill costs $1.50 and an equally effective generic costs 5 cents, why would anyone prescribe the pill with the $1.45 markup? "Most doctors aren't prescribing generic medicines because there are rewards to be had from the pharmaceutical industry," says Evan Levine, MD, author of *What Your Doctor Won't (or Can't) Tell You.* Federal law prohibits companies from blatantly compensating doctors, but there are loopholes. "They take the doctors to an expensive dinner or a strip club and bill it as a 'teaching' seminar," says Dr. Levine.

Get the truth: Ask and you shall receive. Doctors will acquiesce to patients who demand a generic drug (if one is available; about 40 percent of drugs on the market have generics). Don't worry about quality: Generics have to have the same potency and active ingredients as their brand-name brothers. Note: Beware of free samples. While they can save you a few bucks

UNSEAL YOUR MEDICAL RECORDS
Your doctor is writing your body's biography. Have you read it?

Until 2003, there was one secret your doctor didn't have to divulge: the contents of your medical records. But thanks to the Health Insurance Portability and Accountability Act (HIPAA), federal law now guarantees your right to review the file. It's easy to do: Ask your doctor's office for a record-release form, fill it out, and submit it. If you're still empty-handed after 30 days, tell your doctor you plan to file a HIPAA complaint. (Find the form at www.hhs.gov/ocr/howtofileprivacy.pdf.)

Once you have the file, check for accuracy—particularly the sections on family risk factors, food and drug allergies, and conditions treated by other doctors. Caught a mistake or an omission? Ask your doctor to make the changes in the original file. If he balks, put your request in writing. He can refuse (in writing), but the HIPAA provisions state that you have the right to have your objection noted in the file. You also have the right to find a new doctor.

PERCENTAGE OF ADULTS WHO LIE OR STRETCH THE TRUTH WHEN THEY TALK TO THEIR DOCTORS:

Almost 50

in the short term, they can also get you started on an expensive drug with no generic equivalent.

"I'LL PUSH SURGERY, EVEN IF THAT'S NOT THE BEST TREATMENT."

"In many doctors' value systems, surgery is the default," says Christopher Meyers, PhD, head of the Kegley Institute of Ethics at California State University. But research indicates that surgery often isn't the best option. A Baylor College of Medicine study showed that chronic knee pain didn't change after surgery, while another study found that taking a wait-and-see strategy with hernias may be as effective as going under the knife.

Get the truth: "You should always ask what the alternatives are to surgery, including an approach that most physicians feel uncomfortable offering: to do nothing," says Dr. Meyers. If your doc is still scalpel-happy, get a second opinion from a doctor of osteopathy. "These doctors take a more holistic approach and are familiar with newer literature that promotes different strategies," says Dr. Houston.

"I'VE BEEN DISCIPLINED BY MY STATE'S MEDICAL BOARD."

Doctors won't post signs on their office doors to inform you of their disciplinary infractions or the number of malpractice claims they've paid. But you need to know.

Get the truth: Go to www.docboard.org—a site with a searchable database from 15 state medical boards and links to the databases of the other 36 boards. If a practitioner you like has been reprimanded, ask him about it. "If a doctor refuses to answer questions about his background or about whether or not patients have sued him, you should run," says Dan Fee, a spokesman for Citizens for Fairness, a coalition of patients'-rights groups.

The 20 Best Meds for Men

Hidden somewhere in the endless aisles of over-the-counter drugs are the pills that will put an end to what ails you

By Ted Spiker

Talk to any user and he'll say the same thing: If you want the inside dope on drugs, you go to a drug dealer. And there's none more knowledgeable about over-the-counter drugs than a pharmacist. Well, there is actually a source that's even smarter: 3,000 pharmacists.

That's how many pill professors the American Pharmacists Association (APhA) contacted for its newest *Pharmacist Survey of OTC Products*. The APhA survey asked randomly selected pharmacists from across the country to name their picks for "best med" in dozens of different categories, based on both their clinical knowledge and their practical experience. From antihistamines to acid reducers, itch creams to cough medicines, an ace reliever was chosen for every ailment.

What follows is our exclusive look at the best of the best—a selection of the OTC drugs that men need most, plus our own advice on how to get even more out of every medication. And because there's often no need to spend the bucks on a brand name when a generic will do just as well, we've also provided a cheat sheet to cheap health. So go ahead and clip it out—then open your medicine cabinet and clean it out.

ALLERGIES, MULTISYMPTOM

Claritin
Why it won: One dose helps halt hay fever and other sinus allergies for up to 24 hours, compared with 4 to 6 hours for other antihistamines. Claritin is also the first OTC antihistamine that's truly nonsedating, which means you can finally operate heavy machinery (or just drive your car). One caution: Claritin-D also contains a decongesting stimulant, so take it at least 4 hours before bedtime, says Paul Doering, an OTC expert at the University of Florida.

Maximize it: Anytime you're anticipating an allergy attack, pop a preemptive Claritin. "This will make your reaction less severe than if you treated it after it began," says Steven Pray, PhD, DPH, a professor of nonprescription drugs at Southwestern Oklahoma State University.

Generic equivalent: Loratadine, 10 milligrams

ALLERGIES, SKIN

Benadryl
Why it won: Whether it's the burning of a bee sting or the itching of poison ivy, skin reactions involve more histamine—the body's allergy-causing

chemical—than sinus flare-ups do. As a result, Claritin may not cut it. "There's some proof that nonsedating antihistamines have an effect on these allergic reactions, but not as great an effect as Benadryl has," says Linda Krypel, PharmD, an associate professor of pharmacy at Drake University. But that power comes at a price: Benadryl can make you too drowsy to drive a forklift.

Maximize it: Mix Benadryl with Tagamet, an OTC antacid. Tagamet contains cimetidine, what's known as an H2 histamine blocker. Benadryl uses an H1 blocker. "Take an H1 and an H2 together, and you get more relief because they affect different parts of your allergy-response system," says Michael Roizen, MD, a professor of medicine at SUNY Upstate Medical University.

Generic equivalent: Diphenhydramine, 25 milligrams

ATHLETE'S FOOT

Lamisil AT

Why it won: "Lamisil AT inhibits an essential component of the fungal cell membrane," says Donnie Calhoun, RPh, owner of Golden Spring Pharmacy in Alabama. "Without its membrane, the fungus will die." In an Australian study of 217 people with athlete's foot, researchers found that terbinafine, the active ingredient in Lamisil, cleared up the symptoms in 85 percent of people who used it for 1 week, compared with only 56 percent of those applying clotrimazole.

Maximize it: Use Lamisil until your symptoms disappear—and then keep on using it for an additional 2 weeks. "Fungal infections are extremely hard to get rid of," says Dr. Krypel. "Even if you can alleviate the symptoms, the underlying infection may still be there."

Generic equivalent: None

BURNS

Solarcaine

Why it won: It uses the king of the 'caines: benzocaine. In addition to being a powerful painkiller, benzocaine may be safer than other anesthetics, such as lidocaine, which can cause side effects, such as blurry vision and dizziness, says Michael Oszko, PharmD, an associate professor at the University of Kansas. Another advantage of Solarcaine is that it's an aerosol; creams can hurt when you rub them in.

Maximize it: Before you reach for the benzocaine fire extinguisher, run your scorched skin under cool water to prevent blistering (don't use cold water because the drastic temperature change can aggravate your epidermis). "The heat starts breaking down the proteins on the surface of your skin, and that's what results in your blister," says Dr. Pray.

Generic equivalent: Benzocaine, 20 percent

CONCOCTIONS FOR KIDS

Five more picks to fill out the family pharmacy

Like movies and music, over-the-counter meds come with different ratings for adults and children. Usually, a product with "pediatric" in the name is alcohol free and contains a low dose of the active ingredient. But, as with adult versions, their individual efficacy varies. Here's what pharmacists would feel confident giving their own kids.

Cough: Robitussin Pediatric Cough
Congestion: PediaCare Decongestion Drops
Diaper Rash: A + D Original Ointment
Multisymptom Cold and Flu: Children's Dimetapp
Pain and Fever: Children's Tylenol

CANKER SORES

Zilactin Cold Sore Gel

Why it won: It leads a double life at the drugstore. Though Zilactin is marketed as a cold-sore medication, pharmacists chose it for canker sores because it contains benzyl alcohol. Like a liquid bandage, benzyl alcohol temporarily seals off the sore, protecting it from the irritation caused by eating. Minimize the irritation and you'll maximize the healing.

Maximize it: Apply Zilactin about 10 minutes before dining in order to create the strongest possible seal, says Doering.

Generic equivalent: Benzyl alcohol, 10 percent

CARDIAC CARE

Ecotrin

Why it won: It may save your life and your stomach, thanks to a special slow-disintegration coating. "Ecotrin is dissolved and absorbed in the intestines, so it lessens the risk of stomach irritation that can occur with regular aspirin," says Janet Engle, PharmD, a clinical professor of pharmacy practice at the University of Illinois at Chicago College of Pharmacy. But use only the low-strength version—81 milligrams. A study in the journal *Circulation* determined that taking less than 100 milligrams aspirin daily offers the greatest level of cardiovascular protection and that higher doses may actually increase the risk of heart trouble.

Maximize it: Don't take Ecotrin and drop an antacid at the same time. The antacid will cause the special coating to dissolve too quickly, turning Ecotrin into regular aspirin.

Generic equivalent: Enteric coated aspirin

COLD SORES

Abreva

Why it won: Since cold sores are caused by the herpes virus, the only way to knock the disease back into dormancy is with an antiviral medication. Abreva is presently the only topical antiviral treatment available over the counter. A study of 737 people published in the *Journal of the American Academy of Dermatology* found that docosanol (the active ingredient in Abreva) helped heal cold sores 19 percent faster than a placebo (in 4 days instead of almost 5).

Maximize it: After you apply Abreva, rub on a little Zilactin Cold Sore Gel. The Zilactin will help relieve the pain while the Abreva fights the virus, says Dr. Pray. Otherwise, it's hands off. The cold sore will heal faster the less you touch it, says Dr. Roizen, because when you touch it, you can reinfect it with the virus.

Generic equivalent: None

FOREIGN PHARMACEUTICALS

No prescription necessary, but a passport would help

Despite the mind-numbing number of OTC medications lining drugstore shelves, there are actually a few medicines missing. They're the nonprescription products that, for a variety of reasons, aren't currently sold in the United States. The sampling below shows what becoming well traveled can do for your well-being.*

Ambroxol: If if ever shows up stateside, this cough medicine could give Robitussin a run for its money. In a recent *Men's Health*–sponsored survey of cough suppressants sold in Germany, independent pharmacists found that Ambroxol halted the hacking better than other OTC medicines. A German company has a US patent on Ambroxol-coated cough drops. Available in most of Europe.

Ebastine: It's a more powerful off switch for allergies than Claritin, according to US clinical trials. "It was an extremely effective drug," says Paul Ratner, MD, a trial researcher. "But the company chose not to seek FDA approval." One explanation: Ebastine would have had to begin its life as a prescription product at a time when Claritin's switch to OTC caused a spike in the co-pay for prescription antihistamines. Available in Finland and Sweden.

Topical ibuprofen: A recent study in the *Journal of Rheumatology* showed that 84 percent of people using topical ibuprofen felt relief from knee pain, compared with 40 percent of those using a placebo salve. Unfortunately, there isn't the demand to justify a supply. "Topicals are just more popular in places like Germany," says David Spangler, with the Consumer Health Products Association. Available in the United Kingdom, Canada, and most of Europe.

* It isn't exactly drug smuggling, but it is illegal to bring medicine—OTC or prescription—that isn't sold in the United States into the country.

CONGESTION, NASAL

Sudafed

Why it won: It's like nasal Drano. While most other decongestants only reduce sinus swelling, Sudafed also loosens the mucus, thanks to the inclusion of the expectorant guaifenesin. Pharmacists also point out that when Sudafed is combined with a spray decongestant, such as Afrin, it can prevent a person's ears from clogging up during air travel.

Maximize it: Take ibuprofen, too. A new study published in the *Annals of Allergy, Asthma & Immunology* showed that stuffed-up subjects who took ibuprofen with pseudoephedrine—the main ingredient in Sudafed—had 22 percent less congestion than those who took pseudoephedrine by itself.

Generic equivalent: Pseudoephedrine hydrochloride, 30 milligrams, and guaifenesin, 200 milligrams

COUGH

Robitussin

Why it won: This cough remedy edges ahead for what it doesn't contain as much as for what it does. Whether you choose Robitussin guaifenesin to loosen the mucus in a congested chest or Robitussin DM to also help quiet a cough, neither formula contains alcohol. "Alcohol swells bronchial tissues, which could make the cough worse," says Calhoun.

Maximize it: Take up drinking—water. "If your body's cells are hydrated, it will be easier for the medication to work at the receptor sites and provide relief," Calhoun says. "Proper hydration will help you get better faster."

Generic equivalent: Guaifenesin, 100 milligrams (Robitussin Guaifenesin); dextromethorphan hydrobromide, 10 milligrams, and guaifenesin, 100 milligrams (Robitussin DM)

CUTS AND MINOR WOUNDS

Neosporin

Why it won: Three reasons: bacitracin, neomycin, and polymyxin. A recent University of Virginia study showed that ointment containing this antibiotic trio eliminated 96 percent of bacteria in 6 hours, while a salve sans neomycin killed 14 percent. That said, if your gash or rash becomes more inflamed after you apply Neosporin, you may be allergic to neomycin. Instead, go with a double-antibiotic ointment, such as Polysporin.

Maximize it: Even the best bandages can become unstuck, allowing the Neosporin to rub off and the wound to dry out. (Moisture speeds healing time.) If the cut is in an inconspicuous place, Dr. Roizen suggests sealing it with a piece of Saran Wrap and two rubber bands instead. "Saran Wrap really protects the wound because it stays tightly pressed against your skin," he says.

Generic equivalent: Bacitracin zinc, 400 units; neomycin, 3.5 milligrams; and polymyxin B sulfate, 5,000 units

DIARRHEA

Imodium A-D

Why it won: Imodium A-D puts the reins on the runs by slowing down the movement of your intestines; other products focus only on decreasing "fluid production." However, if the cause of your distress is payback from a certain Aztec emperor, reach for Pepto-Bismol instead: The active ingredient, bismuth subsalicylate, can help kill off stomach bugs.

Maximize it: Drink a milk chaser. "Calcium increases your body's ability to slow the intestines," Dr. Roizen says. Down one glass of skim milk twice a day for the necessary 600 milligrams of calcium.

Generic equivalent: Loperamide, 2 milligrams

GAS

Gas-X

Why it won: Gas-X contains the ingredient proven to stop explosive gas leaks fast: simethicone. "It breaks the surface tension of small gas bubbles, helping them pass quickly through the body," says Dr. Krypel.

Maximize it: Besides altering what you eat—less soda and beans—change how you eat. Specifically, slow the heck down. You swallow more air when you eat quickly, thus increasing the number of gas-producing air bubbles in your system, says Dr. Pray.

Generic equivalent: Simethicone, 125 milligrams

HEADACHE

Regular Strength Tylenol

Why it won: Tylenol held a slight edge in a clinical cage match with Aleve. Research published in *Cephalalgia* showed that 37 percent of people who took 1,000 milligrams of acetaminophen saw their headaches disappear after 2 hours, compared with 32 percent of those who popped 375 milligrams of naproxen. However, if the pain is between your eyes, skip both meds and see a doctor. "In almost every case, this is a sinus infection with a sinus headache," says Dr. Pray.

Maximize it: Don't delay. "Most headaches are caused by vascular spasm—a tightening of blood vessels in your head—or the release of that spasm," says Dr. Roizen. "Take medication early and you can stop the spasm from reaching its worst level."

Generic equivalent: Acetaminophen, 325 milligrams

HEADACHE, MIGRAINE

Excedrin Migraine

Why it won: In addition to acetaminophen, it has the proven pain-busters aspirin and caffeine. In a recent study presented to the International Headache Society, researchers compared the equivalent of two Excedrin Migraine tablets with a prescription headache med. Their finding: Eighty-seven percent of people on the acetaminophen-aspirin-caffeine combination reported complete or partial symptom relief after 2 hours, versus only 75 percent of those given the prescription drug.

Maximize it: Make Excedrin's job easier. Researchers at the University of Miami determined that migraine sufferers who received two weekly 30-minute head massages reported decreases in headache pain.

Generic equivalent: Acetaminophen, 250 milligrams; aspirin, 250 milligrams; caffeine, 65 milligrams

HEARTBURN, ACUTE

Mylanta

Why it won: Mylanta combines two balms for the burn: aluminum hydroxide and magnesium hydroxide. "They work immediately, but their duration is short," says Dr. Oszko. Still, it's a longer reprieve than other antacids offer; University of Oklahoma researchers found that Mylanta's ingredients neutralized acid about 22 minutes longer than calcium-based products did.

Maximize it: Stick with liquid Mylanta. "If you take the tablet form, you have to chew it well and drink water to make sure it's absorbed," says Dr. Krypel. "With liquids, you're already there."

Generic equivalent: Aluminum hydroxide, 400 milligrams, and magnesium hydroxide, 400 milligrams

HEARTBURN, CHRONIC

Prilosec OTC

Why it won: It contains omeprazole, a chemical that can slow your stomach's acid pumps. Just one pill can decrease acid production, but a 2-week course is necessary for lasting relief; a new University of Michigan study showed that 43 percent of people on omeprazole for 2 weeks stayed heartburn free for 3 months.

Maximize it: As you're popping Prilosec, try dropping pounds. "Weight loss changes the angle of the esophagus," Dr. Roizen says. "A sharp angle makes it harder for the acid to come back up."

Generic equivalent: None

HEMORRHOIDS

Preparation H

Why it won: Hemorrhoids are just dilated blood vessels, which are best treated by chemicals called vasoconstrictors. Preparation H contains a vasoconstrictor—phenylephrine—while other brands have only anesthetics. Caution: If your hemorrhoids bleed or last more than a week, see a doctor.

Maximize it: Drink eight 8-ounce glasses of water and down 25 grams of fiber daily. The water and fiber will correct the cause of the hemorrhoids—straining too hard—as well as help promote healing, says Dr. Roizen. "It usually has an effect within a day."

Generic equivalent: Phenylephrine HCl, 0.25 percent

JOCK ITCH

Lotrimin AF

Why it won: The fungus in your Fruit of the Looms needs to be treated differently than the type between your toes. The combination of the warm, moist environment in your underwear and the ease with which you can scratch the itch ups the odds of a bacterial infection. Enter Lotrimin AF. In addition to fighting fungus, "the clotrimazole in Lotrimin may help prevent a secondary infection," Dr. Krypel says.

Maximize it: Buy the cream and rub it in well. "The skin protects the fungus, so you need to spend enough time rubbing it into the affected area," Dr. Krypel says.

Generic equivalent: Clotrimazole, 1 percent

JOINT PAIN

Advil

Why it won: Advil owes it all to ibuprofen. When French researchers recently studied 222 people with osteoarthritis, they noted that those who took 400 milligrams of ibuprofen had 23 percent more pain relief during the following 6 hours than those who swallowed 1,000 milligrams of acetaminophen. What's more, after 2 weeks of treatment, the people popping ibuprofen still reported less pain and stiffness.

Maximize it: Employ a pincer move: Use Advil to attack the pain from the inside and a heat wrap to hit it from your skin in. Wraps, like those made by ThermaCare, are better than ointments, says Dr. Pray, because they penetrate deeper and last longer (8 hours).

Generic equivalent: Ibuprofen, 200 milligrams

POISON IVY

Cortaid

Why it won: Steroids. Not the Jason Giambi variety, but a topical steroid called hydrocortisone, which helps relieve both the itching and the inflammation that are caused by an ivy attack. Other topical creams, such as Benadryl and Caladryl, work only to soothe the itch.

Maximize it: Soak in oats. Before you rub on the Cortaid, immerse your itch-afflicted area in a mix of warm water and colloidal oatmeal for at least 15 minutes. One Australian study showed that patients who were treated with colloidal oatmeal for minor burns reported less itching and needed less medicine than those treated with another anti-itch ointment.

Generic equivalent: Hydrocortisone, 1 percent

Who's Got Your Back?

We sample six back-pain treatments to find out which one will make your pain go away fastest—and for good

By Mike Zimmerman

Six a.m.: The pain just winks at first, barely a thumbtack in an acre-wide corkboard—until I roll out of bed and try to stand. Then agony blooms just north of my butt, locking every muscle up to my shoulder blades. I drop to one knee and whisper, "Oh, God." Nothing else to say, really, when your spine feels like it's just been ripped out of your flesh like a tab torn off a FedEx envelope. I think, "The kid. It had to be the kid." The previous evening, I had inadvertently turned my lower back into a fulcrum when I'd extended my arms and lifted my youngest son out of his high chair. I knew I'd tweaked something at the time, but it didn't hurt much. Not like this. This is voodoo-doll pain. Ex-girlfriend-plunging-an-ice-pick-into-a-handheld-Mikey pain.

Every morning, back pain erupts across the land. It's the second-most-common reason for missing work, behind the common cold. One in six American adults lives with back pain every day, according to a recent survey by the North American Spine Society. And those who aren't in agony at this moment probably will be in the future—the NASS estimates that 80 percent of all adults will experience back pain during their lives.

Of course, suffering on that scale doesn't go unnoticed by entrepreneurs. Type in "back pain" at Amazon and you see more than 800 results for self-help books on the topic. Google it, you get more than 21 million hits. (By comparison, "Jessica Simpson" nets a scant 3 million.) And that doesn't take into consideration all the back braces, heating pads, cooling packs, vibrating massagers, pillows, mattresses, and anything labeled "lumbar support" that are available to the afflicted. Nor does it account for the doctors, orthopedists, spine surgeons, chiropractors, acupuncturists, physical therapists, and psychotherapists out there treating said afflicted. Various surveys peg the annual budget for back pain at anywhere from $28 billion to $80 billion a year. But never mind the money. For all of us ice-picked people, it comes down to just one question: Does anything out there really work?

To find out, I decided to become the Odysseus of lumbago and explore all the major back-pain treatments. I'd find answers to the classic questions: Is acupuncture effective? Is my mind making the pain worse (and can it make it better)? Are chiropractors the spinal saviors they claim to be? And would my wife allow me to visit a geisha for some world-class back walking? (Quick answer: No.) My goal was twofold: to uncover the secret to easing my ache and to find a lasting way to keep it from creeping back.

THE FAMILY DOCTOR

Stephen Shore has been my go-to MD for several years, but I've never visited him for anything other than an annual physical. He just smiles and nods knowingly when I tell him about my back; a fit man in his 50s, he's heard thousands of back-pain complaints over the years. "The spine is a tricky machine," he says. "Standing straight, a man can deadlift 900 pounds. But lift a baby the wrong way and *bam.*"

Dr. Shore pokes and prods to determine whether I have any numbness or weakness in my legs from the injury. I don't. He asks if the pain shoots down the back of my legs. It has, but not now. Do I have any loss of appetite or weight? No. Any loss of bladder or bowel control? Not since my wedding day. He has me bend forward. Bend back. Twist left, then right. It's uncomfortable, but I can do it all.

His diagnosis: a lumbar-sacral strain ("lumbar" meaning the bottom five vertebrae in my spine; "sacral" meaning sacrum, the bone between the lumbar and the tailbone). The worst of the pain has passed, so Dr. Shore doesn't prescribe anything other than Advil as needed. "We could stick a needle in there with some medicine," he says, "but you're improving, so I don't think you need it."

In the end, Dr. Shore sends me for an MRI to see what else is going on in my lumbar region, instructs me to use my legs as much as possible when

INSTANT SPINE SAVERS

Five quick tips for taking a load off

Short of a corset, there's nothing that will do more to give a back a break than these tips from Arnie Kander, PT, head physical therapist for the Detroit Pistons.

Check your mirror. It's easy to slouch on long car trips or tense up on stressful ones. Angle your rearview mirror just a little too high so that every time you check it, you remember to relax your shoulders and sit up straight.

Steal a towel. Sitting for long periods pummels the disks in your lower back. A rolled-up hand towel tucked between the small of your back and your chair or car seat will help take the pressure off. Keep one towel at your desk and one in the car.

Lose the laptop. It's designed for portability—and poor posture—because the keyboard is connected to the screen. If you can't work without one, use a detached keyboard, such as the Stowaway Bluetooth ($150, www.thinkoutside.com).

Know squat. Whenever you lift anything, think of Charlize Theron and say to yourself, *Nice stems.* This will help you remember to squat and lift with your legs and never, ever bend at the waist.

Take the time. Shortcuts brutalize backs. Take the extra time you need to correctly lift a shovelful of dirt or snow . . . to walk a message to a coworker instead of e-mailing it . . . to allow frequent breaks when hunched over a household project.

lifting, and he suggests I add core-strengthening exercises into my workouts (more on that later). Other than that, I should "move at whatever speed is comfortable."

A nurse calls a few days later with the MRI results. I have "degenerative disk disease and three small lumbar herniations." Holy crap, I think. Disk disease? She assures me that this is all normal and part of the "aging process." Aging process? I'm only 35.

The Verdict: Confusion. Do I have a lumbar-sacral strain or a disk problem? The only thing I know is that I hurt my back, it got a bit better, and the disks in my thirtysomething spine are degenerating as we speak. As for the treatment advice, trying to wait out the ache while popping Advil is what I usually do anyway, and I find it only somewhat effective.

But what if I had opted for the injection—a combination of lidocaine, an anesthetic, and Depo-Medrol, a long-acting steroid? It wouldn't have been practical, according to Robert H. Haralson III, MD, executive director of medical affairs for the American Academy of Orthopaedic Surgeons. For one thing, Depo-Medrol can take as long as 48 hours to kick in. Plus, he explains,

DO YOU NEED SURGERY?

Our spinal answers to your operation FAQs

What kind of doctor should I see? A spine surgeon. This can be either a neurosurgeon or an orthopedic surgeon who concentrates on backs and ideally has completed a fellowship in spine surgery, says David A. Ditsworth, MD, a neurosurgeon in Los Angeles. Either way, you want someone who does at least 100 spine operations a year, says Zoher Ghogawala, MD, a professor of neurosurgery at the Yale University School of Medicine. Start your search for a surgeon at www.spine-health.com.

What will he do? Take x-rays and an MRI and look for anything that may be inflaming nerves—misalignment, narrowing disks, bone growths called osteophytes, but especially a herniated disk. That would mean the rubbery nucleus of a disk is protruding through its fibrous casing, the annulus, possibly compressing a nerve.

How will he know if surgery is needed? "It's pretty obvious" in most cases, Dr. Ghogawala says—for instance, if a large piece of extruded disk is pressing on nerve endings and your pain is continual. If it's a slight herniation, he may suggest waiting to see if it subsides.

How serious is the operation? Spine surgery is always serious. But if just a small part of the nucleus protrudes, ask about less-invasive endoscopic surgery, in which the nucleus is trimmed through a tiny tube inserted between muscles.

How long will I be laid up? Dr. Ditsworth says he routinely has patients going home the day after endoscopic surgery. "Open" operations typically mean a night or two in the hospital, a return to work in a few weeks, and several months of rehab before resuming athletics.

"there's not much evidence that a onetime shot of Depo-Medrol is any better than just taking the oral anti-inflammatories."

All that said, your family doctor should still be the first stop. In some cases, back pain can signal a serious malady, such as kidney stones or even cancer. ("A slow, progressive onset suggests you may have a tumor," says Dr. Haralson. "Kidney-stone pain is severe and unrelenting.") Your GP is also a gateway doc, leading those with unremitting pain to various specialized tests and treatments, including pain medications, referrals to orthopedic surgeons, and prescriptions for physical therapy (the only way insurance will pay for PT in some states). Just understand that your GP is a jack-of-all-trades, not a spine specialist.

THE ACUPUNCTURIST

"Call me Feng."

I'll remember those three words for a long time. I first hear them in an exam room at a pain-management clinic on the Lower East Side of Manhattan. Ping Feng, LAC, is a fortyish Chinese acupuncturist who is 5-foot-3, a hundred pounds at most. Feng orders me to strip to my Skivvies and lie facedown on the exam table, which has one of those holes for my face, so I see nothing but tile floor.

"Afraid of needles?" she asks with a thick accent.

"Not yet," I reply.

She gives a little *heh heh.* "You not feel anything."

All I hear is a loud snap with each needle, like a rubber band hitting a steak. (Feng, I'd find out later, uses her fingers to snap the needles into skin. Others tap them in through a tube.) I don't feel most of the needles. The others, I do. The one she sticks in the middle of my back feels . . . like a needle stuck in the middle of my back. A few others aren't painful, just creepy. They strike nerves. The muscles quiver for a few seconds, then stop.

Feng sticks me 15 times. Near as I can tell, she inserts a pair along each hamstring, three or four in the top half of my butt, the rest in the bottom half of my back. I've been lying in the same position for 5 or 10 minutes, so I shift slightly. Feng's hand clamps on my arm. "No! Don't move!"

Okay, then.

"Now we start electricity," she says.

"Um, we start what?"

"Electricity through needles. Help relax muscles."

I hear soft plastic clicking, like untangling stereo wires. I'm dying to peek. She fusses with the needles, then flips a switch. I imagine my back and butt lighting up like an old electric subway map—*thrum, thrum, thrum* come the rhythmic shocks. Freaky.

"Okay," says Feng. "Don't move. Twenty minutes, I be back."

She turns off the light, switches on classical music somewhere near my head, and bolts. Sheesh. Twenty minutes. Can't move. *Thrum, thrum, thrum.* Man, that needle in the middle of my back hurts.

The Verdict: As I walk uptown afterward, my back does feel better. Loose. Practically pain free. Acupuncture works. In fact, many studies support its use specifically for back pain. "You can believe or not believe; it's still going to have the same effect," says Keith DeOrio, MD, *Men's Health*'s alternative-medicine advisor. "They've shown through electroencephalograph testing that an acupuncture needle actually changes brain waves."

Exactly how much acupuncture you need depends on the severity of your condition, Dr. DeOrio says. Most patients have lasting relief after three to six sessions. In other words, acupuncture isn't a once-and-done deal, which explains why 30 minutes into my bus ride home, that ice pick returns to my lower right lumbar. But I don't go back for additional sessions. Even without Feng's shock treatment, aka transcutaneous electrical nerve stimulation, a technique usually reserved for patients with more extreme pain, I found the whole process uncomfortable and unnerving. If you want to give it a try, you can find a licensed acupuncturist in your area at www.medicalacupuncture.org.

THE CHIROPRACTOR

The treatment table is so cool. It stands straight up, and I have to step into it face-first. Then, with a flip of a switch, the whole thing lowers on hydraulics till it's horizontal. The unspoken promise: After an adjustment, I'll rise as Darth Vader once did. Reborn. Alive.

We'll see.

First, Stephen Kulik, DC, a pleasant, dark-haired gentleman in his forties, reviews the MRI that I've brought to his office just up the road from where I live in Macungie, Pennsylvania. He also checks out the x-rays he has shot. He shows me the herniated disks on the MRI. Dark patches mark degeneration in the third, fourth, and fifth lumbar disks.

According to Dr. Kulik, my x-rays show a spine and pelvis out of whack. He draws a straight line in grease pencil from my sternum down through my pelvis, and I see where the alignment deviates off center by a quarter inch. "Your pelvis is torqued a bit there," he says. "We'll adjust you to get that back in line." He also points to more grease-pencil lines on a side-view x-ray. "See the angle of these vertebrae? They come together at a 33-degree angle and pinch the disk. We can open up that angle to give the disk some relief."

I take my first table ride. Dr. Kulik runs a thumb along my back, nudging vertebrae as he goes down my spine. Then he lifts the section of padding beneath my pelvis by about half an inch. Abruptly, he jerk-pushes down on my left buttock, and the pad snaps back into position. Again. A third time. No cracks.

He then puts both hands on the middle of my back and shoves forward as if trying to dislodge a piece of shrimp. My spine offers a lame click. Next, I lie on my right side with my left knee lifted halfway to my chest. "Relax and look at the ceiling," he says. I do, and I see a sign tacked there asking, "Have you told a friend about chiropractic today?" Then he leans into me and jerks. My spine lets loose a gratifying crack.

The table lifts me—Rise, Lord Vader!—and I'm done. "See you next Wednesday," Dr. Kulik says. My subsequent visits grow even shorter—3 minutes on the table, and out the door. After my second visit, I get a treatment schedule: three times a week for 4 weeks, then twice a week for 4 weeks, then once a week for 4 weeks.

The Verdict: Chiropractic is effective. After eight visits, my pain improves substantially, almost completely. But I'm told that to get lasting relief from chiropractic, you'll need to ask your doctor one simple question: "What's the plan?" says Tim Maggs, DC, a sports chiropractor who's cracked the backs of the New York Giants. There should be a conditioning element beyond the series of adjustments, otherwise you're doing nothing to prevent the bones from shifting back into their pain-producing position. "The thought that a pill, a shot, or an adjustment is going to keep an unconditioned person out of pain is illogical," he says. "Ultimately, you have to get back into shape." It's advice that I would hear again.

That's one reason I stop going to Dr. Kulik—there's been no mention of conditioning. The other reason: He wants me back for 24 visits over 12 weeks. No can do. My health insurance covers only 20 visits a year, not including a $20 co-pay for each one. I want to save some visits in case I hurt myself again.

THE PAIN BRAIN DOCTOR

The day I visit the Mind/Body Medical Institute in Boston, the city is paralyzed by nearly 4 feet of snow. My flight home is canceled.

It takes more than an hour to travel less than 5 miles from my hotel, so I'm late, and my back's barking. And let's top it off: I'm in town the week before the Super Bowl—an Eagles fan in an unholy land. It's enough to stress a guy out . . . which is exactly why I'm here.

Back pain—and the injury itself—gets all the press, says Ellen Slawsby, PhD, codirector of the chronic-pain program at the institute. However, the stress response we experience—elevated cortisol levels, increased blood pressure, tightly clenched muscles—actually makes the physical pain worse. She calls this "pain distress." Sometimes the distress can cause more pain than the physical injury.

Fortunately, just as we produce stress responses, "our bodies can produce a relaxation response," says Dr. Slawsby. "People just don't do it." The relaxation response reverses the effects of stress. Levels of cortisol and norepinephrine (a neurotransmitter that elevates heart rate) fall, while levels of nitric oxide, a blood-vessel-dilating chemical, jump.

Meditation is the quickest and easiest way to elicit a relaxation response, so Dr. Slawsby wants me to give it a shot. Her favorite advice to reluctant male meditators? "Humor me."

So we try it right there in her snowbound office. Dr. Slawsby speaks in a low, slow voice, methodical, repetitive (a critical element of meditation, she tells me later). "Your right hand feels warm," she says. "Your right hand feels heavy." She completes a series of similar statements for my right arm, then my left hand and arm, and both legs and feet. Shutting my eyes feels unnatural, so I zone on the industrial carpeting, a utilitarian combination of dull light and dark shades that soon becomes a flowing river of color. I'm in it, baby. She tells me to look up.

"How long was that?" I ask, blinking.

"About 20 minutes," she says.

Twenty? Felt like 5. I shift in my seat, trying to find the ice pick. It's there, but I have to search for it. I look at Dr. Slawsby and chuckle.

The Verdict: Useful. I try it again on the plane ride home. When I open my eyes, 20 minutes have evaporated. Whoa. I feel as if I've napped. Have I? I can't tell. But, no lie, the rest of my flight is relaxed and pain free.

The key here is distraction, says Alan Schatzberg, MD, a professor of psychiatry and behavioral science at the Stanford University School of Medicine. "Focusing on other things is extremely helpful" for people with chronic pain, he says. Meditation is one form of focus, but any quiet activity that absorbs your attention can reduce the stress response.

One warning from Dr. Schatzberg: Almost half of all clinically depressed people have chronic pain, so watch for depression-related symptoms like insomnia and difficulty concentrating. The fix could be as easy as taking one of a new generation of antidepressants called selective serotonin-norepinephrine reuptake inhibitors (SNRIs). Last year, a study published in the journal *Psychosomatics* found that the SNRI Cymbalta significantly reduced back pain, compared with a placebo.

THE BACK SURGEON

I'm wearing a pair of sneakers with high-tension springs embedded in the heels. Every time I take a step, my whole body bounces an extra inch or two. These things—called Z-Coil shoes—look ridiculous, but they achieve a key objective in the fight against back pain: unloading your spine. Stephen Hochschuler, MD, the stocky, 65-year-old cofounder of the Texas Back Institute, and my host, has a pair himself. "I didn't wear them today because I was in surgery this morning, and I didn't want to get blood on the heels," he says.

There's a palpable try-everything vibe at this suburban Dallas stronghold, which is the leading spine research and treatment center in the country. Staffers see between 17,000 and 19,000 new patients each year. They do the spinal-research equivalent of three universities. Yet, even though two surgeons founded the place, less than 10 percent of patients go under the knife. "If you can live with it, we don't cut," Dr. Hochschuler says.

After a round of x-rays, he examines me much as Dr. Shore did, testing for any nerve or motor damage. I'm normal. Then he disappears to check my film. When he returns, he asks me to lie on my stomach.

"Okay. This will probably hurt if I'm right, so get ready."

I've been to Feng, I think. *Bring it on.*

He jabs his thumb—hard—into the right side of my lower back. I grit my teeth. There's the ice pick! "Is that it?" he asks.

"Oh, yeah," I grunt. He nailed it.

He nods, smiles, and lets me up. "Come out here, Mike. I want to show you something."

My backlit MRIs and x-rays cover the wall outside the exam room. Dr. Hochschuler shows me my three dark disks. "You have some bulging there, definitely," he says. "And while it's possible your pain could be coming from one of those, I doubt it."

He directs me to another x-ray. "See those sections? Those are your facet joints. You have one on each side of each vertebra. Now, take a look at that one."

He points to the right facet joint on my fourth lumbar vertebra. Compared with the others, it looks . . . off.

"My guess is you have a small bone spur," he says. "That's exactly where I put my thumb just now. I think that's causing the pain."

I believe him. Of everyone I've seen, he's the only one who literally put his finger on the problem. His prescription, however, jars me: "Get in shape." Get? I run 15 to 20 miles a week, play hoops every Wednesday, and lift weights. I'm no Adonis, but I ain't Belushi.

"You're carrying more weight than you should," he says, and damn it, I know he's right. "Your core is deconditioned. You have very little flexibility." Again, all true. And all bad for my back, he explains. In short, if my muscles were stronger and the connective tissues more flexible, my facet joint would be better supported and the bone spur would no longer aggravate surrounding tissue.

The Verdict: "Stretching and strengthening are absolutely the keys to treating lower-back pain," says Dr. Haralson. "It really doesn't matter what the diagnosis is." And that raises another question: Is there an advantage to seeing a spine surgeon first? While Dr. Haralson acknowledges that research has

PAINPROOF YOUR BACK

Two workouts to help you avoid the agony

If you don't have back pain and you desperately want to keep it that way, follow one of these preemptive plans from Michael A. Clark, DPT, president of the National Academy of Sports Medicine. Both improve the strength, stability, and flexibility of the most important muscles for pain prevention—abs, glutes, hamstrings, hip flexors, and lower-back muscles. Perform either routine at the start or end of your regular workout or on off days. Do one set—12 to 15 repetitions—of each move if you're new to weight lifting, two sets if you've been lifting for a year, and three sets if you've been lifting longer.

Warmup

Lie faceup on a foam roll and move your calves, then your butt, back and forth over it. Turn onto your side and repeat for your thighs and lats. Next, perform static stretches (stretch and hold) for your calves, thighs, hamstrings, hip flexors, and lats. The warmup should take 5 to 7 minutes.

Workout One

Lateral tube walk. Loop exercise tubing around your ankles. Stand with your knees slightly bent and position your hands next to your hips. Pull your belly button toward your spine and sidestep 12 to 15 times to your right, then to your left.

Swiss-ball squat. Place a Swiss ball behind your back and up against a wall. With your weight against the ball, slowly lower your body until your thighs are parallel to the floor. Pause, then push yourself back up.

Swiss-ball crunch. Lie faceup on a Swiss ball with your feet flat on the floor and your arms folded across your chest. Your head, shoulders, and back should be in contact with the ball. Raise your shoulder blades off the ball. Pause, then slowly lower yourself.

shown that the faster you visit a specialist, the better off you are, he urges patience.

Seek a specialist only if your pain isn't better after at least 3 weeks of conservative treatments. "Sixty percent of back pain goes away after 3 weeks, no matter what people do," he says. "Don't do anything expensive or dangerous. The best treatment—and we have excellent data to support this—is activity."

THE PHYSICAL THERAPIST

Some spirit-sucking truths: You're never in as good shape as you think. You're aging faster than you realize. As your core goes, so you go. I know all this after one session with Dennis Duerring, DPT, ATC, my physical therapist

Swiss-ball glute bridge. Lie faceup on a Swiss ball with your feet flat on the floor and your head and upper back on the ball. Draw in your abs and raise your hips so your body forms a straight line from your knees to your shoulders. Squeeze your glutes, then lower your hips.

Swiss-ball back extension. Place a Swiss ball near a wall. Lie with your stomach on the ball, your feet pressed against the wall, and your fingers touching your head behind your ears. Keeping your abs tight, raise your upper body until you form a straight line from your heels to your shoulders. Pause, then slowly return to the starting position.

Workout Two

Lateral tube walk. Described in Workout One.

Cable lift. Attach a handle to a low-pulley cable and stand with the outside of your left foot toward the weight stack. Bend your knees to lower your body into a squat. Reach across your body with straight arms and grab the handle. Keeping your abs tight, stand up and rotate your torso, bringing the handle above your opposite shoulder. Then slowly return to the starting position. After a set, repeat on the other side.

Cable chop. Attach a handle to a high-pulley cable and stand with the outside of your left foot toward the weight stack. With your feet shoulder-width apart and your knees slightly bent, reach across your body with straight arms and grab the handle. Keeping your abs tight, pull the cable down toward your right hip as you pivot your back foot to the right. After a set, repeat on the other side.

Cable rotation. Attach a handle to a midlevel-pulley cable. (If you don't have access to a cable station, you can use a resistance band.) Stand with the outside of your left foot toward the weight stack and reach across your body with straight arms to grab the handle. Keeping your abs tight and your arms straight, rotate your body away from the weight stack, moving your arms across your body. Your left foot should pivot to the right. Pause, then slowly return to the starting position. After a set, repeat on the other side.

at Good Shepherd outpatient rehabilitation in Allentown, Pennsylvania. Duerring is 31 but still has a college athlete's body—about 6-foot-2, broad-shouldered, lean as a swimmer. I try not to hold it against him.

Working from Dr. Hochschuler's prescription, Duerring starts me off with an exam that's much like what I've gone through before. The only difference: While I'm lying on my belly and lifting my legs one at a time, he notices something interesting. "I can see the muscles on the lower left side working, but not the ones on the right." His theory: My body compensated for the facet-joint injury, and the muscles on that side atrophied. Apparently, I also have some of the tightest hamstrings he's ever seen.

We start with some basic stretches: hamstring, quad, calf. I'm supposed to hold them for 30 seconds and do three reps for each side. "Feel pull, not pain," says Duerring. Then come 13 trunk-stabilization exercises, but they go fast. Within 15 minutes, I do 160 back and core repetitions, and no exercise requires a range of motion of more than a few inches. "That's it," says Duerring. "Do the stretches every day and the exercises every other day. I'll see you in a week."

The Verdict: A revelation. The other treatments offered me pain-free moments. But after three sessions of therapy and daily stretching on my own, I'm having my first pain-free *days* in a long time. The reason, says Michael A. Clark, DPT, president of the National Academy of Sports Medicine, is that I'm reactivating and retraining the deepest layer of muscle in my core. "That layer attaches to the joints and creates stability," he says. "A lot of research shows that these muscles shut off when you have back pain, and they don't turn back on."

The secret to training those muscles? Small, deliberate movements. "You want quality of movement, not quantity," says Clark. "If you work too fast, the big muscles will compensate for the small muscles." Examples: leg lifts on your back to work lower abdominals, leg lifts on your belly to work the lower back, and crunches.

If you take anything away from this story, take this: Acupuncture and chiropractic and meditation and medication can be powerful—and often necessary—pain-relief tools. But if you don't use that relief as an opportunity to rebuild your body, you're doomed to future bouts of back pain.

I think of the dozens of patients I've seen during my odyssey: all ages, all weights, all kinds. And all limping, using canes, crutches, and walkers, frowns etched in their Easter Island faces. They're learning what I've learned. I'm 35, and I've let my ignored core and bone-spurred facet joint rule my life for long enough. If some evil force jabs me with that ice pick again, I have tools to pry it out. Until then, I'll spend an extra 15 minutes three times a week doing what I should've been doing for years.

Small price for a normal life.

NEED TO KNOW

Don't Worry Yourself Sick

Stress can decrease the effectiveness of your flu shot, according to a study published in *Psychosomatic Medicine*. Among 83 healthy adults who received influenza vaccinations, those with high stress in the days following the shot had 12 percent to 17 percent fewer virus-fighting antibodies than their calm counterparts. "Stress influences the immune system's ability to respond to challenges posed by the vaccine," says study author Gregory Miller, PhD. So plan your shot for a low-stress week.

Wood to the Wise

Enjoy nature—just watch where you sit. Avoiding prolonged contact with trees, branches, and logs may help you dodge Lyme disease. Researchers at the University of California at Berkeley found that sitting on logs resulted in tick exposure 30 percent of the time; sitting against a tree led to exposure 17 percent of time. Ticks feed on animals, and lurking on logs and leaves may "put ticks in a position where they're likely to find a host," says study author Robert S. Lane. Wear light-colored clothing as well; ticks can hide on dark garb.

Skip This Stone

New research shows that upping your intake of unsaturated fats can help prevent gallstones. When University of Kentucky scientists analyzed the diets of 45,000 men for 14 years, they discovered that the guys who ate the most unsaturated fat were almost 20 percent less likely to develop gallstones than

PERCENTAGE OF MEN'S YEARLY SICK DAYS CAUSED BY STRESS: 15

were those who took in the least unsaturates. "Linoleic acid was significantly associated with this decreased risk," says study author Chung-Jyi Tsai, MD. A polyunsaturated fat, linoleic acid is thought to prevent bile from crystallizing into stones. One excellent source: flaxseed.

TREATMENT

Cause Fewer Effects

Medication for chronic tension headaches can leave you dizzy and dry mouthed. Now researchers have identified a drug that treats tension headaches with fewer side effects. In a German study, patients who took the antidepressant mirtazapine daily reported a 34 percent reduction in headache length and intensity, compared with those popping a placebo. Mirtazapine may also protect against future headaches. "Sometimes taking the drug can break a bad cycle of pain and tension, tension and pain," says study author Lars Bendtson, MD. If you experience headaches triggered by fatigue or stress, ask your doctor about the drug.

Positive Feedback

Researchers writing in the journal *Chest* report that biofeedback can reduce the need for asthma drugs. In the study of 94 asthmatics, those who used biofeedback to increase their heart-rate variability—the difference between heart rates during inhalation and exhalation—ended up needing 22 percent less medication than those using no biofeedback. When the asthmatics with greater heart-rate variability did have asthma attacks, they were less severe. "Biofeedback helps modulate the body's reaction to all kinds of asthma triggers, such as allergens and fatigue," says study author Paul Lehrer, PhD. Visit the Biofeedback Certification Institute of America's Web site, www.bcia.org, to find a doctor.

ALLERGIES

Lay Low

Don't head for higher ground to escape allergies. People living on the upper floors of buildings are at increased risk of pollen allergies, say Spanish researchers. After analyzing more than 17,000 people, researchers found that the risk was almost 17 percent higher for those on the eighth floor of a building than for those on the first four stories. "Convection currents transport pollen particles upward," says study author Alicia Armentia, MD. Rather not relocate? Add a high-energy particulate air (HEPA) filter to your air-conditioning system.

No, Thanks, I'm Stuffed

Don't blame the pollen. A recent Italian study found that a common food preservative may cause chronic nasal congestion. After identifying 226 people suffering from persistent congestion, researchers removed all preservatives from the subjects' diets and then added them back one at a time. For a small number of people, reintroducing monosodium benzoate made them stuffed up again within hours of eating. Study author Maria Pacor, MD, suggests avoiding foods with high levels of monosodium benzoate, such as colas, jellies, and salad dressings, to see if symptoms improve.

GUM DISEASE
Toxic Teeth

Normally, having all of your teeth is a good thing. But researchers at the University of North Carolina School of Dentistry discovered that holding on to your wisdom teeth increases your risk of gum disease. By analyzing dental data from a survey of 5,831 Americans, researchers found that those who still had their wisdom teeth were twice as likely to suffer serious gum disease as those who had had them pulled. If you still have any of your wisdom molars, head to a dentist before the migration of gum-disease-causing bacteria in your mouth begins. "Once bacteria set up back there, they tend to move forward," says study author Ray White, DDS.

DOCTOR'S ORDERS
Splitting, the Difference

If you need to take 30 milligrams of medication, you might be tempted to split a 20-milligram pill in half. Bad idea. Splitting prescription pills can lead to incorrect doses of medication. Rutgers University researchers split 90 muscle relaxants of 10 milligrams each and discovered that the "halves" contained anywhere from 2.49 milligrams to 7.48 milligrams of the active ingredient, says study author Thomas J. Cook, PhD. Splitting tools were more accurate than kitchen knives, so if you must divide, invest in a VitaMinda tablet splitter ($6 at www.cvs.com).

WHAT'S NEW

Another Shot

Biotech company Vaxin hopes to avoid another flu-vaccine shortage like the one 2 years ago. Instead of incubating the virus in chicken eggs—a slow process with a low yield—they use only relevant genes from the virus to mass-produce the vaccine in cell cultures in a lab. More tests are planned.

Find Allergies Fast

People currently have to wait 4 to 5 sneezy weeks for the results of allergy tests. But German researchers have created a test with faster results. Doctors combine drops of a patient's blood with a solution, then spread the mixture onto an allergen-spotted membrane. After half an hour, doctors can see which allergies the patient suffers from. The test is available in Europe and could come to the States as early as this year.

Sniff Out Germs

University of Pennsylvania doctors are testing an electric "nose" that can detect sinus infections and pneumonia. As a patient exhales, a sensor on the "e-nose" analyzes his breath. The results are displayed on a computer.

Spitting Image

Blood tests could soon become as rare as house calls, thanks to new evidence that saliva tests may work just as well. Doctors often draw blood because it's the only way to measure protein levels that can indicate disease. But now Oregon researchers have shown that 67 of these proteins also exist in human saliva. There are still more proteins to be identified, but the FDA has already approved a saliva-based test for HIV.

Top Banana

UK researchers have discovered that an extract of the plantain can help soothe symptoms of irritable bowel syndrome. The large bananas contain a unique form of fiber that prevents the intestinal lining from attracting the bacteria that contribute to inflammatory episodes. Clinical trials are under way.

Fishing for Information

Not only do trout possess the ability to foment frustration in hip-wader-clad humans, but they're also able to secrete mucus that battles bacteria. British researchers are studying this mucus in the hope of someday turning it into medicine. Currently, they're conducting lab studies to see which bugs it can beat. So far, the fishy fluid has stopped both E. coli and salmonella, with more tests ahead.

THE COST OF . . .

. . . Not Getting Outside

Your parents were right: It's not healthy to stay cooped up all day. You have to get some fresh air this winter, or . . .

You'll need . . .	The research shows . . .	It'll cost you . . .
Diet books and new pants	People who participate in outdoor activities have less risk of being overweight than those who don't.	$155
Allergy shots and an air purifier	You think pollen's bad? The dust and mold in your home and office aggravate allergies and asthma.	$530
To make up for losing your annual bonus	Stale office air and sick building syndrome lower productivity levels. You won't hit your numbers this year.	$1,500
Therapy, Prozac, or a light box	Too little time outdoors can trigger seasonal affective disorder—depression caused by lack of sun exposure.	$3,403
Extra sick days	When you get sick, the more vitamin D you absorb from sunlight, the sooner you'll get better. D deficiency also puts you at risk of colon, prostate, and pancreatic cancers.	$568
Blood-pressure medication and regular office checkups	Vitamin D from sunlight can lower blood pressure almost as well as drugs can.	$204
A bone-mineral-density test and medication to stop bone loss	Sunlight helps your body absorb calcium so you don't join the 2 million men with osteroporosis.	$405
TOTAL		$6,765

FAST FIXES

Sick of getting sick? Then don't. Bypass the latest bugs and avoid aches with these germ fighters and pain-proofers. Already under the weather? We also have your prescription for feeling better fast.

1. Know your pain. Ninety percent of people suffer from headaches, most of which will disappear with aspirin. But sometimes head pain is a warning of a bigger problem. "Anytime you experience a new or different headache pattern, you should pay attention," says Lisa Mannix, MD, of the National Headache Foundation.

People with migraines, for example, often think they have sinus headaches, which prevents them from receiving the best treatment, say Mayo Clinic researchers. When 100 patients who said they suffered from sinus headaches received neurological evaluations, 86 percent actually were found to have migraines, says study author Eric Eross, MD. If you're plagued by headaches, use these clues to help you pinpoint the cause of your pain. Your best bet, though, is to visit a neurologist, who can give you a more accurate diagnosis than a family doctor or allergist.

Temples or face. Throbbing on one side of the face or head often indicates a migraine. "There's a misconception that migraines always cause nausea, but that's not true," says Robert Kaniecki, MD, director of the University of Pittsburgh Headache Center. "If the pain interferes with your daily tasks, it's probably a migraine."

Triptans, a class of prescription drugs, offer many people relief. With over-the-counter remedies, compare carefully. Advil Migraine is just the regular formula with different packaging, says Dr. Mannix.

You should be concerned if the pain is fairly persistent or if the muscles in your face droop, tingle, or feel numb, says Dr. Mannix. This could be an indicator of a brain tumor, and fast diagnosis is key to treatment.

Behind the eye. Pressure behind or under the eyes is often a sinus headache. Antibiotics can treat the infection that causes them. It also could be a cluster or migraine headache. "These are more prevalent in men who smoke or have type A personalities," says Dr. Kaniecki. The pain is usually around one eye and paired with congestion. If these happen over several weeks, see your doctor for treatment options.

Stiff neck. Generally, pain in the back of the neck is a tension headache; however, it could also be a migraine, says Dr. Mannix. Painkillers work well, but taking them twice or more a week puts you at risk of rebound headaches. If the pain comes on suddenly and severely, and you're vomiting, see a doctor soon to rule out an aneurysm.

2. Get your back on track. Speaking of pain, backaches strike millions of Americans each year. Here are two easy ways to ease the ache.

Be on the ball. Researchers at the University of Waterloo, in Ontario, studied eight men who sat on either a Swiss ball or a wooden stool and found that sitting on a Swiss ball may help alleviate back pain. "It will wear out some people but will be therapy for others," says study author Stuart McGill, PhD. Give it a try. If you like it, alternate between a ball and a chair. He also suggests standing when you're on the phone to give your back a break from sitting.

Seek support. If sitting on a ball is not for you, try a lumbar support cushion on your desk chair. The natural curve of your back decreases by as much as 30 percent when you sit down, and a protruding backrest at lumbar level helps preserve that curve. But it'll work better if you're able to adjust your office chair so the back part of the seat tilts down a few inches (18 degrees, to be exact), says Mohsen Makhsous, PhD, an assistant professor of physical therapy at Northwestern University. His study showed that con-figuration to be the most effective at preventing back pain.

3. Disinfect your desk. Your office—and especially your desk—can be a breeding ground for germs. "People eat at their desks and spill crumbs and coffee, which promotes bacteria growth," says Charles Gerba, PhD, a pro-fessor of microbiology at the University of Arizona. In fact, in his analysis of the office petri dish, Dr. Gerba found that, square inch for square inch, the highest concentration of bacteria isn't on the communal copier or fax machine but, rather, on individual desks, keyboards, and phones. Have a look at the numbers, then do some downsizing with disinfectant.

Office Equipment	Bacteria per Square Inch
Phone	25,127
Desk	20,961
Keyboard	3,295
Mouse	1,676
Fax machine	301
Photocopier	69

PERCENTAGE OF PEOPLE WHO WASH THEIR HANDS AFTER SNEEZING OR COUGHING: 58

4. Avoid cabin fever. Whether you're traveling for business or pleasure, stick with bottled or canned drinks, and hold the ice. The Environmental Protection Agency says that the water on commercial airplanes may be tainted with bacteria. The EPA examined the water supplies on 158 US flights and found that one in eight was contaminated. "Planes refresh their water every time they stop, and some countries don't have the same standards as the United States," says Tom Skinner, an EPA official. The water can harm people recovering from illness or those with weak immune systems. If that's you, skip coffee and tea, which use onboard water, and wash your hands with sanitizing wipes.

5. Quiet your cough. Next time you're hacking up a lung, don't reach for cough medicine. Pennsylvania State University researchers found that cough syrups are no more effective than a placebo. Sick kids received syrup containing either cough medicine or plain sugar. Later, both groups reported similar improvement. "Reviews of the medical literature conclude that these medicines are not effective for adults, either," says Ian Paul, MD, the study author. Instead, use a saline nasal spray to help thin the mucus in your lungs.

6. Soothe the sting. More than 1 million Americans are treated for insect stings and animal bites every year. Here's what to do once you've had a too-close encounter.

Bees and wasps: Yank stingers left behind—they continue to pump venom—wash the area, and watch for allergic reactions, such as nausea or labored breathing.

Mosquitoes: Slather on anti-itch lotion (your athlete's-foot spray works) and pop an antihistamine.

Spiders: Black widow and brown recluse bites are the most common. Look at the spider before you smoosh it; knowing which bit you is key info for the doc.

Snakes: Do not suck the venom out. Remove constricting jewelry, elevate the bitten area above your heart, and call for help. Remember the snake's face.

Ticks: Use blunt-tipped tweezers to pull the tick out, head and all. Douse the area with hydrogen peroxide.

Cujo: Any bite from a frothy mammal may call for an immediate shot of PEP (postexposure prophylaxis). Wash the wound and call for help.

7. Survive a grilling. When it comes to cookouts, most of us remember the citronella candle but forget to ward off the most dangerous barbecue bugs: those on the grill. Here's how to make sure your next picnic isn't your last.

Shop wisely. Ohio State University researchers recently found that only about half of all batches of contaminated meat are recalled quickly enough to avert food-poisoning outbreaks. By analyzing federal data from 1996 to 2002, the study determined that just 62 percent of contaminated meat was discovered within a month of distribution to grocery stores. Much of the blame goes to large, overextended meatpacking plants, says lead researcher Neal Hooker, PhD. "Smaller plants tend to manage a recall better," he says, due to their localized distribution networks. Cut the middleman entirely by buying your beef directly from suppliers at your local farmers' market.

Check the temperature. As many as 78 percent of Americans just eyeball steaks to see if they're done. With that kind of sloppy chef work, it's no surprise that cases of foodborne illness double during the summer months. Make a meat thermometer part of your grilling gear, and you won't need to have your guests sign a waiver. Simply insert the thermometer into the thickest part of the meat without touching bone and make sure the minimum internal temperature is as follows:

- For beef burgers, lamb chops, pork loin, beef or pork ribs: 160°
- For chicken legs or wings: 180°
- For chicken breasts: 170°
- For turkey burgers, bratwurst, kielbasa, and other precooked sausages: 165°
- For steaks (any cut): 145°

OUR FINAL ANSWERS

Aleve It Alone

With the news that Aleve and similar drugs cause heart problems, should I stop taking it for headaches?

—J.B., Denton, Texas

Yes. In a large study on Aleve's use in people with Alzheimer's disease, scientists noted a 50 percent increase in heart-attack risk. Vioxx and Celebrex, similar to Aleve, have also been associated with cardiac risks. Stick to acetaminophen, aspirin, or ibuprofen for pain.

Shake the Flu

I didn't get a flu shot this year. So, aside from washing my hands, taking vitamins, exercising, and sleeping enough, how can I stay healthy?

—B.W., Portland, Oregon

Put whey protein into your postworkout shake. Whey boosts your body's levels of the antioxidant glutathione, or GSH, and recent research shows that GSH may help keep a flu virus from taking hold. Or meditate. In a new study at the University of Wisconsin, people who took an 8-week program in "mindfulness meditation" showed significant increases in flu-fighting antibodies.

Get Your Zzz's

When I take Nyquil, sometimes I wake up after 3 or 4 hours. How come?

—J.K., Missoula, Montana

Nyquil uses the "shotgun approach" to cold relief. It contains a pain reliever, a cough suppressant, an antihistamine, a decongestant, and 10 percent alcohol. You get lulled to sleep by the alcohol and the sedating antihistamine, and you wake up when the alcohol wears off. The decongestant may also act as a stimulant. Try single medications to treat your specific symptoms.

Head off the Pain

Is there anything I can do to prevent a migraine?

—T.M., Franklin, Tennessee

Avoid your triggers. Certain foods (like chocolate and aged cheeses), sleep deprivation, changes in the weather, and bright lights are common ones. (We even know a guy who gets a migraine whenever he skips a shower.) Another theory: Migraines are caused by a serotonin deficit in your brain. Without enough serotonin, the blood vessels in your brain swell, creating pressure that causes pain and other symptoms.

If you get migraines more than twice a month, your doctor may prescribe antidepressants, which can boost serotonin levels, or another drug like Imitrex. If you feel a migraine starting, take these steps: Lie down in a dark, quiet room; use a cold compress on your forehead; massage your scalp; and apply pressure to your temples. If these tactics don't help and you worry about the side effects of antidepressants (decreased sex drive is one), try melatonin supplements. New research shows that they can reduce migraine frequency. Patients who took 3 milligrams of melatonin every night for 3 months saw a 50 percent decrease in headaches. If migraines did strike, they were shorter and less intense, says study author Mario Peres, MD.

Doctor Your Eyes

My allergy meds dry out my eyes. What can I do?

—B.R., ST. Louis

If your symptoms are primarily nasal, you might talk to your doctor about a nasal steroid like Flonase. But if the problem is more widespread, consider artificial-tear solutions like Hypo Tears, Tears Naturale, or Ultra Tears. Or try

PERCENTAGE OF PEOPLE WHO ARE RESENTFUL WHEN A COWORKER MISSES WORK BECAUSE OF A MIGRAINE: 35

nonmedicated ointments like Accu-Tears and Lacri-Lube, though they're harder to administer than drops and can cause blurred vision.

Breathe Easier

I have asthma and use two inhalers multiple times daily. How can I simplify?

—M.R., Arlington, Virginia

What you're most likely inhaling is a bronchodilator (such as albuterol) and another medication to reduce inflammation (a corticosteroid). One new product, called Advair Diskus, contains both in a novel inhaler. Most patients using it control their asthma well with one inhalation twice daily.

Reaction Time

How long does it take to know if a drug is going to have a side effect for me?

—P.T., Merrick, New York

Usually it's within 24 hours or after taking a couple of doses. But occasionally, side effects or toxic reactions can take longer than a week to develop. Tell your doctor as soon as you notice a reaction. Watch out especially for severe diarrhea or skin rashes.

Bad Medicine?

How long can I keep a medication around before it's no good?

—A.D., Aurora, Colorado

Over time, medications break down, and you may get only a portion of the intended dose—and that can be dangerous. Trash all OTC meds after the expiration dates, and ask when to toss prescriptions.

FIVE

BEAT THE MANKILLERS

READ UP ON IT

Putting Up Resistance

Twenty million men are on the verge of diabetes because their bodies have forgotten how to use insulin. Here's how to tell if you're in danger

By Jim Gorman

Mike Nevin was always a big guy. Big but fit. Back when the 39-year-old architect was snapping footballs at the University of Idaho, he was able to comfortably carry 305 pounds—much of it muscle—on his 6-foot-1 frame. In 2002, 15 years after being the biggest big man on campus, Nevin was still expanding, though by exactly how much was a mystery, since he never felt the need to weigh in. "My energy levels were good. I never felt tired," recalls Nevin, who by then was newly married and living in Boise. "I was still pretty active, skiing, playing softball, golf, flag football. I could physically do what I had to do without having a heart attack."

As the pounds piled on, Nevin adjusted his life by increments. He had his ski boots reshaped to fit his expanded calves. He traded up in pants size. His was a strategy of "gain and compensate," and it helped him build a wall of denial as thick as his thighs. Then, in 2002, one part of Nevin's body grew at a rate that alarmed even him: his lymph nodes. They were enlarged, and he had no choice but to see a doctor. And a scale.

"It turned out the lymph thing was no big deal, but one of my doctors was worried I might be a candidate for diabetes," says Nevin. "He recommended I visit an endocrinologist." For a guy used to posting huge numbers in the weight room during his prime—500 pounds on the bench, 650 in the squat— Nevin was blown away by the stats in the specialist's report. Weight: 345 pounds. Body-mass index: 45. Triglycerides: 300. Glucose: 145. By every measure, Nevin was twice the man he should be. "The doctor scribbled down the words 'obese' and 'insulin resistant,'" he says. "Then he told me if I didn't do something fast, my next step could be full-fledged diabetes."

WHAT'S IN A NAME?

For a syndrome with deadly consequences, insulin resistance is saddled with a pretty wimpy name. Which might help explain why so few people have

THE PATH OF LEAST RESISTANCE
Five ways to stay off the road to diabetes and syndrome X

1. Keep your morning commitment. From now on, think of skipping breakfast as skipping a dose of medication. In an 8-year Harvard study, researchers discovered that people who ate breakfast every day were half as likely to develop syndrome X as those who skipped it. Also, obesity rates were more than one-third lower among regular a.m. eaters. The reason? Exactly what you'd imagine: "Filling your belly in the morning might help control hunger and prevent overeating at lunch and dinner," says Linda Van Horn, PhD, one of the study authors. But instead of eggs and bacon, pour a bowel of whole-grain cereal: High-fiber foods lowered the risk of developing syndrome X by an additional 15 percent.

2. Enjoy the daily grind. Coffee can clear the cobwebs from your head and, apparently, your insulin receptors. In a Swedish study published in the *Journal of Internal Medicine,* researchers determined that insulin sensitivity improves in direct correlation with coffee consumption. For each cup you drink daily, you decrease your risk of insulin resistance 16 percent. Echoing the finding, a separate study found that men who drank regular coffee daily significantly reduced their risk of type 2 diabetes. Johan Arnlov, MD, PhD, lead author of the Swedish study, believes that the antioxidants present in coffee may be at work. And while sugar is out, milk may maximize the effect. (See number 5.)

3. Try sensitivity training. New Zealand researchers found that insulin-resistant people who paired intensive endurance exercise with dietary changes improved their insulin sensitivity by about 20 percent after 4 months, compared with almost no improvement in those who also ate smart but invested less sweat. Rather lift weights to see your diabetes risk drop? A Finnish study showed that circuit training (performing a series of exercises one after another without rest) was as effective as aerobic exercise at boosting insulin sensitivity. Do five moves for your upper and lower body, such as a squat, chest press, row, triceps pulldown, and Swiss-ball crunch.

4. Order a wine chaser. Next time you wine and dine, have your last glass as dessert. Building on the finding that light alcohol consumption—one to two glasses of wine daily—enhances insulin sensitivity, Australian researchers sought to determine whether the timing of the imbibing mattered. Their finding: One and a half glasses downed shortly after a meal plunges insulin back to premeal levels. More research is needed, but this seems to show that alcohol beneficially alters glucose disposal, says study author Simon F. Crowe, PhD. Avoid syrupy-sweet dessert wines, such as port or sherry, and ask for a Riesling instead; it's sweet but won't boost blood sugar.

5. Be a dairy king. Already packing a paunch? Swap 500 calories' worth of nutritional no-shows in your diet for 500 calories of dairy products. According to a *Journal of the American Medical Association* study of more than 3,000 overweight people, those who consumed the most dairy products each week were 72 percent less likely to develop syndrome X than the folks eating the least. Researchers suspect that the high calcium content in milk and foods made from it is behind the finding. And it seems even a small amount is beneficial. Eating just one serving of dairy per day was associated with a 21 percent reduction in risk of syndrome X.

heard of it, let alone given it the respect it deserves. Basically, insulin resistance short-circuits the body's system for burning and storing fuel—even in people who aren't Nevin heavy. In fact, being just 10 to 20 pounds overweight can land you in the physiological frying pan. "It's possible to be lean and insulin resistant, just as it's possible to be overweight and not be," says Robert H. Eckel, MD, director of the endocrinology lab at the University of Colorado Health Sciences Center. "But the general rule is, the heavier you get, the more resistant you become."

To comprehend the level of mischief-making caused by insulin resistance, it first helps to understand how a healthy body converts food into energy for cells. A rice-and-bean burrito that goes down your gullet is digested in the intestine, where much of it turns into glucose, or blood sugar, the simple energy source that powers cells. But because glucose can't penetrate cell walls on its own, the party doesn't get started until insulin, a hormone secreted by the pancreas, arrives on the scene. Insulin flows quickly throughout the body, attaches at receptors lining the surface of certain cells, gives the secret handshake, and escorts glucose through the door.

Now, if that burrito you snarfed happened to be, say, a grande deluxe with cheese and you washed it down with 20 ounces of soda, then you've just inhaled more potential energy than your body can possibly use at the moment. No problem. Ever-thrifty insulin steers the surplus glucose to the liver, where it's shelved as glycogen, and to fat cells, where it's rejiggered into triglycerides for safekeeping until, oh, the next famine rolls around. "When insulin drops low enough, we can metabolize our fat," says Dr. Eckel. "Most of us with normal fat stores could live for months without eating."

In a healthy body, glucose and insulin coexist in dynamic equilibrium, sort of like the NASDAQ and the Dow. Glucose goes up, insulin trails right behind. As glucose drops, the pancreas ratchets back insulin output. It's a brilliantly engineered system, particularly if you happen to belong to a nomadic tribe of hunter-gatherers. For cubicle dwellers who forage at the Gas 'n' Go and hunt at Burger World's drive-thru window, it can be murder.

For reasons not entirely understood, cells in the liver, as well as in muscle and fat tissue, can begin to ignore insulin when it comes knocking. This indifference—or loss of sensitivity—is the cornerstone of insulin resistance and the trigger for a sequence of major health problems to follow. (See, fellas, sensitivity can be a good thing.) With access denied, glucose begins backing up in the blood. The always-alert pancreas reads the growing imbalance and responds by cranking out extra insulin. Eventually, insulin succeeds in breaking down the doors to resistant cells and starts stashing glucose, but it might require three times the normal amount of the hormone. Not to mention excessive wear and tear on the pancreas.

As long as insulin gains the upper hand and the pancreas can meet the extra demands placed on it, the diagnosis is confined to insulin resistance. Should the pancreas start to sputter and glucose skyrocket, then all hell breaks loose. Sugar begins spilling into the urine and barging into random cells, unescorted and unwanted. Diagnosis: type 2 diabetes. Most people who have insulin resistance will progress to diabetes, unless they take charge of their health. Untreated, type 2 diabetes can lead to blindness, kidney failure, impotence, and amputation.

Still, insulin resistance is more than just a precursor to diabetes, even though the American Diabetes Association (ADA) now calls it exactly that— "prediabetes." All of that free-roaming insulin will sabotage your body's system for using and storing fats. Specifically, excess insulin jacks up triglyceride levels in the blood and lowers the level of HDL cholesterol by encouraging the liver to overproduce dangerous substances called very low-density lipoproteins (VLDL). (Quick refresher course: HDL is good cholesterol, LDL is bad cholesterol, and VLDL is Osama bin Laden–bad cholesterol.) The combination of high triglycerides and low HDL levels is a major risk factor for heart attacks, since it signals that the coronary arteries are likely being layered with plaque.

The deadly duo of high triglycerides and low HDL is also a key indicator of a recently discovered metabolic disorder known as syndrome X, which goes by the alias "insulin resistance syndrome." Other markers of syndrome X include inflammation of the blood-vessel walls and high blood pressure. Researchers aren't entirely certain whether insulin resistance causes syndrome X or whether it's guilty by association. This much is known: If you have syndrome X—and as many as 25 percent of people do—your risk of a fatal heart attack doubles.

PUBLIC ENEMY NUMBER 1

If insulin resistance were a contagious disease, there would be no end to the hand-wringing news accounts about "the deadly scourge sweeping our nation. Details at 11." An astounding 41 million Americans have insulin resistance, according to a newly revised estimate by the ADA. Think about it: One out of every three people in your office, stuck in traffic around you, or cruising the aisles at the Hefty Mart has put himself on a collision course with diabetes and heart attack. "We're not on the cusp of a public-health emergency. We're in it," says M. James Lenhard, MD, an endocrinologist and the

HOW MANY TIMES MORE LIKELY YOU ARE TO DEVELOP TYPE 2 DIABETES IF YOU EAT A LOT OF RED MEAT: 2

director of the weight-management program at Christiana Care Health System in Wilmington, Delaware. Insulin resistance strikes especially hard in the 40-to-74 age group, where the rate hits 40 percent, although the real boom market of late is among men and women in their 30s.

How did insulin resistance snatch so many bodies while we were busy minding J. Lo's love life? Some men run a higher risk of the condition simply because they didn't choose their parents carefully enough. Diabetes in the family tree raises the odds; so does being African-American, Native American, Latino, Asian-American, or a Pacific Islander. By one estimate, half of the risk of insulin resistance is hereditary. "Genes may put the bullet in the gun, but it's the environment that pulls the trigger," says Dr. Lenhard. And chances are, the finger on the trigger is a pudgy one.

The connection between fat and insulin resistance is powerful and consistent. Among obese individuals, 85 percent have some degree of insulin resistance. Conversely, even minor weight loss leads to an immediate improvement in insulin function. But exactly how flab fosters the decline in insulin sensitivity is unclear. The scariest theory: Our lard is somehow alive. "Fat is not an inert storage depot. It produces resistin, which has a negative effect on muscle tissue's ability to respond to insulin. The more overweight a person is, the more resistin will be produced," says Erik J. Henriksen, PhD, a professor of physiology at the University of Arizona College of Medicine. "Fat also releases adiponectin, which has a positive effect on insulin response. But as individuals become more obese, they produce less." In effect, fat begets more fat in a negative-feedback loop.

Inactivity, and not just its fat by-product, may also play a crucial role in causing insulin resistance. We already know that insulin serves as a sort of ticket scalper that gains glucose entrance to a cell. But once inside the gate, hapless glucose can't find its seat without the help of chemical ushers called IRS-1 and GLUT-4. And this is where inactive men get into trouble. "Physical inactivity lowers the levels of IRS-1 and GLUT-4 and decreases their effectiveness," says Dr. Henriksen. Lack of exercise may also increase free fatty acids in the blood and step up the storage of visceral fat, both of which are leading suspects in the mystery of what causes insulin resistance, according to Dr. Henriksen.

IT'S IN YOUR HANDS

As complex as the origins of insulin resistance are, stopping it in its tracks is surprisingly straightforward: Exercise, lose weight, and eat smart. Even modest effort in these areas yields big health dividends. Take what the Diabetes Prevention Program found when it carried out a major clinical trial involving more than 3,000 insulin-resistant people. The researchers showed that a 7 percent weight loss (about 14 pounds for a 200-pound man), coupled

FROM SUGAR DADDY TO MR. SOFTEE

How a case of untreated diabetes can mean a bittersweet end to erections

1. Normally, when you become sexually aroused, nerve signals are sent from your brain through your spinal cord to the autonomic nerves in your penis. These nerves then holler at blood vessels to dilate and flood the inner chambers of your penis, aka corpora cavernosa, with blood. Presto: An erection!

2. It's theorized that diabetes derails this love train at the autonomic nerves. These nerves are sheathed in the appropriately named Schwaan cells, which act as a sort of insulation for your wiring; they help protect the nerves and improve signal conduction. And like most other cells in the body, they also take glucose from your blood and convert it into sorbitol for energy.

3. Unfortunately, the Schwaan cells' appetite for glucose is endless. This means that if your bloodstream is flooded with glucose, as it is with untreated diabetes, the Schwaan cells will continue to convert the extra sugar into sorbitol—even if the little buggers are full. As large amounts of glucose continue to be converted, the Schwaan cells try to dilute the excess sorbitol with water, causing them to swell. This swelling, in turn, puts pressure on the autonomic nerves.

4. Eventually, the swollen Schwaan cells begin to pinch the nerves, weakening the signal for the blood vessels to dilate to produce an erection. Even worse, if glucose continues to fill your bloodstream, the swollen Schwaan cells and the nerves they surround will die. No more nerves, no more erections. This process is slow—10 to 20 years after the onset of diabetes—but the result is permanent.

with walking for half an hour 5 days a week, reduced the risk of diabetes by 58 percent. "The bright side of insulin resistance is that it's like an early warning signal," says Cathy Nonas, RD, director of obesity and diabetes programs for North General Hospital in New York City. "Catch it quickly, make the necessary lifestyle changes, and you can avoid diabetes, cardiovascular disease, and stroke."

Mike Nevin heeded the warning. It took him a few days to recover from the one-two punch of being labeled obese and insulin resistant. Then he directed the mental toughness that had earned him a starting position on a Division I college football team toward the challenge of drastically improving his health.

"There was no way I was going to end up with diabetes, having a needle stuck in me several times a day," he says. Nevin immediately committed himself to a workout routine that included lifting weights 6 days a week and running 3 to 8 miles three times a week. "The first day I ran, I made it about a block and a half without stopping," he says. "The next day, I could run two squares farther on the concrete sidewalk. That's how I measured my progress."

While making his cells ravenous for energy through exercise, Nevin also overhauled his diet. He quit the gut-busting lunchtime routine of burgers and fries, stopped drinking beer, and swore off baked potatoes and white bread. Instead, he began eating a lot more vegetables and fruit, low-fat cheeses, and whole grains. He also substituted fish for some red meat. "This was the first time in my life that I combined diet and exercise. I lost nearly 20 pounds a month in the first 4 months," says Nevin. "When I saw my doctor, he couldn't believe the change." The improvements could be seen in Nevin's blood profile, too: His triglycerides plummeted below 100, his LDL dropped, his HDL rose, and his blood sugar sank to 85. He eventually carved his weight down to 225 pounds, with a lean 17 percent body fat.

Not surprisingly, once he whipped himself back into shape, Nevin also rediscovered his need to compete. This past year, he ran his first half-marathon and earned a black belt in tae kwon do. "I'm proud of what I've done," he says, "but I'll tell you, the easiest way to lose 120 pounds is never to gain it."

Sun Starved

Dangerously low vitamin D levels may be the next national epidemic—increasing the risk of heart disease, colon cancer, and prostate cancer. The solution? Catch some rays

By Tom McGrath

Frankly, I didn't really want to die at age 37.

That was the first thought I had three summers ago, when my dermatologist told me that the small pink lump on my left cheek was, in fact, skin cancer. He quickly went about assuring me that, despite the funeral dirge playing in my head, death wasn't really an option here. I had the mildest form of the disease, basal-cell carcinoma, which hardly ever causes long-term problems. What's more, removing it would be a simple slice-and-stitch procedure. And that's just what it was. In the end, the root canal I'd had 2 months earlier was probably more of a near-death experience.

That said, ever since that moment, I—like so many guys nowadays—have become far more conscious of protecting myself from the sun. I slather sunscreen on my fast-burning Irish skin and outfit myself in a series of grimy baseball caps (my fedora phase, thankfully, has passed). Having cheated death at age 37, I'm not about to let it win at age 47.

There's just one hitch: My attempts to save my skin may ultimately cost me my life. At least that's the warning a group of researchers is giving sunphobics like myself. They're suggesting we've grown dangerously leery of the sun and, specifically, that we need more of the ultraviolet vitamin, vitamin D. As evidence, they point to an alarming number of people—particularly those living in the northern part of the United States and those with dark skin—who are running close to "E" when it comes to D.

In 2002, for example, a study of otherwise healthy 18- to 29-year-olds in Boston found that one-third had significantly low vitamin D levels by the end of the winter. A recent article in the journal *Nutrition Reviews,* which looked at five separate studies, concluded that "prevalence of vitamin D insufficiency is higher than anticipated in North America." Meanwhile, one noted expert on bone and calcium believes that the problem is even bigger than that. "I admittedly have a liberal standard," says Robert Heaney, MD, of Creighton University in Nebraska, "but I estimate that as many as 80 percent of people in the United States don't get enough vitamin D."

Now, granted, "You need more vitamin D" sounds like what your grandmother might say if she were named Surgeon General (right after she proclaimed beets the national vegetable). But there's reason to pay attention, since researchers believe that a lack of D—a substance that helps our bodies use calcium and is crucial to bone strength—could be behind much of what ails us here at the dawn of the 21st century, including heart disease, colon cancer, and prostate cancer. Indeed, a 2002 study in the journal *Cancer* speculated that vitamin D undernourishment may lead to more than 23,000 cancer deaths each year.

"I think this is a major unrecognized epidemic in the United States," says Michael Holick, MD, a researcher at Boston University Medical Center and the most high-profile member of the vitamin D research community. "It affects children and adults of all ages, all races, and both sexes. It's very significant."

WHY WE'RE COMING UP SHORT

The way God drew it up, getting enough vitamin D ought to be a cinch, since the process is as unconscious as breathing. When you're outside in the sunlight, UVB rays from the sun activate an enzyme in your skin. Presto, vitamin D is created and goes to work in your body.

Unfortunately, in practice several things can interfere with the process. First is geography. The farther you are from the equator, the less direct the sunlight is and the weaker the UV rays become. Above 42° north, for example—picture a line stretching roughly from Boston to northern California—it's difficult for many people to produce vitamin D during the winter. African-Americans, Latinos, and others with dark skin are at a further disadvantage, since their pigmentation limits the UV light they can absorb and slows vitamin D synthesis.

The final obstacle in vitamin D production is, or at least can be, the environment—the cause of the last big vitamin D crisis, in the early 1900s. As the industrial revolution kicked into high gear, more people moved to the cities and hunkered down in dark, dank tenements; meanwhile, pollution from bustling factories clouded the skies. The result was far fewer UV rays touching people's skin—and a lot more vitamin D deficiency. "At the turn of the last century," says Dr. Holick, "more than 80 percent of the kids in Boston had rickets."

While fortifying milk with vitamin D eventually solved the rickets problem, it may have given us a false sense of security. Research has shown that our milk supply, for all the trust we put in it, is remarkably unreliable. A 1992 study published in the *New England Journal of Medicine* showed that, of 42 milk samples tested, 26 contained less than the 400 international units (IU) of vitamin D per quart listed on the label. Some of the skim milk tested contained no D at all. In 2001, Cornell University researchers analyzed 648 samples of milk sold in New York State and found that 46 percent were underfortified.

But even if milk came as advertised, it still might not cover our bodies' needs. While the current recommended daily intake is 200 IU for adults up to age 50, there's a growing consensus that we need five times that—1,000 IU—to keep our blood levels where they should be. (An editorial in the *New England Journal of Medicine* several years ago argued for just such an increase.) And that's nearly impossible to get solely through diet, particularly since cold-water fish is the only food naturally high in D. As Dr. Holick puts it, "You'd have to take a multivitamin, drink two glasses of milk, and eat salmon every day just to begin to satisfy your vitamin D requirement."

THE D-BATE

On a recent morning—a warm, sunny one, it's worth noting—I am sitting in Dr. Holick's office at BU Medical Center. Lean and wiry, with shaggy white hair and lively blue eyes, Dr. Holick has been studying vitamin D since he was a graduate student at the University of Wisconsin 30 years ago. Lately, he's also become one of the most controversial vitamin D researchers. Earlier this year, just prior to the publication of his new book, *The UV Advantage*, Dr. Holick was asked to resign from BU's dermatology department by the chairwoman, Barbara Gilchrest, MD.

"She'd been e-mailing me for more than a year, saying her dermatologist friends had been questioning how I could be a professor of dermatology and suggest that people be exposed to some sunlight for their health," says Dr.

AN UDDER DISAPPOINTMENT
You "got milk"—but how about vitamin D?

Cows aren't vitamin D machines. That's why commercial dairies doctor fresh milk with 400 international units (IU) of D per quart—or at least they try to. As recently as 2001, a study found that what's in your cereal bowl may be decidedly low in vitamin D.

To see how dairies are doing today, we sent eight milk samples from four states—California, Illinois, Pennsylvania, and Tennessee—to a lab for vitamin D testing. The results: Six samples contained the correct amount of vitamin D, and two were actually overfortified. (One contained 6,000 extra IU, prompting us to notify the dairy.) Not bad, but the amount of milk tested was, statistically speaking, a drop in the bucket, which is why we also looked at the latest state data. Of 33 milk samples from the five largest dairies in Tennessee, 13 were underfortified. And in California, 21 out of 93 samples were found to contain less than the required amount of vitamin D. (Data from Pennsylvania and Illinois wasn't available at press time.)

This isn't to say that milk—the low-fat kind—isn't worth working into your diet; Harvard research suggests that dairy calcium can help you stay slim by forcing your body to burn more calories during digestion. For the time being, however, we've been soured on milk as a reliable source of vitamin D.

Holick, who still holds several positions at the university. "Then, in February, she told me she would like me to resign. Which I did."

Dr. Gilchrest declined to be interviewed for this story, but when one newspaper asked what she thought of Dr. Holick's recommendations, she answered, "I read better things in ladies' magazines." Her criticism was echoed by the American Academy of Dermatology, which likened the advice to "smoking to combat anxiety." (Dr. Holick's critics also say that he accepts money from the indoor-tanning industry. He doesn't dispute the charge, but claims the amount is small and comes with no conditions.)

In a way, it's tough to blame dermatologists for their hard-line zeal. In 1980, roughly 400,000 cases of skin cancer were diagnosed in the United States; this year it will be more than a million. Little wonder that the US government recently added UV radiation to the list of known human carcinogens.

Dr. Holick tells me he doesn't deny that skin cancer is a problem—in fact, he says that after a few minutes in the sun, people should cover up or use sunscreen. But he also believes that the zero-tolerance approach of many dermatologists could be just as dangerous.

Two large population-based studies seem to lend credence to his concern. A few years ago, a NASA physicist named William Grant, PhD, noticed that residents of New England were $1^1/_2$ to two times more likely to get prostate, colon, or breast cancer than those living in the Southwest. Intrigued, Grant began comparing the UV levels in 500 US cities and counties with the rates of cancer in those areas.

"I found a correlation between lower UV levels and a higher incidence of 12 different types of cancer," says Dr. Grant, who launched the San Francisco–based Sunlight, Nutrition and Health Research Center to further study vitamin D. More recently, Dr. Grant redid his study (which was published in the journal *Cancer*), this time controlling for other cancer risk factors, such as smoking and alcohol intake. The new research, which hasn't yet been published, confirmed his findings.

A similar geographic link has been found between sun exposure and multiple sclerosis: Cases of MS in the United States increase the farther north you go. And a new UK study found that those with skin cancer have half the rate of MS of those without cancer. Dr. Grant says the link is inescapable. "I estimate that half of the 400,000 with MS in the United States would not have MS if they had the same UVB doses as those living in the southern states."

THE EVIDENCE MOUNTS

If vitamin D were on trial in a court of law, Dr. Grant's findings would be circumstantial evidence—compelling but not enough to convict. A stronger case can be made for the connection between vitamin D and bone health. Not only does research show that low levels of D can increase your risk of osteoporosis by as much as 300 percent, but new research also is finding a link to unexplained bone pain. A study from the Riyadh Armed Forces Hospital in Saudi Arabia found that 80 percent of back-pain sufferers were light on vitamin D.

Less concrete—but more alarming—is exhibit B of D's relationship to cancer. Lab studies have shown that cancer cells have difficulty growing when D levels are normal; meanwhile, a study published 2 years ago in the *Journal of the American Medical Association* found that those with diets high in vitamin D were 40 percent less likely to develop potentially cancerous colon polyps.

Researchers have also discovered a link between vitamin D and heart health. Studies have shown that the farther you live from the equator, the higher your blood pressure is likely to be, and that people tend to have lower blood pressure during the summer, when UV rays are stronger. (The hormone that controls BP is regulated by vitamin D.) And a study in the *Journal of the American College of Cardiology* found that low vitamin D levels may be a factor in congestive heart failure.

Still, the idea of vitamin D as a possible panacea has some people, including many dermatologists, skeptical. James Spencer, MD, director of dermatologic surgery at the Mount Sinai Medical Center in New York City, says Dr. Holick and his colleagues remind him of the late Linus Pauling, the Nobel Prize–winning researcher who became obsessed with the idea that vitamin C could ward off everything from colds to cancer. "Dr. Holick got religion on vitamin D the same way Dr. Pauling got it on vitamin C," says Dr. Spencer. "It's a very appealing notion: Just take this pill, or spend more time in the sun, and everything will be fine. But come on, is life ever that simple?"

Vitamin D researchers, ironically, argue that it's the dermatologists who are oversimplifying things. "A tendency we all have is to focus on the disease in our specialty," says Dr. Heaney. "The dermatologists have looked at the rise in melanoma and panicked. But they aren't looking at the whole human being."

Dermatologists have also exaggerated the actual risk that skin cancer poses, say D experts. They note that, while skin cancer is the most frequently diagnosed cancer in the United States, more than 90 percent of cases are either basal-cell carcinoma or squamous-cell carcinoma. Both are relatively harmless if detected early. Granted, nearly 8,000 deaths per year from melanoma are not to be dismissed, but from a public-health standpoint, that makes skin cancer less of a problem than vitamin D deficiency is, says Bruce Hollis, PhD, a vitamin D researcher at the Medical University of South Carolina. "I tell my medical students that if I were going to have cancer, I'd rather have basal-cell carcinoma than breast cancer, colon cancer, or one of the other cancers linked to vitamin D deficiency."

ARE YOU D-FICIENT?

Find out if you're short on the sunshine vitamin

There are only two ways to detect low levels of vitamin D: Go for a blood test, or wait until a bone breaks. Our advice? Choose the first method: It's quick, it's covered by insurance, and it can be piggybacked onto the cholesterol panel you should be getting annually anyway. The specific parameter you want tested is called 25-hydroxy vitamin D, and your level should be at least 20 nanograms per milliliter (ng/ml), with 45 to 50 ng/ml being ideal. If you aren't at least at the lower limit, consider buying a vitamin D supplement, one labeled "Vitamin D_3," aka cholecalciferol. A Creighton University study showed that when men took a single vitamin D_3 supplement, it raised their levels of 25-hydroxy vitamin D and kept them elevated for 2 weeks, compared with a spike and then a dramatic drop with vitamin D_2. GNC sells a D_3 supplement that comes in a 700-international-unit daily dose.

DEALING WITH THE D-LEMMA

So in the end, are we simply left with a grim choice—dying of either too much sun (skin cancer) or too little (prostate cancer, MS)? Not necessarily. In the short term, those most at risk—African-Americans, people living in the northern part of the United States, the elderly—can get a blood test to see whether they have adequate levels of vitamin D. (See "Are You D-ficient?") We can also be judicious about which parts of our bodies get exposed to the sun: Since basal- and squamous-cell cancers most often appear on the face and ears, Dr. Holick suggests protecting those areas with sunscreen, while still exposing your arms and legs.

Of course, the ultimate solution would be to find some way to get the vitamin D we need while limiting our exposure to the sun. And those possibilities exist—from broader, more reliable fortification of the food supply to more powerful D supplements. (Right now, most multivitamins contain just 400 IU, even though toxicity only becomes a concern at 10,000 IU and above.) Or perhaps there's some other way.

"I'm a fan of Stanley Kubrick and the film *2001: A Space Odyssey*," Dr. Holick tells me as we sit in his office. "And in there, he has the astronauts being exposed to simulated sunlight to make vitamin D. I think that one day indoor lighting will be developed so you could actually be exposed to small amounts of UVB rays to get your vitamin D."

Vitamins from the lights? Maybe our future isn't as dark as it seems. But in the meantime, I've never been happier that I like salmon.

Scope Things Out

Three humiliating tests. Three ways to beat cancer and other mankillers. Our man bent over and tried them all so you don't have to

By David Brill

Imagine, if you will, that every flatulent offering you've leaked into the world since birth has somehow been captured and sadistically forced back into your colon.

Imagine, further, that a middle-aged guy sporting a goatee and designer glasses is orchestrating this by pumping you up through what feels like a kiddieland plastic straw he's inserted into your rectum.

Weirder still, imagine that his staff includes a female dominatrix-cum-med tech who barks, "Are you miserable yet?"

If your sexual fantasies play out along these lines, I say, glove the one you're with. But to me, this scenario represents just one particularly unpleasant episode in my mission to evaluate the range of tests—from the miraculous to the medieval—for assessing the health of the 30-foot-long link sausage known as the gastrointestinal (GI) tract.

GI complaints affect 70 million Americans, and colon cancer is the number-two cancer killer in the United States, behind lung cancer. It will eventually snuff nearly 40 percent of those who get it.

Many GI cancers are relatively easy to cure *if they're detected early,* says Douglas O. Faigel, MD, an associate professor of medicine at Oregon Health and Science University in Portland. Polyps—cancer incubators—can easily be removed from the colon wall before they turn nasty. But once they go south, you will, too.

So the answer is, yes, you need to have it checked, especially if you're over 50 or have a family history of colon cancer.

But among the multiple possibilities for bowel exploration, which way is best? In this mission, I'm GI Joe, on recon behind the lines of gastrointestinal diagnostics and determined to answer that very question.

I am under the command of Kent Farris, MD, a gastroenterologist with Gastrointestinal Associates in Knoxville, Tennessee, and, notably, a Bronze Star recipient in Vietnam. My tour of doody: swallowing a tiny video camera, having my rectum probed by a 5-foot-long colonoscope, and making that rendezvous with the sadistic med tech for a "virtual" colonoscopy. In the end, we'll all know which one serves best.

LIGHTS, CAMERA, DIGESTION

Though I've never been particularly discriminating about what I eat, I've never knowingly ingested an electronic device. So when Susan Cox, Dr.

Farris's petite, energetic medical technician, preps me to swallow a video camera, I feel my mouth go dry.

"Okay, down the hatch," she says, handing me the flashing pill—about the size of a large vitamin tablet—and a glass of ice water. It's not a perfect breakfast, but I'd rather accept the technology at the front door of my alimentary canal than at the service entrance in the rear. And the M2A, as it's called, is not a hard pill to swallow. A couple of sips and it slides down my gullet as easily as a raw oyster and begins its transit through my gut. During its 8-hour cruise, the pill will scan for polyps, blood, irritation, ulcers, blockages, cancer, Crohn's disease, and other abnormalities in my upper GI tract and send movies to a bulky pack strapped around my waist.

THE ELECTRIC KOOL-AID GASTRIC TEST

The camera pill's real strength lies in its ability to visualize the 20-foot-long small intestine—what Dr. Farris calls the "last frontier" of the digestive system. "Traditional studies can view the esophagus, stomach, and large intestine, but they can't explore the small bowel," says Dr. Farris. "You can't reach it from the mouth or the anus." (Making it one of the few areas safe from telemarketers.)

The camera has three primary weaknesses: It won't spend enough time in my stomach to scan it effectively; if it does spot a problem in my small intestine, a traditional scope or even surgery may be required to confirm or treat it; and because the camera's batteries will give out after it clears my small intestine, my colon-cancer prognosis must wait for another day.

The prep is a simple fast, and 4 hours after swallowing the pill, I'm allowed to drink clear liquids. Eight hours after ingestion, at 4 p.m., I return to the doctor's office, where Cox removes the monitors. The pill, which is not recyclable, will remain in my system for 24 to 48 hours before stealthily entering the Knox County wastewater-treatment system.

A couple of days later, Dr. Farris and I sit in front of a computer screen to watch the world premiere of I Am Dave's Digestive System. It begins with a fleeting cameo appearance by my tongue and the back of my teeth, segues in seconds to the pale pink folds of my stomach, and continues through the murky, mucus-coated tucks and folds of my small intestine. Projected on a bedsheet, the roiling and churning images produced by the M2A might be enough to incite drug-dosed hippies to start meadow dancing.

Though my GI system is, for the most part, healthy, Dr. Farris has detected two abnormalities: gastritis, erosions of the stomach lining caused, in my case, by the bacterium H. pylori; and celiac sprue, an underdiagnosed disorder of the small intestine that can result from an allergy to wheat gluten. Thanks, M2A.

(BOWEL) MOVING VIOLATION

Traditional, or optical, colonoscopy relies on a long, flexible tube called a colonoscope that's inserted through the rectum. If all goes well, it snakes in 3 or 4 feet, to thoroughly check out the juncture of the large and small intestines.

GI SPY

Five ways to stop colon problems before they stop you

Test	What is it?	How do I prepare?
Colonoscopy	The gold standard for colon-cancer screening. A telescoping tube takes colon pictures. Built-in tools snip problem tissues.	Fasting and colon cleansing with laxatives. Astronomical flatulence afterward as the inflated colon returns to normal.
Flexible sigmoidoscopy	A tube the size of a finger is inserted into your rectum, inflates it with air, and takes pictures of the lower colon. Can biopsy suspicious-looking tissues.	Liquid diet for 2 days. Two enemas before the exam. No sedation, and the procedure takes about 15 minutes. Lots of post-test flatulence.
Fecal occult blood test	A chemical test that detects occult ("hidden") blood in your feces, which can be a sign of cancer.	Smear a sample of your own stool on special test paper for 3 days in a row.
Capsule endoscopy	The M2A camera pill transmits video of all 20 feet of your small intestine. Used to diagnose Crohn's disease, celiac disease, and intestinal polyps.	Fasting beforehand. While the pill makes its trek, you wear a 3-pound receiving device that relays images from your small intestine. No side effects, and you'll pass the pill in your feces.
Virtual colonoscopy	As in a standard colonoscopy, the colon is inflated. Images are taken with CT scans, not a colon snake. The bad news: You're awake the whole time.	Same as for a standard colonoscopy. Same flatulence afterward, as well.

My prep for the lower procedure is medieval. I devote the day before the test to a purging process that can only be described as epic. At 3 p.m., I begin a fast and start ingesting a 6-hour regimen of three industrial-strength laxatives. They are remarkably fast-acting. Within 45 minutes of downing the first dose, my body is little more than a glorified waste chute, and I remain perched

What's it good for?	How much will it cost?
Explores the entire colon and removes polyps. It's the most accurate test available. Ninety percent of colon cancer is curable if caught early.	$800 to $1,600. Recommended once every 10 years for people of average risk, or more often if you have a family history or have had positive tests in the past.
The scope can't scan the upper part of the colon, where 40 percent of cancers and polyps are found. Must be paired with a fecal occult blood test for complete diagnosis.	$150 to $300, covered by insurance. Should be done every 4 years. Less trouble and expense than a colonoscopy, but less effective, too.
Not all cancers bleed, so the test is by no means definitive. Aspirin can produce a false positive.	Between $10 and $25, usually covered by insurance. Should be done once a year, in conjunction with a sigmoidoscopy.
The gutcam is 70 percent more effective at diagnosing problems in the small intestine than is the traditional endoscope. Not yet proven beyond the small intestine.	$1,000. Some insurance carriers may cover it. The test is most often prescribed to diagnose unexplained bleeding in the intestine.
According to the *Journal of the American Medical Association*, it's about one-half to one-third as accurate in spotting suspicious polyps. If it finds one, they snake 'n' snip anyway.	$950

on porcelain for most of the afternoon and evening, grateful that no one is around to hear the echoing sound effects.

By 6:15 the next morning, I've donned a hospital gown gaping in the rear and await my fate in the examining room. The 5-foot-long colonoscope is poised nearby, coiled like an adder, ready to strike.

Before the procedure, my most fervent hope was that the nurses attending Dr. Farris would be geriatric hags. Tragically, all three of them, including the anesthesiologist, are attractive young women who will regard me from my least flattering angle.

The angel of unconsciousness inserts an IV, and I register the etherlike "smell" of the drug just before I register absolutely *nothing*. Have at me, girls.

I awaken groggy a half hour later with a nurse standing over me, telling me the procedure went well. I'll have to take her word for it.

In 10 minutes, Dr. Farris arrives to give me my report, complete with color pictures. My colon is healthy, he tells me, and he was able to examine the entire 4 feet. Had he detected any polyps, he could have clipped them and sucked them out through a tube. It's a simple procedure, yet vitally important: "A polyp can become a cancer in a few years," Dr. Farris says.

That's why colonoscopy remains the master plumber of your nether regions: You can search and destroy with one bowel invasion.

DO IT TO ME ONE MORE TIME

While most healthy men have 10 years to recover before they undergo a second colonoscopy, I submit to two in as many hours. Heck, my colon's already cleansed; bring it on. I'm still groggy from the first procedure, so my girlfriend drives me to a nearby radiology lab.

This rectal probe will be "virtual" and "minimally invasive," according to the brochure. My colon will be inflated with enough air to pull tight any folds and creases in its wall. Two CT scans will then build detailed 2-D and 3-D images of the colon, revealing polyps and other diseases.

It sounds very cool and noninvasive, but an article in the *Journal of the American Medical Association* makes me wonder if I'm wasting my time. They sent people to get both tests, and the results were eye-opening: The virtual method spotted only 55 percent of the suspicious polyps that the standard colonoscopy found. The virtual procedure did even worse with smaller tumors. And even if it does spot a polyp, they'll need to go back in with the standard colonoscope to snip it out. So, as my appreciation for the sensitivity of my rectum rises, my doubts about the virtual scanner's sensitivity rise right along with it.

As I lie on yet another gurney—unanesthetized this time—the Marquis de Med Tech inserts a plastic tube into my rectum and begins squeezing a large bulb to infuse air into my colon. A female associate enters the room and asks, "Are you miserable yet?" I say yes, in a whining voice, but they keep on going.

I imagine the blessed relief that will come when my colon ruptures, glazing the technician's glasses with fetid yellow slime.

Despite my concerns about an exploding colon, the major risk of the procedure is from exposure to radiation. According to the radiation tech, I'm about to be dosed with 1,000 millirems—a hundred times more than you get from a chest x-ray. You don't do that for fun. The benefit: a radiological image from anus to esophagus that can show problems—chiefly tumors—in other organs as well.

The photo session is over in 10 minutes, and soon I'm sprinting toward the restroom, where I experience the sustained, violent, and wall-shaking release of gas as my grossly distended colon returns to normal.

The virtual scan is clean, confirming the findings of the earlier optical scan. My graphic description of the procedure elicits a knowing laugh from Dr. Farris. "They don't do a very good job of preparing patients for the discomfort," he says. A standard colonoscopy inflates the bowel as well, but they have the decency to knock you out before they gas you up.

What follows is a recovery day of binge eating and spontaneous releases of colonic gas. There's added comfort, as well: However ill-advised my dietary choices might be, I know that my healthy digestive tract has, of late, been through much, much worse.

NEED TO KNOW

DRUG NEWS

Pills That Kill

Two common heart medications may have a fatal effect when mixed, according to the *New England Journal of Medicine*. Researchers analyzed hospital records of 1.3 million patients and found that admissions for dangerously high potassium levels increased $4\frac{1}{2}$ times after doctors started treating heart failure with a mix of ACE inhibitors and the drug spironolactone. If you're popping these meds, don't stop—yet. "Have your doctor make sure they're right for you, and ask how often he should check your potassium levels," says study author David Juurlink, MD.

Dead Man Walking

A drug that's used to keep you up could knock you out for good. Provigil, a new medication for increasing alertness, can be bad for your heart, say Vanderbilt University researchers. In a study of 12 healthy people, one 400-milligram dose of Provigil caused a 10 percent increase in heart rate and similar rises in diastolic and systolic blood pressure. For those with heart disease or hypertension, these spikes could be dangerous, says study author Indu Taneja, MD. If you fit that description and you take Provigil, talk to your doctor.

Can You Bayer It?

People scheduled for heart surgery are often told to stop taking aspirin because its blood-thinning properties could lead to deadly blood loss on the operating table. But this precaution can also cost lives: Research shows that heart patients who take aspirin during the week prior to surgery have a 45 percent higher survival rate. Which way to go? Don't stop popping. Japanese researchers recently found that it's safe—and beneficial—to take aspirin until 3 days before heart surgery. In the study of 22 heart-surgery patients, the researchers noted that the patients' clotting ability returned to normal within 3 days of going off aspirin, says Koijiro Furukawa, MD, the study author. Of course, other seemingly benign pills, such as vitamins and herbal supplements, can cause trouble, so always tell your surgeon what you're swallowing.

A Stroke of Bad Luck

A common blood-pressure drug provides significantly less stroke protection than previously thought. Although the beta-blocker Atenolol lowers blood pressure, patients who take it have an 18 percent greater risk of stroke than do patients taking other BP drugs, according to a *Lancet* review of eight studies. "Beta-blockers are often the first line of treatment for high blood pressure, and Atenolol is one of the most popular," says study author Lars Lindholm, MD. "But this suggests that other drugs perform better." Ask your doctor about other options.

The Wonder Drug

Statins can reduce the risk of heart attack by as much as 60 percent—reason enough to fill the prescription. But research indicates that these little cholesterol-busting wonders may also perform several other lifesaving tricks, thanks in part to their anti-inflammatory properties. Here are some of the possible fringe benefits of a daily dose.

Statins may reduce the risk of . . .

- colon cancer by 51 percent

- macular degeneration by 50 percent

- stroke by 17 percent

- glaucoma by 40 percent

- prostate cancer by 56 percent

- erectile dysfunction by 30 percent

- rheumatoid arthritis by 50 percent

TREATMENTS

Exercise to Your Heart's Content

Sweat or stent? German researchers say exercise is a better treatment than angioplasty for heart disease. A year after 101 men with coronary-artery disease either had a stent angioplasty or began riding a bike 20 minutes a day, 88 percent of the cyclists had had no cardiac events, versus 70 percent of stent recipients. Exercise, unlike surgery, benefits the entire network of blood vessels, says study author Rainer Hambrecht, MD. "Stents will remain the therapy of choice but should be combined with aggressive lifestyle changes," he says.

Insulin Intervention

A "crash course" of insulin may help treat type-2 diabetes, say Canadian scientists. A year after newly diagnosed patients received 2 to 3 weeks of intense insulin treatment, seven patients no longer needed diabetes medication, eight needed only glucose tablets, and only one required daily insulin injections. More tests are still needed.

TESTS

Get Results in a Snap

Sometimes snoring is simple noise pollution. But at other times, it signals sleep apnea, which can increase the risk of heart disease and erectile dysfunction. How do you know if the wood you're sawing is a coffin in the making? Go to a sleep lab. Or, even better, test yourself for sleep apnea. When US Air Force researchers monitored 20 patients with both the SNAP home test and traditional laboratory equipment, they found that the results were almost equal. The SNAP test is available by prescription.

The Scope of the Problem

It's literally a pain in the butt, but a colonoscopy is worth the lifesaving potential. Colonoscopies can sometimes fail to spot cancer, however, say researchers in Toronto. In a study of nearly 5,000 people who had colon-cancer surgery, 4 percent had had clean colonoscopies despite the presence of cancer. Though the miss rate is low, it's still troubling. To ensure an accurate exam, prep exactly as instructed. "If you don't, there's a chance that the bowel won't be cleaned out, and that makes it difficult to examine," says study author Linda Rabeneck, MD.

PERCENTAGE OF MEN AGE 50 AND OLDER WHO HAVEN'T HAD THEIR PSA LEVELS CHECKED THIS YEAR: 43.3

CANCER NEWS
Not Worth the Wait

Men diagnosed with early-stage prostate cancer often employ "watchful waiting," in which treatment is used only if the disease progresses. But for many men with prostate cancer, early action may be a better strategy than watchful waiting. Swedish researchers assessed 223 patients who had watched and waited for 20 years. Those men had triple the mortality rate of those who sought treatment. "Before this study, there was no evidence that early treatment conveyed any survival benefit," says study author Hans-Olov Adami, MD, PhD. If you're diagnosed with prostate cancer at age 60 or younger, consider a radical prostatectomy, advises Dr. Adami.

In related news, many prostate-cancer patients who delay radiation treatment are prescribed hormone therapy while they're waiting. But when researchers at Fox Chase Cancer Center analyzed the medical records of almost 1,500 patients, they determined that men who receive hormone therapy to treat prostate cancer before radiation have the same recovery rates as those who skip the hormones. If your doctor insists on hormone therapy, consider finding another doctor.

Harmful Hormone?

Rather than keep men young, supplemental testosterone may escort them to an early exit. Research from Johns Hopkins University indicates that testosterone associated with hormone-replacement therapy (HRT) is linked to an increased risk of prostate cancer. HRT increases blood levels of free testosterone, and in a study of 794 men, those with the highest levels of naturally occurring free testosterone had an 88 percent greater risk of prostate cancer than men with the lowest levels. Men considering HRT should proceed with caution until more data about the link between HRT and prostate cancer is available, says J. Kellogg Parson, MD, the lead study author.

Your Breast Defense

While it's not the epidemic that it is in women, breast cancer in men is on the rise. Researchers at the University of Texas M.D. Anderson Cancer Center studied 25 years of data and found that breast-cancer rates in men increased by 25 percent from 1973 to 1998. The study also showed that survival rates for men were lower than for women, and that men were more likely to be diagnosed with late-stage cancer. In other words, guys don't spot the disease soon enough. "If a man finds a lump under one of his nipples, he should see his doctor and potentially have a mammogram or a biopsy," says Sharon Giordano, MD, the study author.

NUTRITION NEWS

Sometimes You Feel Like a Nut

The storehouse of selenium in Brazil nuts has already been shown to protect against prostate cancer, and now, new research confirms that selenium may help ward off colon cancer. University of Arizona researchers found that men with high blood levels of selenium are six times less likely to develop colon cancer than men with low levels. The mineral causes cancer cells to self-destruct. "If a cell senses damage to itself, it can begin a process that will result in the cell's death—good news if it's a cancer cell," says lead researcher Beth Jacobs, PhD. Eating just one nut a day will keep you at optimum cancer-fighting levels.

Fishing for a Healthier Heart

Eating more seafood is one of the easiest and most effective ways a man can reduce his chances of having a heart attack. In a recent study that analyzed the eating habits of more than 220,000 people for more than 11 years, scientists at Northwestern University figured out just how much you can tip the scales in your favor.

Servings of fish	Heart-disease risk reduction
1 to 3 per month	11 percent
1 per week	15 percent
2 to 4 per week	23 percent
5 or more per week	38 percent

SAFETY

Pack Your Bags

Turns out side air bags are not optional. A study at the University of Alabama found that in frontal collisions, side air bags protected the head and neck as well as seatbelts and better than front air bags. Side air bags also reduced head injury by 75 percent in side collisions.

WHAT'S NEW

Butt Out

Smokers may soon be able to kick the habit for good. Two drug companies—one in the United States and one in Britain—are racing to develop the first FDA-approved smoking vaccine. The vaccines work by blocking nicotine molecules from reaching the brain. So when smokers light up, they don't get the high. The vaccine won't, however, take away the craving. With funding from the National Institute on Drug Abuse, Nabi Pharmaceuticals' product—called NicVax—has already gone through phase 2 trials. Results are promising: Thirty-three percent of the smokers receiving the highest dose of NicVax quit smoking for a month or more. And even the folks who didn't stay smoke free on NicVax lit up a lot less.

Easy to Swallow

You know that popping an aspirin during a heart attack can save your life and prevent damage to heart muscle. But carrying a bottle of aspirin in your pocket ruins the drape of your gabardines, and loose pills gather pocket lint. Enter John Higgins, who, after reading a *Men's Health* article on aspirin's powers, created the Re-Pillable card—a slender device that fits in your wallet's credit card slot and holds five aspirin. Available at www.repillable.com.

Go for the Shock Value

You used to need a doctor's note to purchase a lifesaving defibrillator. Now the FDA has approved the sale of home defibrillators without a prescription. "I would love to see them in every home," says P.K. Shah, MD, a *Men's Health* advisor and the director of cardiology at Cedars-Sinai Hospital. "But they should at least be in the homes of individuals with or at risk of heart disease."

PERCENTAGE OF MEN WHO DON'T KNOW THEIR CHOLESTEROL LEVELS: 40

Perhaps where Little Leaguers play, too: A defibrillator can save a child who collapses from a ball to the chest. Look for the Philips HeartStart model ($2,000).

Be on the Level

After analyzing more than a dozen studies, researchers writing in the *Journal of the American College of Cardiology* determined that the healthiest LDL cholesterol level is in the 50- to 70-milligrams-per-deciliter (mg/dl) range—almost half of the current "safe" range. Even lowering LDL to 79 mg/dl reduces levels of C-reactive protein (CRP, a marker for the inflammation that's a precursor of heart disease) by an average of 36 percent, says study author James O'Keefe, MD. When LDL is lowered to 110, CRP drops by only 5 percent. Zap high LDL with foods rich in soluble fiber and monounsaturated fats.

Lung Cancer Cure

A vaccine developed at Baylor University Medical Center leads to a decline in tumor growth among patients with advanced non-small-cell lung cancer (NSCLC). Created with cells from the patients' tumors and a gene called GM-CSF, the vaccine alters the surfaces of cancerous cells so the immune system can find and destroy them. The drug could be approved for use sometime in 2006.

THE COST OF . . .

. . . Smoking

You know tobacco is a killer, and you know how hard it is to quit. The average smoker dies an average of 10 years sooner than his fresh-lunged friends and risks skin cancer, ulcers, and even blindness. Debilitation and death not convincing? How about money? Here's what 1 year of smoking can cost you.

You'll have to . . .	The research says . . .	It'll Cost You . . .
Pick up 365 packs of smokes	The average adult inhales 7,300 cigarettes a year.	$1,431
Take a lower bid on your house at resale	One-third of house shoppers said the smell of smoke was their biggest turnoff. And nearly 40 percent said they'd offer less on a house that smelled smoky.	$5,100
Work on your smile with tooth whitening or veneers	Tobacco yellows teeth and restricts bloodflow to the gums, causing eventual tooth loss.	$2,500
Treat your stomach to Pepcid, Tums, and a trip to the gastroenterologist	Lighting up incites heartburn and peptic ulcers. It can also damage the liver and may cause gallstones.	$285
Take lutein supplements for your eyes	Smokers are four times more likely to go blind from age-related macular degeneration.	$122
Visit a dermatologist and likely have a surgery or two	Puffers have a higher risk of developing skin cancers.	$110
Swallow some little blue pills for the bedroom	Men with high blood pressure who smoke a pack a day are 60 percent more likely than nonsmokers to suffer from erectile dysfunction.	$180
TOTAL		$9,728

FAST FIXES

Recently, more and more studies have shown that a substance called C-reactive protein (CRP) is a valuable predictor when it comes to forecasting heart disease. Though it was discovered in 1930, doctors now know that CRP helps measure chronic inflammation and the overall health of your arteries. The higher your CRP level, the more at risk you may be for heart disease—even if your other indicators look normal.

"Half of all heart attacks and strokes in the United States each year occur among people with essentially normal cholesterol levels," says Paul Ridker, MD, a professor of medicine at Harvard Medical School. "There's more to heart disease than just lipids. In addition to the problem of cholesterol, there's the problem of the immune system or the inflammation response."

A heart attack occurs when plaque ruptures inside your blood vessels. But that rupturing hinges not just on how much plaque you have but also on the degree of inflammation, Dr. Ridker says. Your level of CRP—measured by a simple blood test—helps detect this condition so you can predict whether you're in danger of cardiovascular disease and stroke. "You can be at quite a high risk of both despite having normal cholesterol," Dr. Ridker says. "Even people with low cholesterol but high CRP are at high risk."

Luckily, just as you can with cholesterol and body fat, you can take steps to shrink your CRP. "If you have your CRP measured in your twenties and thirties, you can prevent heart disease and strokes in your fifties and sixties," Dr. Ridker says. Ask your doctor to piggyback a "high-sensitivity CRP test" on top of any other blood test. Ideally, you'll want it measured whenever you have a cholesterol check, or at least every 5 years. You're at low risk if your CRP is less than 1 milligram per liter (mg/l), moderate risk if it's 1 to 3 mg/l, and high risk if it's above 3 mg/l. Aside from drugs such as statins, lifestyle changes—like the eight lifesavers that follow—are the best way to whittle down your CRP. Start doing these now so you'll never end up in the ER clutching your chest.

1. Pop a multivitamin. A *grande* cappuccino isn't the only thing you'd better slug down before you go to work. A study in the *American Journal of Medicine* showed that people who popped a multivitamin each morning for 6 months decreased their CRP by 0.7 milligrams per liter (mg/l). And a University of California at Berkeley study found that people who took 500 milligrams of vitamin C saw a 24 percent drop in CRP after just 2 months.

Arch Mainous, PhD, a professor of family medicine at the Medical University of South Carolina, says CRP levels are connected to the amount of stress caused by free radicals in your body. "Vitamins C and E decrease the oxidative stress," he says.

Take 500 milligrams of a vitamin C supplement, or a multivitamin like GNC Men's Mega Men, which contains one of the highest levels of vitamin C (300 milligrams) in a multi. Another way to swallow more C: cherries. In a small study published in the *Journal of Nutrition,* people who ate two daily servings of cherries lowered their CRP by 16 percent.

2. Trust your Greek friends. Whether for your car, your uncle's hair, or your arteries, the right kind of oil can make everything run smoothly. A recent study at the University of Athens in Greece found that people who most closely followed a Mediterranean diet—one rich in olive oil—had CRP numbers 20 percent lower than those of their less oily brethren. "We believe olive oil helps turn off the gene that makes the pro-inflammatory molecules that attach to your arteries," says Michael Roizen, MD, a professor of medicine at SUNY Upstate Medical University and author of *Real Age: Are You As Young As You Can Be?* Dr. Roizen suggests taking in 25 percent of your daily calories from monounsaturated fats, with an emphasis on olive oil as the source. One way to sneak it in: breakfast. Take a tablespoon of olive oil and mix in the spice of your choice—oregano if you like Italian food, red pepper if you like things spicy—then spread it on your toast, bagel, or English muffin. Or use it instead of butter when you're cooking eggs.

3. Floss like a fiend. There's a price to pay for a dirty mouth. One study in the *Journal of Periodontology* shows that the inflammatory effects of periodontal disease also cause inflammation of your arteries; signs of disease in multiple spots in your mouth can hike CRP by 14 percent. "The bacteria that cause gum disease, we think, set up an immune reaction that attacks your arteries," Dr. Roizen says. Floss daily and make regular dentist appointments so hygienists can remove plaque.

4. Build a salmon burger. Yet another bullet point to add to fish oil's already impressive résumé: "Lowers CRP." In a new Harvard study, people who consumed the most omega-3 fatty acids (1.6 grams per day) had 29 percent lower CRP readings than those who ate the least. "Omega-3 fatty acids may decrease hydrogen peroxide, which plays an important role in the inflammatory process," says study author Esther Lopez-Garcia, PhD. Good sources of omega-3s include flaxseed, walnuts, sardines, tuna, and, of course, salmon. And though wild salmon is tops for taste, the canned kind is better at lowering CRP. "Canned salmon is packed in vegetable oils that also contain omega-3s," says Dr. Lopez-Garcia. Here's how to get your health on a roll: Drain the liquid from a 6-ounce can of pink salmon and dump the fish into a bowl. Mix well with one Eggland's Best egg (fortified with 150 milligrams omega-3s), $1/4$ cup of diced red onion, and a tablespoon of bread crumbs. Form into two patties and dredge in additional bread crumbs. Bake at 350°F for about 20 minutes. Slip the patties inside whole-wheat buns.

5. Cut the fuel supply. We already know what kind of damage fat can do—both to your body and to subway turnstiles. Losing that fat by cutting calories is an important way to put the squeeze on CRP. In a Wake Forest University study, those who cut calories and lost weight reduced their CRP by 6 percent over an 18-month period, says study author Barbara Nicklas, PhD. She speculates that the body reduces inflammation because it's not being stoked with excess calories.

Dr. Nicklas says that firing up your metabolism with interval training can also help decrease inflammation. Try this track workout: After warming up, run a quarter of the way around a track (about 100 meters) at close to sprint pace. Rest until you recover, then run 200 meters as fast as you can at a near-sprint pace. Rest, then do 300 meters. Rest, then do 400 meters. Now come back down the ladder—300 meters, then rest; 200 then, rest; and finally 100 meters.

6. Eat fiber, fiber, and more fiber. Leave the Froot Loops for the kids and reach for the All-Bran. In a study published in the *Journal of Nutrition,* the odds of having high levels of CRP dropped by 40 percent for those people who had the most fiber during the day. Possible reasons include fiber's impact on insulin and its ability to bring down cholesterol and blood pressure. "It's also possible that fiber may have an independent effect through other processes," says study author Umed Ajani, MD. Whatever the reason, consume your recommended 20-plus grams of fiber with the ABC method: Each day, eat an apple (3 grams), two slices of whole-grain bread (4 grams), and a large bowl of fiber-rich cereal such as All-Bran (13 grams).

7. Go out with the guys. Catch *Monday Night Football* together and the social interaction may help you beat another CRP booster: depression. According to a Johns Hopkins University study, men who were depressed had a 64 percent chance of having higher levels of CRP, and a new Duke study showed that people with moderate symptoms of depression had two times higher CRP numbers than their light-hearted counterparts. The causes aren't clear, but depression may boost norepinephrine, a stress hormone that trig-

PERCENTAGE OF MEN WHO WOULD WAIT A FEW DAYS BEFORE GOING TO A DOCTOR FOR CHEST PAIN OR DISCOMFORT: 37

gers chronic inflammation. Bonus: Down a beer with the boys and you may lower your CRP even further, according to a study published in the journal *Atherosclerosis*.

8. Then sleep in the next day. A Harvard study reports that skimping on sleep can ratchet up your CRP. Two groups slept either 8.2 or 4.2 hours for 10 consecutive nights. The latter group experienced a fourfold increase in their CRP levels. The spike that sleep deprivation causes in the stress response may increase CRP. "If you feel that you aren't getting sufficient sleep, a diagnostic sleep study may be warranted," says Janet Mullington, PhD, one of the study authors. Visit www.aasmnet.org/listing.asp to find a sleep clinic.

OUR FINAL ANSWERS

Bruise Clues

I'm on aspirin therapy and bruise like a peach. Should I be worried?

—L.U., Salem, New Hampshire

Maybe. Some bruising is normal, since aspirin reduces blood clotting. But excessive bruising can be a sign of bigger problems, like liver disease. If your gums bleed or there's any blood in your urine, tell your doctor immediately.

The Heart Never Forgets

I've heard that statins can cause memory loss. Should I really take them if this is a side effect?

—J.S., Corpus Christi, Texas

The experts are watching this; there's some concern about possible memory loss associated with statins. A large study is under way to evaluate this prospect. We do know that statins dramatically reduce heart attacks and strokes—both of which certainly have an adverse impact on memory. So until we have conclusive evidence that states otherwise, continue taking your statin.

Prostate Panic

I read that the standard PSA test for prostate cancer is now considered to be flawed. What's going on here? I thought that was the most reliable measure of a man's risk.

—J.K., Columbus, Ohio

Conventional wisdom has always said that if you have a PSA (prostate-specific antigen) score above 4.0, you could have prostate cancer. (A biopsy would confirm it.) But in a recent *New England Journal of Medicine* study, prostate cancer was found in 15 percent of participants whose PSAs were less than 4.0. The knee-jerk reaction: Uh-oh. The intelligent reaction: "There's no cause for alarm," says Alan W. Partin, MD, PhD, a professor of urologic oncology at Johns Hopkins Medical Institutions. The PSA test is not obsolete. Dr. Partin's advice: Have a PSA test when you hit age 40, especially if you're African-American or have a family history of prostate cancer. If your PSA comes in at 0.6 or lower, you don't have to be checked for another 5 years. If your score is between 0.6 and 2.5, go back for annual checks. But if your PSA is 2.6 or greater, talk to your doctor about two other prostate-cancer markers: Free PSA shows how much PSA is bound to proteins in your blood (unbound is better). If your free-PSA level is less than 10 percent, you're due for a biopsy, says Dr. Partin.

The other marker, PSA velocity, measures the change in PSA over time. Since PSA levels rise more rapidly in men with cancer than in men without it, an increase of 0.75 points or more in a year means it's biopsy time.

The Pressure's Off

Do those blood-pressure machines at the drugstore really work?

—D.M., Pottsville, Pennsylvania

No. *Men's Health* advisor P.K. Shah, MD, director of cardiology at Cedars-Sinai Medical Center in Los Angeles, is skeptical about the accuracy of these machines. "They do not use the Gold Standard for Blood Pressure Measurement, which is the most reliable machine for blood-pressure measurement," says Dr. Shah. "Drugstores' machines are not regularly checked or calibrated and depend heavily on how correctly the cuff is placed on the arm." Definitely avoid the ones that take a measurement from your finger; they are notoriously unreliable.

Chew on This

If I chew nicotine gum to help me quit smoking, won't I become addicted to the gum?

—D.P., St. Joseph, Missouri

You might, but it would still be better than smoking. The gum slowly reduces the dosage of nicotine and keeps you from inhaling all the other toxins that come in cigarettes. The gum also helps you break the psychological addiction because it doesn't provide any of the sensory associations (the feel of the cigarette, the smell of tobacco, the sound of a lighter) that kick your brain into craving a smoke.

PERCENTAGE OF ADULTS WHO FIB TO THEIR DOCTOR ABOUT WHETHER OR NOT THEY SMOKE AND HOW MUCH: 22

Happy to Quit

Why do doctors prescribe antidepressants for smokers trying to quit?

—M.U., Boulder, Colorado

You're asking about bupropion, which is found in both Zyban, a smoking-cessation drug, and Wellbutrin, an antidepressant. Bupropion replaces the chemical that stimulates nicotine cravings in the brain. It can also relieve some withdrawal symptoms, such as anxiety, depression, and irritability. You don't need to be depressed for this to work—as if you needed a reason to be happy to be smoke-free.

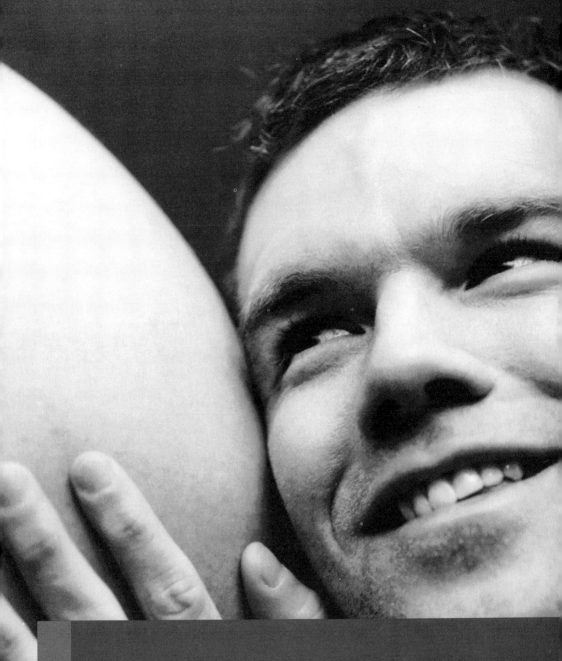

SIX

BE A GREAT DAD

READ UP ON IT

The Last Smith

He wants kids. She doesn't. It's an increasingly common role reversal.
What's a wannabe daddy to do?

By Larry Smith

"**Y**ou have it so good."

This is what friends have been telling me for the past 7 years—since I started dating Piper, the woman who recently became, for lack of a better term, my fiancée. Five seemingly innocuous words describing the evidently enviable situation surrounding my fiancée's views on spawning (as in: Let's not).

Yet I promise you, I don't have it so good. When the love of your life isn't pushing you to impregnate her, your buddies declare her Woman of the Year. But you're left having to make some incredibly adult decisions that even a man who's lived and loved for more than 3 decades thought would be—somehow, some way, by somebody—made for him.

Like: Am I willing to let the family name die on my watch?

THE SEVENTH INNING STRETCH

After 7 genuinely interesting, reasonably committed, sex-is-still-good years with Piper, there's no reason to suspect we won't be together for 60 more. But until recently, much to the astonishment and admiration of my pals, we hadn't spent much time talking about what I always thought was my inevitable segue from late-night *Seinfeld* to mornings with Snuffleupagus. Perhaps I'd avoided the subject because she's always made it quite clear that a child isn't a huge priority for her, nor is giving up red wine for 9 months. (And how could I ask anyone to give up red wine?) She hadn't brought it up, and neither had I. Mutual avoidance was working wonders.

That changed not long ago when we were both having a particularly good time trading funny faces with a dangerously cute 1-year-old in a Mexican restaurant. Riding what was up to that point a perfect two-margarita buzz, I was suddenly sobered up by Piper: "You're not going to turn 42, freak out, and leave me for some 27-year-old who's eager to be a mom, are you?"

Good question. If I were to turn 42 and despair about not being a daddy, the logical solution would be to find a younger woman who wanted kids.

There always seem to be a lot of them around. I'd prefer to avoid that situation, of course, it being bad manners and all. Yet I can't get this notion of daddy destiny out of my head. It's a destiny tied in part to the fun of making goofy faces, but also to some innate and yet completely out-of-character desire to carry on the family name.

I am, after all, the last Smith.

THE FAMILY TREE IS COUNTING ON ME

The first Smith was my grandfather Morris, who died 2 years ago after an excellent run that began in the Russian town of Minsk and ended 91 years later in a tony suburb of Philadelphia. Upon arrival, his family was anointed "Smith," a loose translation of the family name of Blacksmith, an irony not lost on the generations of Smith family men who haven't produced much in the metal shop.

We do, however, like betting on horses.

Smitty had two boys, dad Louis and uncle Ralph. Dad had two girls and me. Ralph got married to Kathy, with whom he shares a travel-rich and kid-free existence. This makes me the only living male in my family still realistically likely to father children. "It's up to you," the first Smith said wistfully 10 years ago at my sister's wedding, as my girlfriend at the time looked on in horror.

When my grandfather lamented the possible end of the Smiths, he was, in a sense, joking. But still: Will I have kids? Everyone seems to need an answer. I hear it from my parents, who bring up the high-school sweetheart who squeezed out her first offspring at 24, an age at which I felt lucky if my cat survived the weekend. I hear it from my older sister (two young boys, one newborn girl, and—one hopes—a vasectomy to be named later), who enjoys cornering my girlfriend at family gatherings and declaring, "I just want you to know that if you have a child out of wedlock, that's okay." Thanks, sis.

UNCHARTED TERRITORY

To Smith or not to Smith? Seemingly the oldest question in the book, and yet to me it's completely new territory. My grandfather and father didn't have to ask these questions. Their lives had expected plans and paths, with relationships that fell into the traditional gender roles of their day. I am part of

NUMBER OF AMERICANS WHO DEFINE SUCCESS BY THE WELL-BEING OF THEIR FAMILY OR HOW WELL THEY RAISE THEIR CHILDREN: **1 in 3** the first generation of men who have to answer these questions with no model to look back upon.

My guy friends picked their partners not because they viewed them as fertile vessels of future momdom but because they are soul mates in life—strong women who can't wait to attack class-four rapids, can figure the re-fi on a condo, and look hot in a tool belt. These are not women likely to stay at home all day finger painting with the tykes, greeting us with a scotch and slippers after a hard day at the office. Nationally, women are waiting longer to spawn: The latest census reveals that the age at which a woman gives birth to her first child has increased steadily for 3 decades. (It's now 25.) And many women are choosing to take a pass entirely; birthrates are down 17 percent since their 1990 peak, according to the National Center for Health Statistics.

For the first time since, oh, the beginning of time, men are being asked to keep their seeds to themselves. (In China, I hear, they even give you a rebate.) So if I or my many friends in similar situations do want kids, not only do we have to make the case, but we may have to agree to become the de facto moms as well. This is serious stuff, in a "custody to the plaintiff" sort of way. I'm fine taking over traditionally female responsibilities like playdates and poopy diapers, but putting my career on hold? Who's got the time? And what if I end up, I don't know, watching porn during nap time? What kind of example is that?

"It's so tricky because traditionally the woman is supposed to bug you about it until you just go off and do it," says my best friend, Lenny, a 35-year-old real live rocket scientist living in San Francisco. "But in the case of my wife, the burden is on me to make the pitch—to actually decide whether I want one or not. And because she's kind of pushing for 'no,' if I make a strong case, we have a child, and we're miserable, then it's my freakin' fault. I can't even blame her."

Plus, at age 35, I'm old enough to have really learned how to enjoy myself. I picture my pop going from college to marriage to family to mortgage—leaving no time or money to hit the trails of Nepal or get gigs with a band on the Lower East Side. Luckily, it all happened so fast that he didn't know what he was missing. Many of my friends have spent a solid decade postcollege trying out a few different careers, exploring their creative sides, traveling all over the globe. "We're so deep into the hedonism, and we're so good at it," says Lenny, "that it's hard to give up."

WELCOME TO PARENTHOOD

Our pal Eddie, 31, wasn't ready to give it up. That was clear to anyone attending the Giants-Dodgers game at Pac Bell Park last summer. Eddie, an Oakland furniture designer, had won a booze cruise outside the ballpark for 30 of his closest friends. His wife was home that night with their 3-week-old boy, Jackson. Eddie's wife, who's 5 years older than he is, had been eager to start a family and convinced the guy known as "Freedom Ed" to come to the plate. "I figured it would take her at least a year to get pregnant, and then another 9 months to have the child, so I was banking on 2 more years," he recalls. Then he hit it out of the park on his first swing. A little more than 9 months later, after countless martinis, Freedom Ed jumped off the boat, swam across San Francisco Bay, climbed onto the pier, flopped into the stadium, and ran across the promenade naked, egged on by the astounded crowd. The police arrested him and threw Jackson's dad in the drunk tank.

My friend Chuck, in his late forties, describes coming home from the hospital with his son and celebrating by smoking a little pot with the kid's aunt. A few puffs later he realized it was time to change his dude's diaper for the first time. Chuck started to get down to business, when his 1-day-old dude projectile-pooped all over himself, the wall, the dresser, and his dad.

"My sister and I were hysterically laughing," says Chuck. "But at that moment I realized *I cannot be high and take care of this baby.*"

THE BACHELOR LIFE OR BABYHOOD?

In one of the few official looks at male decision-making with regard to making babies, a University of Montana study called "Men's Experience of Making the Decision to Have Their First Child" found that men talked mainly about their fears of what they would lose if they had a child—freedom, independence, and intimacy, for starters. "I was really struck by how little difference there was in how they talked about these potential losses, whether the man was 18 or 40," says study coauthor Andrew Peterson, EdD.

My pal Patrick was so fearful he took preventive action: 34 years old and single, he got a vasectomy. The only hard part was The Consultation, in which two thirtysomething women—after triple-checking the master script of the American Dream—closely questioned him about his decision: "Are you sure you want to do this?" Then they played a video of a dad manning the barbecue with three kids on the deck and mom waddling around pregnant in the background. The narrator relayed the importance of making the right decision . . . after you've had a family. "After 2 minutes," Patrick recalls, "I popped out the video and said, 'This doesn't apply to me. I'll sign the papers now.'"

My fiancée has made it clear that unless I'm emotionally prepared for the responsibility, she's not even going to entertain the thought of bringing a mini-me into this world. But how does a person know? Even satisfied customers admit they stepped in blind. I'm fascinated when Sammy, a father of two, says the only thing he really misses is watching *Monday Night Football* in its entirety. I'm amazed to hear Scott, my buddy since second grade, explain that while he's barely gotten any sleep in the 3 months since his daughter, Delanie, was born, he's working off a "baby high." I'm intrigued to hear, over and over, "It's the best thing that will ever happen to you," even if I can't fathom how.

"I do worry I'm missing out on one of life's adventures," says Lenny, who was able to squeeze in a conversation between rock-climbing trips at Yosemite. "Presumably it's the reason we're here—to keep the species going. I don't want people to say, 'Lenny, I can't believe you're not populating the race. You're such a dick, man.'"

There aren't many role models in pop culture for the childless. Typical is Hugh Grant's character in *About a Boy*, who's a lout until he learns he can make a miserable boy happy (largely by buying him cool sneakers, but still). Or Campbell Scott in *Roger Dodger*, a pitiable figure—until he forms a special bond with his nephew. Message: You're a selfish clod, lost and lonely, until a child enters your life.

So what's a Smith to do? One young mom after another keeps telling me that Piper's maternal instinct will kick in and my daddy desire will go into overdrive. If that happens, I suppose we'll spawn, turn into piles of parental mush, immediately declare it the best decision of our lives, and start obsessing about school districts. At least the decision will be made and we'll be able to get back to refinancing our mortgage.

As for the original Smitty, he became more zen about the whole baby notion over the years. Just after his last birthday, with my girlfriend far out of earshot, I asked my grandfather his latest thoughts about the possibility of the Smiths' demise. The first Smith grinned a big grin, and then, with a little shrug, said, "You know, there are plenty of Smiths in the phone book."

Father Really Does Know Best

As a tortured nerd in high school, I sought my tough-guy father's counsel. My dad's surprising advice changed my life forever

By Mike Jollett

When I was 15, I was terrorized by a 12th-grade headbanger. A big, mean S.O.B. who ran with the skinheads, snorted coke before school, and walked the halls with a menacing scowl on his face and a 4-inch switchblade tucked in his vest. I was a nerd. Or, perhaps more precisely, I was an achiever: honor-service-club president, straight-A student, essay-contest winner, track-team captain. I guess all that suburban propriety offended him (hell, it offended me at times), and somewhere along the line he decided that he hated me. He'd sabotage my locker, yell at me between classes, intimidate my friends. He once even slammed my lily-white cheerleader girlfriend's head into a desk. Everyone at the school was afraid of him. I was afraid of him. I had no idea what to do about it.

So, I told my dad. Now, Dad and I were nothing alike. It's fair to say that throughout my childhood, we had a strained relationship. He could be a great guy and all, but because of his ninth-grade education and bad temper, I wanted nothing more than not to be him. He'd been an outlaw in his youth, running drugs to Mexico, writing fraudulent checks, and spending 3 years in prison. These things haunted me. I mean, they were good stories to tell my buddies, whose suburban fathers were typical rat racers. But I felt marked, the child of a felon, destined for a life of mediocrity.

I would literally picture his face as I memorized chemistry formulas at 3 a.m. or rounded the final turn of some track workout, arms flailing, face drawn back in a deathly grimace, driving myself into the ground, running away from what seemed like the destiny he'd created for me.

My dad would've thought this was funny, had I come clean with him at the time. Not because he considered my work pointless, but because he always described prison in the '60s as just another bump on a long road. It was nothing like the modern conception, with murders in the wood shop and gang rapes in the shower. It seemed almost charming, like something out of *Cool Hand Luke*. A place filled with roughneck, blue-collar guys with missing teeth,

AGE AT WHICH THE AVERAGE SON DISLIKES HIS DAD THE MOST: 17

who play poker, get in fistfights, and have trouble with the conjugation of basic verbs.

Everyone in prison thought my dad was crazy. Whenever someone came too close, he'd go berserk, yelling with that incredibly powerful voice of his, intimidating whoever approached him, convincing them that he was a cannon ready to go off. And maybe he was. In any case, it worked. They left him alone. And he got through it. "I did my time, and they did theirs," my dad would say.

Which is why he seemed like the right guy to talk to about the headbanger. I sat him down one morning and told him about the threats, the intimidations, the months spent with my stomach in knots. He listened intently and thought for a moment, furrowing his weathered brow as I did during geometry class. Then he looked up and said, simply, "Well, you're going to have to kick his ass."

THE ANATOMY OF AN ASS KICKING

This was a quandary. Kick his ass? The thought had never occurred to me. I would have been less surprised if he'd told me to quit school and join the circus. I was not a kicker of asses. The SAT, service clubs, track meets—these things I could do. But kick ass? Absurd. I'd never even been in a real fight. But my dad was dead serious: "Just 'cause he's bigger don't mean sh––."

Half an hour later, I stood in the driveway in front of our house with my dad, receiving instruction, like a heavyweight boxer, on how to throw a punch ("Stay on your toes, keep your elbows in, and when you hit, hit hard"), how to scream really loud to intimidate the opponent, how to duck so I wouldn't get punched. He held a pillow while I hit it, and told me things like "There's no such thing as fighting dirty. Once you're in a fight, win." And "You can confuse him by spitting in his face first, then punching him while he wipes it off." And "Walk up to him with a stack of books and toss them in the air, and when he reaches out to catch them, break his nose with your fist." Like the good student I was, I brought a pad of paper and a pen, scribbling notes in the margin: "Kick knee, then punch neck, yell real loud. Break nose." I was advised to carry a roll of nickels to add more power to my punch. I was told to wear loose-fitting clothes and not eat too much for breakfast. He explained these things the way an astronomer might explain to his son the reasons for a solar eclipse—calmly and with a commitment to getting the details right.

The next morning, I went to school, terrified as usual. I was shaking as I walked down the hall, fingering the heavy roll of nickels in my right pocket. The headbanger found me during the morning break, as he always did—standing by my locker, trying to open it despite the heavy dents he'd made in it previously. He walked up to me and pushed me into the wall. "Hey, punk, am I going to kick your ass today?"

The question lingered in my mind for a moment. I'd spent the morning wondering the exact same thing. Then, slowly at first, I felt the thin, precarious strand of sanity that had stretched and stretched for months—begging for moderation, for pacifism, for the easier route of, well, punking out—finally reach some kind of limit, and snap.

I turned toward him, mustered every frenzied, screeching nerve in my body, looked him straight in the eye—and punched him as hard as I could, dead in the face. I threw the punch with my weight balanced, my elbows tucked, and yelled "Come on" real, real loud. Just as Dad had said to do.

And then a strange thing happened. I let loose with the most surreal stream of unending profanities that I had ever uttered in my life. I bounced uncontrollably. I screamed maniacally. My entire body, my entire field of vision, every thought, every muscle, every ounce of fear I'd ever felt for the preceding months became pure, bottomless, unadulterated rage.

"Let's go, let's go! I'll kick your ass. *Come on!*" The headbanger was wearing steel-tipped motorcycle boots and a ring with a nail driven through it. I bobbed and weaved and slammed my skinny fist in his face, 10, maybe 15 times, until blood streamed from his eye, from his nose, from his mouth. It was bizarre. I felt detached, almost calm at the center of it. As if I were watching myself on television.

I remember seeing the faces of my classmates, who stood with jaws dropped, wondering how I could possibly be the same kid who'd been discussing T.S. Eliot in honors English only yesterday. They looked terrified. Surely, I'd lost my mind.

The anger was familiar. I'd heard that voice many times before—that confident, loud, intimidating voice that told you to stay very far away. I'd heard it directed at cars in traffic, at my neighbor when he tried to poison our dog, at anyone or anything that threatened our family. I'd even heard it directed at me a few times. It was my dad's voice. And here I was, having hated that voice for so many years, having resented the life that necessitated it, in the midst of the most terrifying situation of my life, and I was not afraid. The voice had immediately become my ally, just as it had been his.

And then, just like that, the fight was over, the bully left bleeding in the corner. I went home that afternoon and told my dad about the fight. How I'd screamed and wailed and jumped and beat the crap out of the headbanger. My dad took it all in with this enormous smile covering his leathery face. He was hanging on my every word, clarifying details, asking me, What then? What next? and Then what?

Never was my father prouder of me. Not because he wanted me to be a fighter, but because, unlike with report cards and essay contests, this was a success he'd contributed to. It was a sign—perhaps the first of my entire life—that there was a little bit of the old man in me after all.

THE AFTERMATH

I spent the next few months as something of a local hero. High fives and back pats and comments in the hallways like "Damn, Einstein, you messed that dude up." Everyone had hated the headbanger.

And there was a certain poetic justice to his demise. At the end of the fight, he'd told a bunch of his cronies that he was planning to sic some big "skinhead" on me. Word of this got out, and a number of people took great exception to his, uh, social affiliations. He received death threats at his house and never came back to school again. Last I heard, he was working at Target.

The glory of my victory soon faded, but I noticed a subtle change in my standing—surreptitious nods in the hall, a certain stoic deference from even the toughest kids in the school—which seemed to ignore academic standing and future prospects and instead communicated, rather plainly, that I was a person who spoke their language. I was cool.

BACK TO BASICS

In the 15 years since that day, I've never once had to throw a punch again. I've backed down on a number of occasions and have been ready to step out-side on a few others. But cooler heads have always prevailed. I guess it's almost always the case that a difficult situation requires restraint, a soft word, diplo-macy. But occasionally, it requires a left hook to the jaw. On that day, I learned that, if pressed, I could deliver that left hook. It's an important thing for a man to know.

I suppose that's something my dad always understood. It's funny: I've learned a lot from books in my life, things I resented my dad for not knowing. But as I've gotten older, I've realized that the most important things in life can't be memorized from a book. It wasn't that my dad didn't care about my grades; he was more concerned that I be a good person, with a square head on my shoulders. He was interested in basics.

Since that day with the bully, my relationship with my father has con-tinued to mature and grow. Today, we're best friends. He's sick now, with a

NUMBER OF MEN WHO HAVE SEEN THEIR FATHER IN A FISTFIGHT: 1 in 8

PERCENTAGE OF THOSE DADS WHO DUKED IT OUT AND WON: 89

host of heart and liver problems that are partly the result of shooting heroin in his twenties. The doctors have said many times that he's going to die. But he just keeps fighting. Working out. Eating well. Trying to manage stress. Again, basics.

These days, Dad likes to say, "I could've been a contenda." What he doesn't realize is this: He was a contender. *Is* a contender. All that b.s. from his youth never mattered. All that mattered was the attention, the advice, the jokes, the fact that he selflessly gave everything he had to help me solve whatever problem came up in my life.

Because it really is good advice, you know. Whether it's a bully, a tough career decision, a divorce, cancer: "Stay on your toes. Keep your elbows in. Don't be afraid. You may be smaller, but just gather your courage, and when you hit, hit hard."

The Secret Life of Dad

When you were young, your father was Superman. Then you realized he's just a man. Here, we honor vulnerable, flawed, ordinary dads everywhere

By Mark Baker

When you're a kid, your father is a mythical beast—part saint, part action hero, part silverback gorilla. He's bigger, stronger, and smarter than you. He's honest, good-looking, and fiercely protective. He's great at his job and always true to your mom.

As you grow up, the emperor starts shedding his baggy sweatshirts and black socks. You learn that the wizard isn't such a whiz at his finances. Or that the beast has been covertly taking on a second back—his secretary's—at the local Super 8. Under the light of your own maturity, the old man begins looking a bit more human.

Savor it. Only now can you understand what makes your father tick—his motivations, his quirks, his misguided dreams. Only now will you be able to learn from his mistakes or know what genetic predispositions await. What follows are interviews with men between the ages of 24 and 50, guys willing to pull back the father curtain on a public stage. There's not a perfect dad among the fathers here. Perhaps that's why the lessons are so valuable.

DAD SECRET 1: HE GETS SCARED, TOO

When I was 11, my dad asked to speak with me privately. He explained that he was sharing this information because I was the eldest child in the family, and he felt I was old enough to understand. Mom was going to have surgery near her brain, and she might die.

I can remember the uncertainty in his voice. I also remember how proud I was that Dad thought I was mature enough to confide in. It also occurred to me that Dad needed someone to talk to; I'd never seen him so vulnerable before. It was a defining moment in my journey from boyhood to manhood.
Pierre, 47, informatics specialist

When my dad's father passed away, Dad never shed a tear. On the way to the funeral home, he kept punching the accelerator pedal; the car was jerking down the road. We soon realized that he was breaking down, but he was trying his best to hold his emotions in. Eventually, my mother turned around to us kids in the backseat and cautioned us firmly but silently not to say one word.
Paul, 40, clergyman

NUMBER OF MEN WHO THINK THEY ARE BETTER FATHERS THAN THEIR DADS WERE: 1 in 2

I was 9. My pop and I had just gotten back from Disney World. I went to my room, and it was barren. I mean, all my stuff was just gone. I sat there in my empty room, wondering what had happened. He came in and asked me if I wanted to sit on his lap. I did so, expecting him to explain things and tell me everything was okay. Instead, he bear-hugged me and started bawling. Then Mom came and took me away. Their marriage was over.

Paul, 24, pilot

DAD SECRET 2: IF YOU WANT IT, HE WANTS IT FOR YOU TIMES 10

My freshman year of high school, I was competing against a better player for the final spot on the basketball team. At dinner one night, I told my parents I was quitting. "I'm going to be cut anyway," I said.

"You can't quit now," my dad insisted. "You've been practicing for months. You'll regret it."

That evening, I went to the neighborhood hoop to shoot around. A half hour later, Dad showed up wearing jean shorts, white socks, and 10-year-old sneakers. He looked ridiculous. Dad was no athlete, and this became clearer as he launched air ball after air ball.

After about 20 minutes, I lied, "I'm going to practice foul shots now. Coach was screaming about them today. You can go."

"You sure?"

"Yeah, be home in an hour."

Dad walked off, head down, embarrassed and defeated. He'd coached my Little League teams and made some calls to get me on my seventh-grade football team, but this was something he couldn't help me with.

I was cut the next day.

Jon, 35, Web producer

DAD SECRET 3: HE CARES, EVEN IF HE DOESN'T KNOW HOW TO SHOW IT

My dad divorced my mom when I was 2. I didn't see him again until I was 7—and it was only for 4 or 5 seconds. My stepfather was adopting me. They were going through the proceedings at the courthouse. I was waiting for someone to come out of the restroom. The guy who came out happened to be my dad. He walked right past me, didn't say anything, and went on his way. He just kept walking.

The next time I saw him, I was a junior in high school, and my car had broken down. He invited me to one of his houses, opened up his six-car garage, and said, "Take your pick." There was a 911 Turbo, a Corvette, an SL500, a Viper. He said, "Here's the key to the key box. Take whatever you want." That's how our father-son relationship started. Yeah, it was exciting. I was 17. But I was also thinking, "Why isn't he asking me more about myself and how I've been?" He loved being the hero of the moment. More than anything else, he taught me how not to act. In every situation in life, I try to do exactly the opposite of what my dad would do.

Oh, I took the Porsche.

Darren, 27, musician

DAD SECRET 4: HE'S THIS CLOSE TO SMACKING YOU ONE

I must've been about 8. Saturday morning, beautiful day. Dad and I had an errand to run. I don't even remember what it was. But for whatever reason—probably the same inner demon that made me toss tantrums about church, Cub Scouts, Little League, CCD classes, summer swim team, everything—I wouldn't budge. We faced off in the driveway, sun shining, where any neighbor could see. And after about 3 minutes of debate, one of Dad's hands clamped around my throat and pinned me against the car. The other cocked back in a fist. Not an open hand. A fist. I froze. I'd never seen his fist before. He didn't hit me. He didn't have to. I shut up and got in the car.

From that moment on, the threat was there. I'd pushed too far. And Dad was now just a guy who was sick of wasting time on the only Saturday he'd get all week. Now that I have three kids of my own, I've felt that breaking point. I haven't made the fist yet. I hope I never do. But, man, after 3 minutes of debate with my oldest boy about haircuts, allergy shots, or what to eat for lunch, I get what Dad was gettin' at. I really do.

Mike, 34, marketing manager

DAD SECRET 5: ONCE IN A WHILE, HE NEEDS TO ACT LIKE A KID AGAIN

My best friend and I joined the track team in high school. We were slow runners, so they handed us a discus. We brought it home.

We were neighbors, so our dads were good pals, too—always outside on Saturday with their heads under the hood of a car. My dad was a big football and track star when he was in high school, and the guy next door was a high jumper and a discus man. "I haven't had one of these in my hands in years," the neighbor dad said, grabbing the discus. "Let me show you guys how you do it."

He wound up and slung it down the street. There was an old woman down the block whose garage was right at the edge of the property line. The discus hit the side of the garage, splintered the wood, and disappeared inside. We were dumbfounded. He'd been explaining to us how the ancient Greeks said the discus was a weapon of war, you know.

We turned around, and the two men were gone. They'd disappeared. We were just two kids standing in the yard. The dads ran away.

The old lady telephones the house. My mother asks my father about it. He says, "I don't know. Ask the kids."

Bob, 45, musician

DAD SECRET 6: HE'S A DIFFERENT GUY AT WORK

Dad was a corporate lawyer who worked at a clean desk in a sedate office. At home, he was a pipe-smoking Ward Cleaver, kind and helpful, not overly strict, but stern when he had to be. He was unfailingly warm with neighbors, at church, among relatives.

I was an adult, still holding this image, when one of his associates started talking about what my dad was like downtown, at work. How coldhearted he was in business deals, a real hard-ass in negotiations, definitely not somebody you want to cross. My eyes widened. "Oh, yeah," the man said. "We call him Mr. Warmth."

I was knocked sideways. My dad, coldhearted? With a sarcastic nickname? For days, weeks, months, this revelation bothered me. But over time, I became amused by it. Now, I kind of like it. My wonderful dad, the hard-ass.

Brandon, 47, salesman

DAD SECRET 7: HE'S NOT AS TOUGH AS HE LOOKS

My father went to one of the best law schools in the country. He practiced for a while, but then quit to become an accountant for a big restaurant.

The only piece of advice he ever gave me was "Don't become a lawyer."

"But why, Dad?"

He hesitated. "Because you have to lie all the time," he said finally.

My dad wasn't strong enough for this world. He went through life with a soft-on rather than a hard-on. He believed that you have to lie to be a good lawyer, and he couldn't do it, so he decided to walk away.

Frank, 50, book dealer

My dad wanted to wrestle. At Mom's request, we took the match into the yard. I got myself in a bad position. We were facing each other. I was bent over with my head down by his knees, and he had his arms wrapped around my waist. I couldn't move or do much else, so I just stood straight up, which put him up on my shoulders. He grunted, "Put me down." I did. Hard. He got back from the emergency room a few hours later. The diagnosis: a cracked rib and bruised pride.

Mike, 34, telecom engineer

DAD SECRET 8: THERE'S MEANING BEHIND HIS MADNESS

When I was about 10, my dad and I went for haircuts at Lee the barber's. Lee cut my hair first, then cut Dad's. Then we got in the car to drive home. As we pulled into the driveway around dinnertime, my dad realized he'd forgotten to pay for my haircut—3 bucks—and had only paid for his own (4 bucks). So we drove back to Lee's to give him the $3. The trip cost us about 40 minutes, and dinner was cold when we got home. I didn't understand why he couldn't have just paid Lee the next time he saw him.

Thing is, as an adult I've always been very careful about debt. I carry no credit-card debt, no loans. I often borrow $10 for a cab at night, but I always pay it back first thing the next morning. Knowing that I owe someone something is very unsettling. I've always wondered if that evening drive back to Lee the barber had something to do with it. There was never a lesson or a talk around it. It was just my dad doing what he was supposed to do. So that's what I try to do, too.

Steve, 39, stockbroker

DAD SECRET 9: HE CAN STILL APPRECIATE A BEAUTIFUL WOMAN

When my firstborn—a son—arrived, my dad drove my mom halfway across the country to meet him. They arrived late on a winter afternoon, and we gathered in the living room to fuss. My wife and the new granny were taking turns holding my firstborn, talking to him, and fixating on him the way women do.

PERCENTAGE OF MEN WHO WISH THEIR FATHERS HAD BEEN AROUND MORE WHEN THEY WERE GROWING UP: 90

At one point I noticed that my dad's gaze was carrying past his grandson, through the window, and over to the apartment building across the street. And there, in a second-floor apartment, was one of the most amazing, gorgeous, sweaty women I've ever seen, doing some kind of aerobic dance routine in front of the TV set. My dad couldn't keep his eyes off her. Honest to God, it had never occurred to me that he was a horny bastard, just like me!

When I look back on that family dynamic—the mothers cooing over the newborn male, the fathers quietly lusting after the fertile babe—I realize that we're all just playing out our roles in the big reproductive machine that keeps our species going. Men look and crave, and women attract glances and rings and sperm. The system relies on each of us doing our part, and it works.

Pete, 47, novelist

DAD SECRET 10: SOMETIMES HE NEEDS YOU TO BE THE BIGGER MAN

Dad had been sick—both knees were bad, a heart problem flared up, an infection set in—but after 10 months, he was finally healthy again. I stopped by the house one day. He was eating lunch, and we chitchatted. Nice spring, slow Saturday. Then something told me it was time: "Thank you for all you did for us, Dad. I appreciate it. I love you." Nothing big, nothing dramatic. Just words that were better said than held on to.

Francis, 33, architect

DAD SECRET 11: ONCE THE I'S ARE DOTTED, HE'S OUT OF HERE

My father spent 15 hours a day in the family business, 365 days a year, for 2 decades. The business was good. It paid the college tuition for three kids and built a nice nest egg for my parents. By the age of 52, Dad was retired.

His plan was to do all the things he'd never had time for. Except he didn't. He mostly sat on the couch and watched TV. I called him one day, and the conversation turned to the football game that Sunday. "I might miss it," he said.

"Going away?" I was half joking, half hoping.

"No, I think I'm having a heart attack."

It caught me off guard. "Call 911."

"Nah. It'll be okay," he said. "The worst that can happen is that I die."

Dad was 55, and he'd packed it in. His life's work was done. I stayed on the phone with him until my mom came home. She rushed him to the hospital. It was only indigestion.

He died 4 years later, after a freak accident at the house. At least I knew he was ready.

Russ, 37, media planner

My dad and I had our best conversations watching college basketball, usually late at night. I'd get home from the bars and find him in his La-Z-Boy, feet up, watching the West Coast game on ESPN. I'd plop down, and we'd shoot the breeze until one of us gave in to bed.

Our last basketball talk took place in his hospital room. He was dying—he knew it and I knew it, but we never talked about it. Then, suddenly, his tone turned serious: "You okay?"

"How so?"

"You know—house, money, the baby, job—are you doing okay?" I was, thanks in no small part to him. But he wanted to be sure.

"You don't need anything? Nothing at all?"

I didn't, and he was surprised and relieved. And that's how we left it. The conversation turned back to basketball. He died 2 weeks later.

Mike, 35, accountant

NEED TO KNOW

FERTILITY NEWS

Your Clock Is Ticking, Too

Women aren't the only ones who are on a timetable to have children. University of Washington researchers found that after the age of 35, most men start to produce semen riddled with DNA damage. The lower your sperm quality, the more likely your child is to inherit defective genes.

Fat and Infertile

Looks like "big daddy" is something of a misnomer. Scientists at Pennsylvania State University's College of Medicine recently discovered that overweight men have a fat chance of becoming fathers. The researchers measured several fertility markers in 87 men and found that as the men's body-mass indexes rose, their levels of inhibin B, a hormone necessary for sperm production, dropped—by as much as 33 percent in some cases. "Fat tissue converts testosterone to estrogen," says study author Eric Pauli, PhD. "It's reasonable to assume that these hormone rearrangements result in a lower inhibin B level." Changing your body composition—specifically by building more testosterone-producing muscle instead of estrogen-producing fat—will help correct the hormonal imbalance.

Too Hot to Handle

Slide your laptop onto a table. The heat from laptop computers can affect male fertility, according to a new study of 29 young men in the journal *Human Reproduction*. Researchers found that 1 hour with a computer on a

THE POSSIBLE PERCENT CHANCE REDUCTION IN HEALTHY SPERM AS A RESULT OF CARRYING A CELL PHONE IN YOUR PANTS POCKET: 30

man's lap increased scrotal temperature by as much as 5°F. (A computer's internal temp can hit 158°.) Frequent temperature elevations over several years "may affect sperm production and sperm quality—and, eventually, fertility in the future," says study author Yefim Sheynkin, MD, director of male infertility and microsurgery at Stony Brook University Hospital.

Your Dreams of Siring a Son—Up in Smoke

Smoking tobacco may decrease your chances of having a son. Researchers from Denmark surveyed the mothers of 12,000 infants and found that parents who smoked were 20 percent less likely to have sons than couples who didn't. Cigarette smoke appears to damage Y chromosomes, the researchers say.

ON DADDY DUTY

Babe Watch

Watching the kid doesn't have to mean watching Barney all day. Gary Greenberg, author of *Be Prepared: A Practical Handbook for New Dads,* says turning the day into an interesting outing works for both of you.

Pet store. Look at the cats and hamsters (and the toys), but the fish are best. They fascinate babies, and you can put babies' faces up close to the tank. "Plus, the tanks produce white noise that will soothe them to sleep," Greenberg says.

Racetrack. Stimulation everywhere: thundering horses, cheering people, muttering losers. Go to the paddock to let your child see the thoroughbreds close up. He'll be picking trifectas in no time.

Dog park. "It's a fun visual activity for a baby," says Greenberg. Stick with the small dogs. Just don't let big ones "use your kid as a chew toy."

Museum. Young children respond to sculptures and paintings of bold and simple faces and shapes. Think bright modern art; Poussin's subtleties will be lost on the little ones.

Bookstore. Lots to see at eye level in a stroller, and plenty of floor space for roaming. Big stores have kids' areas and reading sessions so you can browse nearby stacks.

Construction site. Cranes, trucks, bulldozers, noise. It's *Bob the Builder,* full size and in real time.

Have a Silent Night

Parents can lose up to 200 hours of sleep a year when a child has poor sleep habits, according to the National Sleep Foundation. And sleep loss is bad for

MINUTES OF SLEEP THAT CHILDREN 3 AND OLDER LOSE PER NIGHT WHEN THEY HAVE JUST ONE CAFFEINATED BEVERAGE A DAY: 30

kids, hurting their memory retention and problem-solving skills. Here's how to get them to conk out.

Slow down. You may think your WWE reenactments will tire him out just before bed. It's more like giving him a double espresso. The best sleep prep: at least 30 minutes of a quiet, soothing activity, such as reading, says Sheila C. Ribordy, PhD, a clinical psychologist and a professor at DePaul University. Also, eliminate caffeine from your child's diet, says Jodi Mindell, PhD, associate director of the Sleep Disorders Center at the Children's Hospital of Philadelphia.

Stay on schedule. Even as infants, children should have a bedtime routine they can count on. Establishing this leads to healthy sleep habits during the childhood years and beyond. Dad can use different routines than Mom, as long as they're predictable.

Unplug. Remove the television and computer from the bedroom, say sleep experts. Movies, video games, and instant messaging busy the mind and preoccupy thoughts. Listen to soothing music instead of watching *Sports-Center* with them.

Talk. Nighttime is when worries surface—and when children are most likely to share their feelings. Use bedtime to talk about your child's day. Teens may be stressed about school or friends, while little ones need reassurance that nothing scarier than dust bunnies lives under the bed. Be their release valve.

Plan. Teenagers generally don't manage time well, hence the late-night projects. Helping them organize time is easier than forcing them to go to sleep, says Ribordy.

Don't compromise. Debating what time the children should go to bed "teaches kids to be good arguers," Dr. Ribordy says. No debates, no changes. When the rule is broken, the consequence is moving the bedtime up the next night, adding more peace and quiet to everyone's day.

Father Time

Quality time with the kids doesn't mean a conversation at a red light on the way to soccer practice. Dads can do things that "reinforce the important sense of 'we-ness' among family members," says Sarah Schoppe-Sullivan, an assistant professor of family science at Ohio State University. Family bonding will "foster healthy social development in children." Here are four easy ways to carve out quality time with the kids.

Eat. A key to family unity is "finding time to eat together," says William Doherty, PhD, a professor of family social science at the University of Minnesota. One option: Call ahead so a pizza's ready when you arrive. "You can eat as quickly as you could at home," he says.

Play. Find a seldom-used table and set up a board game. Then play it, slow-motion-style. "Leave the game out somewhere and together chip away at it little by little, about 10 minutes a day," says Dr. Doherty. The impromptu gatherings are fun. Good choices: chess, Monopoly, or a 3-D puzzle.

Walk. "If your children go to school close to your home, walk home together once in a while," says Dr. Doherty. Or drive them. "The most important thing is to talk." You can then return to work knowing you're a good pop.

Isolate. A little time alone with one child can do as much good as a day with the entire family, experts say. For preteens, "a regular bedtime story or talk is very high-quality time," says Dr. Doherty. When alone with one child, speak well of his mom and siblings and "refer to the family as a unit by using words like 'we' and 'our,'" says Schoppe-Sullivan. You'll reap the rewards of family time without the commotion.

Whine and Dine

Next time you see a kid pitching a fit in the junk-food aisle of the grocery store, just wave a copy of the *Journal of Pediatrics* in his parent's face. Then explain how a recent study from Stanford University followed 150 families for nearly 9 years and found that children who regularly throw tantrums over food are three times more likely to develop weight problems than even-tempered kids are. "The likelihood is that parents feed these children differently, perhaps using food to calm them," says lead researcher W. Stewart Agras, MD. The result: a kid who's spoiled and overweight. Instead, Dr. Agras suggests, try rewarding your child with an activity—maybe a Frisbee session, bike ride, or plain old game of catch—since the chunky kids in the study also tended to be less active. An afternoon in the park probably wouldn't hurt you, either.

Happy Meals

Dad's turn to cook dinner? Don't fall back on pizza again. There are ways to trick your sprouts into eating healthy.

Start over. Serve breakfast for dinner. Kids love the novelty. You can serve healthy scrambled eggs or omelets with cheese and vegetables. "Some whole-grain toast and a glass of milk complete the meal," says Elizabeth Ward, MS, RD, author of *Healthy Foods, Healthy Kids*. Or make pancakes and mix in applesauce to provide a serving of fruit.

Go fish. Try flounder, because it doesn't have a strong fishy taste. Canned tuna also makes a good entrée, especially mixed into regular mac and cheese for a healthy, high-protein meal.

Put them to work. Let the kids build their own meal. Here's fajita night: Buy some whole-grain wraps, grill up chicken strips, and set out peppers, salsa, and refried beans. "Putting a meal together is fun for kids," says David Katz, MD, an associate clinical professor of public health at the Yale University School of Medicine and author of *The Way to Eat*. This can also work for tacos or stir-fry.

Be smart about sweets. Try yogurt for a dessert—add animal crackers or layer some 'gurt on fruit salad or pound cake to trick the kids into enjoying calcium. If they insist on having cookies, Dr. Katz recommends Barbara's brand cookies. "They're not exactly health food, but they don't have trans fats," he says.

Stay rational. If you don't have time to prepare food, pick up a roasted chicken from the grocery store. As a worst-case scenario, it's fine to order a thin-crust pizza with vegetable toppings. You'll limit the fat and unnecessary dough, and you'll all go to bed happy.

Free Wheeling

Junior will toss the training wheels faster by using these techniques to teach your kid how to ride, courtesy of *Bicycling* magazine executive editor Bill Strickland, who's taught 5-year-olds and 21-year-olds.

"Using a hill is better than using the holding-on method because the slope supplies the momentum, which makes the bike more stable and lets your child concentrate on the key thing—balance," says Strickland.

- Lower the seat so your child can put both feet on the ground while sitting. Find a grassy slope about 20 yards long and just steep enough so the bike will coast and hold the bike while he hops on.
- Let go and tell him to lift his feet and coast without pedaling. If he loses balance, he can easily put a foot down.
- After a few successful coasts, raise the seat for some downhill rides. Then go to a flat field to practice maneuvers like pedaling, turning, braking, and starting from a standstill.

PERCENTAGE OF DADS, ON AVERAGE, WHO EAT DINNER WITH THEIR KIDS EVERY DAY: 55

**SPORT THE AVERAGE
GUY PLAYED AS A KID:** Baseball

**NUMBER OF MEN WHO ADMIRED AND RESPECTED
THEIR LITTLE LEAGUE COACH:** 1 in 2

Raise a Good Sport

Chances are good your kid isn't the next LeBron, A-Rod, or Deion, but raising a kid to love sports is priceless. As his first coach, you have a huge impact on how much he enjoys sports and likes himself. Follow these tips from Rick Wolff, chairman of the Center for Sports Parenting, and Joel Fish, PhD, author of *101 Ways to Be a Terrific Sports Parent,* so you don't screw up a kid's love of the game.

Skip postgame analysis. When the thrill or agony of the game is still fresh, he doesn't need you harping on him. The only challenge he should face: sugar or waffle cone?

Play up the positive. Find something specific—stopping a ball, not giving up on a fast break—and tell him it was worth the price of admission. "Kids want to believe parents feel proud of them," Dr. Fish says.

Sandwich criticism. If you want him to stop being a ball hog, wait until the next practice and say, "You're a great ball handler [praise], but if you could dish off when you're double-teamed [constructive criticism], you'd be unstoppable [praise with incentive]."

Ask his opinion. If he stops wanting to go to practice or starts picking grass in the outfield, there could be a lot of reasons. He's the best source. Say, "Help me understand," Dr. Fish suggests. You're acknowledging the situation without claiming to have the answers or giving him the third degree.

Watch yourself. In the stands, meet with other parents and agree to call each other on offensive behavior—pacing, grimacing, arm waving. Your kid will notice this stuff, and it'll suck out all the fun he thought he was having. All you need to do is cheer.

WHAT'S NEW

FERTILITY NEWS

Skip the Snip

You may want to forgo a vasectomy if you have any lingering dreams of being a daddy. British researchers say that even 10 years after a vasectomy reversal, pregnancy rates are 50 percent lower than in couples with other infertility problems.

Stronger Swimmers

The little blue pill may deliver a bonus. New research shows that in healthy men, Viagra makes sperm swim faster and bind better to eggs. In a study published in *Fertility and Sterility,* when researchers in South Africa gave the erection helper to men who didn't need the help, they found that the straight-ahead swimming velocity of the subjects' sperm increased, and that the rate at which the sperm attached to an egg was nearly 50 percent higher than in the placebo poppers. According to study author Stefan S. du Plessis, MD, the trial revealed that Viagra has no adverse effect on ejaculate quality and that with further study, the drug could be used to help men with poor-quality sperm become fathers.

One at a Time

Considering in vitro fertilization? Don't fear siring a stable of kids, says the *New England Journal of Medicine.* Thanks to a better understanding of how to grow viable embryos, multiple births from IVF have decreased by almost a third.

COOL TOOLS

Papa's Got a Brand-New Bag

No need to lug around that pastel, teddy bear-emblazoned diaper bag the wife loves. Kelty has come up with a rugged diaper daypack ($60, www.kelty.com)

that makes daddy day care look macho. It's made of tough black or blue ripstop nylon, with handles fashioned from climbing rope. Inside is a changing pad, so Junior's bottom is protected. It's such a cool pack, you may find yourself using it long after he's potty trained.

DOCTOR DADDY

The Best Medicine

While it's still our favorite mold, penicillin isn't the best cure for strep throat in kids. According to doctors at the University of Rochester Medical Center, antibiotics called cephalosporins are three times as effective as the classic cure.

An Outside Shot at Treating ADD

When kids with attention deficit disorder start climbing the walls, make the walls disappear. University of Illinois researchers discovered that being out-doors helps control ADD in children. After surveying 500 parents of kids with ADD, the researchers found that outdoor activities reduced symptoms by almost one-third. The rates were the same whether the child was reading or playing basketball, which indicates that children are not just "burning off" excess energy. Being outside may somehow replenish neurotransmitters needed for concentration, says study author Frances Kuo, PhD.

Put off the Home Improvements

Australian doctors have found that kids exposed to volatile organic com-pounds (VOCs) given off by paint, new carpeting, and household cleaning products are four times more likely to have asthma than tykes who aren't around VOCs.

THE COST OF . . .

. . . Being an Absentee Father

The number one excuse most men give for not spending more time with their families? Work. Think your kids aren't missing you? A study found that 42 percent of teenagers want to spend more time with their dads. Missing out on time with your kids has a huge hidden psychological—and financial— impact on you and your family. Here's what 6 months of catching up at work, rather than playing catch with your kids, could cost you.

It'll take . . .	Research shows . . .	You pay . . .
Extra supervision for the kids	Your wife can't watch them all the time, so you'll need day care or a sitter.	$4,550
More allowance	Guilty parents tend to become more generous with allowances.	$480
A tutor	Kids whose parents don't take an interest in them tend to perform worse academically.	$1,010
Couch time of 1 day a week—for the kids	Children interpret an unavailable dad as an unsupportive one—which leads to anger and hostility that a therapist will have to work out.	$3,000
A cell phone with instant messaging and Internet service	An electronic connection to the kids is better than no connection at all.	$970
Two new video games and a shopping spree at the mall	Parents set up latchkey kids with the latest games so they can entertain themselves.	$170
Disney World for a week	It's the classic guilt reliever.	$2,300
TOTAL		**$12,480**

TIMES MORE LIKELY A SON IS
TO SMOKE CIGARETTES WHEN HE
LIVES APART FROM HIS FATHER: 4.3

FAST FIXES

Morality is a kind of navigation software kids download from the adults in their lives. The problem is, they have one eye on Dad and Mom, another on Kobe and Britney. The best way to make sure they download your example and delete those others': Teach and nurture a sense of right and wrong, empathy, decency, and equality. Here are six ways to do just that, courtesy of Daniel Amen, MD, psychiatrist and the author of *Change Your Brain, Change Your Life.*

1. Build the bond. If you want your children to share your values, listen to them, spend time with them, and encourage them. In the *Journal of the American Medical Association,* psychologist Michael Resnick, PhD, reported that teenagers who felt loved by and connect to their parents had a significantly lower incidence of emotional distress, drug use, violence, and suicide.

2. Show 'em how it's done. Children do what you do, not what you tell them to do. If you want your children to act with a sense of integrity, you must set an example. So if you tell them not to steal but you have a pirated satellite box, the commandment has less impact. If you tell them to be kind to others but you are frequently rude to your wife, the odds are they will be rude to others.

3. Teach, don't punish. When your kid messes up, your anger won't erase the event; it'll just pile another negative on top of it. After you cool down, go over the incident to see what the child can learn from it. Also, when moral teaching opportunities arise, such as during a television show or when they tell you about the events of their day, use the time to talk about sensitive issues.

4. Write some commandments. It's often helpful for parents to have written rules posted at home, such as "Tell the truth" or "Treat others with respect." First, follow the rules yourself. Second, when children follow the rules, notice it and show appreciation. When they break rules, discipline them with love, not guilt or anger.

5. Edit the guest list. New research indicates that children become like the kids they hang out with. If her friends shoplift or cut classes, she's more likely to do so. Use parent-teacher conferences to inquire about your kids' friends and act accordingly. After school, steer kids toward groups that are properly supervised. Also, arrange events where you'll get to know your child's friends, so you can weed out the bad and encourage the good.

NUMBER OF MEN WHO FEEL THEIR FATHER IS THE PERSON WHO MOST INFLUENCED THEIR LIVES: 2 in 3

6. Maintain the brain. Brain health determines how we think and act. Brain illnesses, such as bipolar disorder and autism, are often associated with difficult behavior, and physical trauma can cause problems with judgment. Protect your children from brain injuries (no soccer headers), educate them about drug and alcohol abuse, and get them help for mood and behavior problems.

OUR FINAL ANSWERS

High Expectations

My wife recently became pregnant. I really want to be there for her. Can you give me any advice?

—C.J. Brattleboro, Vermont

We checked with a pregnant friend who just had her first ultrasound (and is freaking out because her fetus looks like a chipmunk) and another who gave birth to a baby boy 2 months ago. They both agree that you should read the same pregnancy-and-childbirth books your wife is reading. That way you'll know almost as much about what her body is going through as she does. Offering to do "anything" to help when she's experiencing wild mood swings or wicked back pain also would be incredibly sweet—just don't claim to know exactly what would be best for her or she'll bite your head off. Speaking of which, being verbally decapitated is something you should prepare yourself for anyway. The most wonderful, generous thing you could possibly do for your wife, says our prego friend, is to allow her to bite without your biting back. That's love.

Time to Make the Baby

My wife and I are hoping she gets pregnant soon. Is there anything we can do to time it right when we have intercourse?

—G.S. Fredericksburg, Maryland

Buy an ovulation-predictor kit and have your wife check her urine around the middle of her menstrual cycle. When the tester changes color, have sex that night and the next night (2 nights in a row). Abstain from ejaculating a day or two beforehand so you don't deplete your sperm supply.

A Daily Dose

Should I put my kids on a multivitamin?

—J.F., Omaha, Nebraska

There's really no reason not to. Some experts maintain that your children should get all of their nutritional needs from their diet, but there is a good possibility your child could be lacking nutrients. Growing kids can always use a boost. It's generally safe for kids older than 2 to take a children's multivitamin. Read and follow the label carefully. Stick with a reputable brand (like Kirkland Signature or Flintstones Complete) and make sure you keep the bottle in a secure place out of reach of the child.

Don't Keep Your Distance

My wife says I'm a distant father, just as my dad was. I can see her point, but how much does it matter? I turned out okay.

—L.P., Bloomington, Indiana

Having a bond with you is very important to your children's health and development. Ask yourself: Do you spend much one-on-one time with them? Do you focus on what they do right? Do you hug them? Build the connection by spending uninterrupted time with them—which is hard these days. Listen to them without distraction. Spend at least 20 minutes a day doing something each child likes. It's the best investment you can make.

Problem Child

My 11-year-old son screws up all the time. How can I get him to shape up?

—D.S., Phoenix

When kids struggle, you have to figure out why before you can figure out how to help. It could be a lack of discipline. But sometimes they have brain problems, such as attention deficit disorder, that need treatment. Make sure your son has good supervision—at school and on the field—and that you are a positive presence in his life, no matter how frustrating his behavior is. If he still struggles, get him a thorough evaluation by a school psychologist to make sure you're not missing a potentially treatable condition.

Temper Your Temper

Sometimes I just want to slap some sense into my kids. Is this normal?

—B.K., East Lansing, Michigan

Yes. The urge to hit your kids is a normal reaction to irritating behavior—as long as you have control over these urges. I've seen that spanking or hitting will not improve children's behavior and only makes them angry and anxious. When you have to resort to extreme discipline, make them clean out the garage.

Crowd Control

How can I keep my 13-year-old son from hanging out with the wrong crowd?

—S.T., Casper, Wyoming

Forbidding him from hanging out with those cigarette-smoking shoplifters will make him want to hang with them even more, says Myrna Shure, PhD, a professor of psychology at Drexel University and the author of *Thinking Parent, Thinking Child*. Instead, try to let your child make his own decisions. During conversation, casually ask, "What is it that you like about those friends?" Most kids know a bad crowd and recognize the consequences involved. If not, talk about what could happen, then ask, "Do you want that to happen to you?" He may walk away on his own. Be patient and keep your tone neutral. "Eventually he will open up to you because he won't feel threatened or be afraid of punishment," Dr. Shure says. But if drugs or violence come into the picture, it's time to set rules.

Take It Outside

My kids love to play next door, but my neighbor smokes, and I don't like their being around his secondhand smoke. How can I deal with this situation diplomatically?

—S.J., Lawrence, Kansas

When they ban smoking in restaurants and bars, it moves all the smoke outside. Hate to break it to you, but you have about as much legislative power over your neighbor's house as Pam Anderson has over the US Senate. In this case, it's your kids—not the smoke—who'll have to move outside.

Between a Pimple and a Hard Place

My son is depressed about his acne, but I'm afraid he'd get suicidal on Accutane. What should I do?

—R.S., Salem, Oregon

A study presented at the Congress of the European Academy of Dermatology and Venereology found that 66 percent of teens with acne said having it made them depressed. Accutane is a very effective acne remedy, but in rare cases it may worsen depression. Monitor your son for suicidal feelings and warn him about the signs of depression. But chances are he'll feel much better once his skin improves.

The Naked Truth

I found my 13-year-old's stash of *Playboys*, and I didn't say anything about them. It's better for him to sneak those than to look at graphic Web porn, right?

—K.W., Rutland, Vermont

The desire to see nudity is a natural part of brain development. The problem is that he can't develop healthy sexual attitudes unless you let him know his curiosity is normal—your silence doesn't help. Try to have a conversation about all the images he might encounter, rather than both of you being sly.

Full Disclosure

I'm divorced, with an 8-year-old daughter. What's the best way to let a date know about my child?

—L.D., Pine Bluff, Arkansas

You're like a bald guy who shows up for a first date wearing a baseball cap. Why are you so worried about hiding something that she's going to find out soon enough? There's no need to broadcast your situation as you shake hands or to treat it like you're disclosing your herpes virus. You have a daughter and you're proud of her, so you mention it at the moment when it comes up most naturally. Anyone who's going to be turned off by the fact that you're a good dad is probably not someone you want in your—or your daughter's—life anyway.

The Ex Files

My ex isn't allowing me visitation rights. How can I make her let me see my daughter?

—J.B., Santa Fe, New Mexico

It'll help if you're not a deadbeat, but paying child support won't automatically entitle you to visitation rights. Have the lawyer who handled this speak to your ex-wife's lawyer. Maybe they can work it out. If your ex is violating a court order, the next step is to take her to court—which involves court fees. The best method would be to talk it out with cool heads and no lawyers.

SEVEN

TAKE YOUR JOB AND LOVE IT

READ UP ON IT

Contents under Pressure

Simple logic: The bigger your job, the more stress it dumps on you.
Yet here are four successful men with high-stakes gigs who defy that
logic. Learn their secrets, and make anxiety work for you

By Mike Zimmerman and Stephanie Tuck

Successful men feel stress.

Really, they do. They just don't feel it the same way the rest of us feel it.
For us, it's a slow-building rage. For them, it's a buzz. For us, fear. For them,
fuel. But why? What's the formula? For the "average" guys who bust their
butts at work and claw at every next rung on the ladder, the transformation
from stressful to successful might as well be alchemy.

To help explain, we found four men at the top of their respective fields.
They're all-stars (one quite literally). If you ask them how they can do so well
under such huge pressures, they just shrug. It's what they do. Execute, or die.
These guys don't have time for tension. They mine their personal natural
resources and forge tools to protect them from stressors like anxiety, anger, and
lack of time. Put simply, they give themselves every opportunity to succeed.

Here's your opportunity to banish fear and boost confidence. To play like
the all-stars play. Adopt even one of these strategies and you, too, will soon
find yourself achieving success instead of stressing about it.

JAVY LOPEZ

Catcher, Baltimore Orioles

Imagine that you've just left your job of 12 years to join another company
for a lot more money than you were making before. Your previous employer
had an incredible run—10 years of prosperity. This new company, however, is
trying to reemerge from years of mediocrity, with you at the forefront of its
reengineering plan. Feeling the pressure yet?

Well, imagine that on your first day, a monster project is hurled your
way—in front of the entire workforce. Now, let's say you deposit that offering
in the cheap seats, where it belongs. That's precisely what Baltimore Orioles
catcher Javy Lopez did on Opening Day 2004. A sellout at Oriole Park, and

Lopez stepped up to face no less than Pedro Martinez. First pitch: Oh, my. A line drive that never dropped below 50 feet torpedoed the left-field stands. Against Pedro! Sitting in front of his locker in the Orioles' clubhouse, Lopez smiles like a heroic Little Leaguer and tries to shrug it off. "You don't want to look bad in front of 47,000 people."

Not that this is alien territory for the 33-year-old Lopez—who is much taller and leaner in person than the pad-laden backstop you see on ESPN. He'd spent his entire career with the Atlanta Braves and has felt every stress professional sports has to offer, especially the postseason kind (he has a .278 average in 60 playoff games). After coming to Baltimore? He felt a different level of pressure, but he says, "It's not overwhelming me. Sure, people have a lot of expectations of me. It is a different scenario—new team, new

WHAT STRESSES YOU OUT?

Tom Hanks, actor

"The only thing that stresses me out is a ringing telephone. Knowing that I'm going to have to answer that ringing telephone—that stresses me out."

Elijah Wood, actor

"Face-to-face questions. Getting attention all the time. It's nice to be anonymous."

Usher, singer

"Everything. I stress me out. I'm a perfectionist. I like things to be the best they can possibly be."

Regis Philbin, TV host

"When you leave your house in New York City, that's when the stress comes into your life."

Jeff Greenfield, senior analyst for CNN

"Thanks to two loving but compulsively punctual parents, time stresses me. I tend to leave for the airport before the plane is finished being built."

John Salley, former Detroit Piston and TV cohost

"One way I deal with stress is to say, 'It is now 3 p.m., the game will be over at 5:30 p.m., and I'm going to be happy at 6 p.m.' I look past it."

Salman Rushdie, novelist

"A bad day's work."

league, my eyes as big as this," as he makes grapefruit-size semicircles with each hand. "But you know what? You have to deal with the toughest moments, too." Here's how Lopez does just that.

His Anti-Stress Strategies

Change the setting. "When I'm running out to home plate," says Lopez, "I picture myself going to the bull pen in Fort Lauderdale. There's only the pitcher concentrating on throwing strikes and me catching them. Same thing with batting. I picture myself in a batting cage, hitting against a machine." So no matter what test you might be facing, set the stage in your mind. "This is called 'imaginal rehearsal,'" says Allen Elkin, PhD, director of the Stress Management and Counseling Center in New York City. "You tweak the situation to bring up something more supportive and less stressful."

Control the clock. Ballplayers face huge time sucks: rabid autograph hounds, leechy reporters, and endless requests for, well, everything. So Lopez decided early on what his limits were. He established a game-day routine and sticks to it. The result: less aggravation. "Control of my time is never taken away from me," he says. Bottom line: You owe time to an employer, a mate, family, a friend. Do a quick audit—on paper—to see where the minutes go. Then reach a compromise between your ideal and their expectations.

Remember your role. Some numbers: 3 years, $22.5 million. Some scarier numbers: .328 average, 43 home runs, 109 runs batted in last year. To Orioles fans, that adds up to one world championship. But Lopez shakes his head. "I'm not the one guy who will make the team win," he says. "I'll be one of many." Hear that, Superman? "Taking the pressure off yourself to be responsible for every facet of a project will help you perform better on the part you're in charge of," says Kathy Matt, PhD, director of the stress lab at Arizona State University.

HAROLD FORD JR.

US Congressman from Tennessee

"If you let it, stress brings out the best in you," says Representative Harold Ford Jr. as he weaves his new black Cadillac Escalade through the nation's capital—a twisted street layout that he seems to pilot by instinct. His cell phone bleeps, he answers. His BlackBerry flashes, he obeys. Then the phone bleeps again. All to a pulsing mix of Outkast, the Beastie Boys, and old-school Otis Redding. This distinguished gentleman from Tennessee is inside the Beltway in every sense—35 years old and already a four-term congressional veteran—literally working the town as he drives through it. "Stress can push you," he says between calls. "It's part of the job, and I kind of enjoy it."

As Ford parks the SUV and strolls to his office, he describes his day: Out of bed at 5:30 a.m. for 20 minutes on the treadmill as he watches morning news shows. After that, he gives sound bites to the press from Memphis. Then it's meetings. Breakfast meetings, lunch meetings, dinner meetings.

In between, eight to 10 *more* meetings with local organizations and constituents. Then fund-raisers or cocktail parties. And that's not counting House votes and subcommittee conferences—and his mandatory run. "The challenge is to keep my energy up," he says. Hence the nonnegotiable run. "It's a demanding day, but I love the action."

That much is clear. As we walk through a hallway in a congressional office building, everyone gets a hello, a how-are-your-kids—pure political flesh pressing, but that's the job. This innate talent for navigating the Washington labyrinth helped the young rep with the rep for hard work land a plum position—the national cochairmanship of the Kerry presidential election campaign. His ability to turn anxiety into action didn't hurt, either. "I've learned how the process works and how to work that system," he says. "I can handle stressful situations better now."

His Anti-Stress Strategies

Look at your loves. There's tremendous pressure in our society to both settle down and succeed. The result: tension. "I was engaged 4 years ago, and my schedule was a factor in our breakup," says Ford, his voice dialing back a notch. "These days, I'm focused on my [career] goals." The underlying concept here, says Dr. Elkin, is looking at your short- and long-range priorities. "Will focusing on your career now allow you to have the family you want later?" he asks. Making a tough choice today can relieve a pile of pressure.

Get in good. Day to day, there's nothing more stressful than being part of a team that doesn't accept you. Ford knew this going to Washington and, once there, gained his Capitol Hill green card by going where the power is generated—the congressional gym. "[The gym is] where some of the best things happen for people in my district," he says. Even if you've been at your job for years, set up a happy hour or initiate an off-site lunch. There's a spot on the roster; get up off the bench.

Don't waste downtime. Ford knows that being alone is an opportunity to prepare for the crazy times. "I do my best creative thinking on airplanes or when I go for a run," he says. "When I fly, I brainstorm alone and take notes.

THE AVERAGE GUY'S WEEKLY SALARY:

$560

It's quiet, and I can think." This is a terrific way to kill tomorrow's stress, for "most stress is anticipatory," says Dr. Elkin. Ask yourself: Do I know what's required? Have I scouted for pitfalls? Do prep work, and you'll be drooling for 9 a.m., not dreading it.

DONNY DEUTSCH

Host of CNBC's *The Big Idea* and CEO of international advertising firm Deutsch, Inc.

"F––king great to meet you!" says Donny Deutsch, his blue eyes offering a genuine twinkle. The advertising mogul and TV talk-show host hops up from his black leather office chair with the enthusiasm of a man who's had a few Red Bulls for breakfast. He's an impressive guy at first handshake—the can't-argue-with-that greeting, the muscular frame, the casual yet formal uniform of black T-shirt and jeans. From his little corner of his firm's 130,000-square-foot office, Deutsch coolly hosts his guest and handles the deluge of phone calls and messages from his three assistants. This is a guy who has learned to, as he puts it, "maximize the utils from every brain cell."

His record backs him up. In 2000, he sold the controlling interest in his ad agency reportedly for more than $200 million and stayed on as CEO. He also co-owns an independent movie studio, writes books, and hosts CNBC's *The Big Idea,* a kind of hipper, edgier Charlie Rose–style yakfest. Which leaves Deutsch to wonder why his business-as-usual seems so unusual to others. "When people say to me, 'Oh my God, you must be so stressed!' I say, 'No. Stress is when you're worried about the rent.'"

His life 10 years ago—*that* was stressful. Deutsch was unhappily married, at war with his business partner, and 45 pounds heavier—an idea man without a clue how to fix the fix he was in.

"It was the most stressful time in my life," he says. Eventually, Deutsch ended both relationships, created an exercise routine, and got healthy in every area. Today, at age 46, he's happily remarried and ensconced in a lifestyle that's equal parts hard work and hard fun. He helps himself stay calm with a "mental switch," as he calls it: "I tell myself, Nobody has cancer. So the sh–– of 'Oh my God, I'm having problems at home or at work'—you know what? You don't have cancer; you'll figure it out." Here are a few more switches you can flip.

His Anti-Stress Strategies

Muscle out the competition. Boardroom showdowns can make any man quiver, which is why Deutsch uses physical confidence to stifle any psychological doubts. "I like going into a meeting knowing I can beat the other guy up, you know?" he says with a chuckle. His secret: When finalizing a week's schedule, Deutsch reserves morning and evening time slots—all 5 days—with

WHAT STRESSES YOU OUT?

Morgan Freeman, actor

"I stress out when I don't get what I want. Oh Lord, give me the courage to change the things I can, the strength to accept what I cannot change, and the wisdom to know the difference."

Dean Winters, actor

"Downtime. I'm not good with downtime. I like to work."

Mark McGrath, lead singer, Sugar Ray

"Being a singer who can't sing. Don't tell anybody."

Michael Kors, designer

"Looking at my calendar."

Tony Hawk, skateboard champion

"When skating took a downturn in popularity and I was trying to make a living and raise a family. That was stressful because nobody cared about my skill."

Carson Kressley, *Queer Eye* Guy

"Stress stresses me out. It's a vicious cycle: Which came first, stress or being stressed? Airports stress me. Split ends stress me. And polyester stresses me . . . the fiber, not the movie."

Darius Rucker, singer, Hootie and the Blowfish

"My kids asking for the 50th time in a row if I will take them to Chuck E. Cheese."

his trainer for weight training and running. This lets him double his exercise investment when time allows.

Kill your internal editor. To Deutsch, anything that filters your instincts causes stress. "Nothing is bottled up," he claims. "I try not to be inappropriate, but the key is to be who you are as much as possible." Easy for a CEO to say. "Not everyone can express himself freely at all times," says Dr. Matt. So find a place where you can let loose—at the bar, in the gym, at a game—and you'll lessen the stress of self-censorship elsewhere.

Embrace failure. If you fear failure, you're under the kind of constant, slow-burning stress that hollows you out. But Deutsch asks, what's the big deal about failure? "Russell Simmons and I tried to start an urban advertising agency, and it didn't work out. So what?"

He's right; most anxiety is based on personal perception, says Paul J. Rosch, MD, president of the American Institute of Stress. "The Chinese word for 'crisis' consists of two characters: danger and opportunity," he says. If you see failure as exactly that, the menace evaporates.

JON FAVREAU

Actor, writer, director (*Swingers, Elf*)

"I'm a worrier," Jon Favreau insists, as he sits in a posh new office space smack in the middle of the Sony studio lot, smack in the middle of the most vicious industry humanity has invented.

Sure, the chair is leather, the desk is new, but that's what you get when you direct a film that tops the $100 million mark the way *Elf* did. For the 37-year-old Favreau, he of the close-cropped, wavy hair and gentle big-lug looks, success doesn't make the stress go away. All it does is let him spread it around. "Right now, I have four or five people worrying for me. I know they're going to do a better job worrying about their areas than I will."

The pressures have been there throughout his career—breaking in with small acting gigs (*Rudy*), fighting to make low-budget films (*Swingers*). But each new project was a little bigger than the last: *Made,* in which he directed himself in the lead role; *Rocky Marciano;* and then *Elf.*

Favreau knew everyone was watching how an indie guy handled a big-budget, big-star holiday movie. Now that he's knocked it on its ass, everyone is watching even more closely to see if he can follow up. The pressure's on, the lights are bright, and the drool is running down Hollywood's chin.

Favreau forces himself to ignore it. "My life is an endurance run," he says. "Making a movie, being an actor, being a writer, it's all about long distance." That philosophy has helped him handle not only big-budget studio success but also cult-hit cable-TV accolades for his show, *Dinner for Five,* and the responsibilities that come with a booming family life (3-year-old son, 1-year-old daughter). And he just finished gearing up for his most recent directorial gig, *Zathura,* a sci-fi action flick.

This is the kind of stress that sends others in the industry searching for a pharmaceutical fix they can use and abuse. But not Favreau. "You have to be able to control your anxiety. And you shouldn't do it with tranquilizers."

NUMBER OF MEN WHO FEEL STRESSED OUT BY THEIR JOBS: 1 in 2

His Anti-Stress Strategies

Do what you doodle. Say again? Let Favreau explain: "When I was in school, I would end up doodling a picture of a toy I wanted or whatever I was obsessing about. Now I've made my life about the things that used to take my attention away from 'work.'" That, friends, is doing what you love. First step: Look at your own doodle daydreams. Second step: Ask yourself very seriously why you're not making them reality.

Limit your projects. In Favreau's line of work, it's common for a player to have a dozen projects "in development." Not Favreau—to him, it's needless stress. "In life, you have a limited resource as far as your energy and focus is concerned. I'm doing it more like a sniper," he says—one shot, one kill at a time.

"Limiting yourself to one project where you can most effectively use your talent will prove far more rewarding and act as a powerful stress-buster," says Dr. Rosch. Audit your own to-do list, and you'll pinpoint the things you neglect. Are they worth it?

Grow it slow. One of Favreau's biggest successes—*Dinner for Five,* now in its fifth season—came not from thinking big but from exactly the opposite, and that led to a stress-free birth. "I held the *Dinner for Five* idea for a year and a half," he says. "We were able to maintain it because I wasn't trying to make a splash, a headline, or a payday."

Indeed, aiming too high can paralyze you, says Dr. Elkin. "Perfection is overrated. If you start with 'okay,' you can build on it."

Think Fast

Your six-step plan for becoming the sharpest guy in the office

By Ted Spiker

Office life is violent.

And we don't mean in the employee-tenders-resignation-with-12-gauge-Mossberg sense. White-collar work is more of a mental firefight. Every a.m., your colleagues walk in with brains cocked and loaded with brilliant ideas, gunning to get themselves ahead and leave you behind in a corporate body bag. Bang! You're demoted.

Want to be the last man standing? Pack a bigger brain. Fortunately, you don't need an FBI background check to own some high-caliber gray matter. "The lifestyle decisions we make day by day can profoundly influence whether or not our brains work at their peak potential," says Jeff Victoroff, MD, a professor of clinical neurology at the University of Southern California medical school and author of *Saving Your Brain*. And peak potential equals promotion. So go ahead, squeeze the trigger on these simple get-smart strategies. You're guaranteed to blow away the competition.

While they're stuck in traffic . . .
Take a new route to work.

You probably won't pull into the parking lot any sooner, but at least you'll show up smarter. When British researchers used MRIs to measure the brain sizes of London taxi drivers, they found that cabbies with the most experience had the largest posterior hippocampi—the area associated with memory. Because taxi drivers have to memorize the detailed layout of a geographically complex city and need to recall that information every day, they literally "build bigger brains," says Dr. Victoroff. Don't have a hack license? Any activity in which you push the intellectual envelope in a similar way—exploring new routes to work, hiking unfamiliar trails on the weekends, even taking on more new projects at work—will, over time, act like Miracle-Gro for your mind.

While they're eating bagels . . .
Have a protein shake.

Swiss researchers found that of three different breakfasts—high-carbohydrate, high-protein, and a balance of both—the high-protein meal helped men score highest on a computer memory test (similar to the electronic game Simon). "Short-term memory can be better after a protein-rich meal because the food increases your levels of the amino acids tyrosine and phenylalanine," says Karina Fischer, PhD, the lead study author. To re-create the 4:1 protein-to-carbohydrate ratio used in the study, pick up a can of Nitro-Tech whey protein (available in chocolate, vanilla, and strawberry flavors, at www.muscletech.com and most gyms). Dump 1 scoop of Nitro-Tech into a glass, followed by $^1/_4$ cup skim milk and $^1/_4$ cup water. Stir and gulp. You'll maximize your memory for 3 hours. (An alternative you can chew: turkey jerky, which also has the right ratio.)

When they b.s. at the watercooler . . .
Make noise.

The white kind. Studies show that listening to white noise—such as a constant whooshing sound—while you work may actually *improve* your concentration. "A steady, smooth sound of a constant intensity and regularity reduces the impact of unpredictable noises by making it harder for the brain to process them," says Mary Anne Baker, PhD, a professor of psychology at Indiana University Southeast. In non-geekspeak: Since white noise is produced at a constant low level, it can screen out random, distracting sounds without being a distraction itself. The result: Your mind is free to home in on the task at hand. Before you spring for a white-noise generator, try it out by turning your computer into one with free demonstration software from www.nch.com.au/tonegen.

When they pop antacids . . .
Swallow some E.

And some vitamin C, too. In a study of 3,385 older men published in the journal *Neurology*, those who took vitamin E and C supplements daily per-

DON'T PLAY DUMB

Being smart doesn't do any good if you just end up acting like an idiot. Take it from Clare Spiegel, president of Your New Image, a career consulting company; she makes a living helping office types create the appearance of intelligence. Here's your free consultation.

Talk like Bill. Gates, not O'Reilly. Speaking at midvolume during a speech or presentation projects more intelligence, says Spiegel. The reason: You come off as calm and authoritative, rather than desperate to convince everyone of your point. "Plus, talking too loudly can be perceived as boisterous and obnoxious," she says.

Mingle. Whether you're at the company party or at the cafeteria salad bar, try to talk with people from different levels of the corporate hierarchy, as well as those with different specializations. "The ability to talk effortlessly about a variety of subjects with different people is perceived as a sign of intelligence," says Spiegel. So for every 5 minutes you spend chatting up a VP about first-quarter earnings, spend 5 talking fly-fishing with the guy in accounts receivable.

Tone it down. Smart guys dress the part. That means no more Hawaiian shirts on casual Friday. "If you wear a colored shirt, make sure the shade is dusty or muted," says Spiegel. "Bright colors give off the image of someone who's not in the know." Joseph Abboud makes shirts that are subdued without being bland.

formed 20 percent better on tests of concentration, memory, and reasoning than those who didn't pop any. Researchers believe that the antioxidants in the vitamins protect neurons from oxidative damage that causes a dumbing down. "You could assume that if it works in older men, it would be even more beneficial if you started sooner," says Helen Petrovich, MD, one of the study authors. Since most multivitamins are light on E, take a separate 400-milligram supplement twice a day, recommends Guy McKhann, MD, a professor of neurology at Johns Hopkins University. And stick with a brand that contains tocotrienols, a type of vitamin E that studies suggest is better at delivering oxygen from your heart to your brain.

While they're pounding martinis . . .
Drink white wine.
Everyone else in the office drinks to forget life, but you're going to have a happy hour to remember. Three large European studies recently revealed that people who down one or two alcoholic drinks a day retain their memories better than either teetotalers or heavy drinkers. "Alcohol can lower your cholesterol, so you'll have better bloodflow and more glucose and oxygen reaching your brain," says Dr. Victoroff. But why sip Chablis? "Red wine gives many people headaches, hard liquor sometimes contains toxins, and beer can sabotage your waistline," he says. "But a glass of white wine may be a great way to keep your brain cells running strong."

When they reach for the remote . . .
Grab your joystick.
Not that joystick, but the one attached to your kid's Xbox. British researchers found that the longer people play video games, the higher their levels of concentration, sometimes equaling a trained athlete's ability to focus. "Playing video games requires a high level of concentration to be successful, and that seems to transfer to the real world," says Jo Bryce, PhD, the study coauthor. The researchers didn't look at which games were more effective, but if you want to blast and zap on your lunch break, go to www.c-eon.com and download Arcade Park to your handheld. For $15, you get pocket versions of six classic low-tech games: Arkanoid, Asteroids, Black Shark, Digger, Lode Runner, and Pac Man.

Survive Judgment Day

Criticism can put anyone on the defensive. Here's how to turn those put-downs into praise

By Laurence Roy Stains

It's Friday afternoon, just past 5:00, when your boss calls you into his office. He's agitated. You're numb. This has been coming all week.

"What happened on that project?" he asks, and before you can answer, he begins whaling on you for a recent failure that has your name attached. Like a lot of managers, your boss didn't get where he is by being the world's most understanding guy. In fact, upper management sent him away to "charm school" last summer, and he came back wearing a stiff smile for about a day and a half. Then he went back to his gruff ways.

Most managers know that if they don't want to waste their breath, they'll sandwich their criticism between positive comments. But, being the impulsive, self-centered bastard that he is, your boss seems mostly concerned with getting this off his chest. So he blasts away, and you leave his office feeling as if you've been hit by a shotgun at close range.

With any luck, later he'll regret his performance. I don't want you to regret yours.

You can start by not feeling bad about feeling bad. "Everybody is exquisitely sensitive to negative feedback—that's a given," says Robert A. Baron, PhD, a professor of management and psychology at Rensselaer Polytechnic Institute. "If you accepted everything that everybody said about you, you'd be a chameleon," says Rick Snyder, PhD, a professor of psychology at the University of Kansas.

We all have our flaws. But you won't exactly advance your career by smiling wanly and saying with a shrug, "Hey! Nobody's perfect!" That would be a perfectly stupid response. And so would most of the other responses that come naturally when you're under fire, such as the following:

Arguing. Debating the point makes you look defensive and therefore guilty. Debate too long and you can practically see a thought bubble with the word "weasel" forming above your boss's head. If you deny your mistake with words that echo his ("I did not roll my eyes"; "I did not hit on the client's daughter"), you actually corroborate the accusation by calling to mind the very image you want to negate.

Explaining. When people complain, don't explain. It only extends and escalates the argument. I recall once, long ago, being called on the carpet for failing to meet profit goals. I was young and clueless; I didn't pick up on my mentor's bottled-up anger. When I launched into my carefully crafted defense,

NUMBER OF MEN WHO PLAN TO WORK PAST RETIREMENT AGE: 1 in 3

he snapped, "I don't want to hear your pathetic excuses," and our relationship was never the same thereafter.

Getting insulted. Even though your boss is agitated, he's not criticizing you. He's criticizing your action (or lack of it). He's agitated because he waited days to say something, and so he stewed about it. That's his fault. Now all you can do is listen. Don't react.

So, what do you do? You can take a few tips from all those long-suffering folks on the front lines of criticism: flight attendants, bartenders, cashiers, receptionists, waiters, and any clerk who's handling your botched reservation. These people hear criticism all day, every day. Once in a while, they catch a break: Their bosses send them to workshops where they trade war stories and learn how to deal with difficult people.

Chances are, they take a workshop from Sam Horn; Horn has taught negotiation to more than 150,000 people. Several years ago she distilled her wisdom in *Tongue Fu! How to Deflect, Disarm, and Defuse Any Verbal Conflict*, a book that gives you the words to handle all kinds of criticism, fair and unfair.

If the criticism you're hearing is basically true and you're basically responsible, here's what Horn says to do:

Agree. Let your boss have his say, and then quickly respond with, "You're right. I messed up." "Instead of outlining what went wrong, acknowledge what they've said and move on to what can be done about it," writes Horn. Explanations only further annoy your already irate boss.

Apologize. Be humble. Show contrition. Take responsibility. Anything else will come off as arrogance or denial.

Act to make amends. Offer a solution. Use the words "us" and "we." This is really what your boss wants—just as you want the waiter to comp your overcooked entrée. When you're given what you want, don't you feel better about the business than if nothing had gone wrong in the first place? Wouldn't it be great if your boss ended up feeling that way about you?

If your boss bats away your attempts at damage control, then either he's taking an extra-long time to vent his frustrations or he's a deeply troubled guy. In which case, Horn has a nifty idea: Look him in the eye and ask, "So, what do you suggest?" Then stop talking. You can be comfortable with the verbal vacuum that ensues, because now you have him on the hook.

Psychologists Baron and Snyder have found that people are more accepting of criticism if it's delivered by someone of high status whose authority is respected. No surprise there. But whoever may be doling out the hard news, Dr. Snyder says most of us put harsh words through a process he calls "reality negotiation." To put it simply, we somehow reconcile the negative feedback with our preexisting concepts of ourselves. "We are wired to protect our view of who and what we are," he says. "When information deviates from that, we engage in different kinds of negotiation strategies to make it more consistent with what we already thought about ourselves."

For example: When the boss says you really blew that project, you finesse it in your mind. Yeah, I did blow that, but listen, it won't happen again. Good move? Absolutely, says Dr. Snyder. "You're cutting off that one negative performance and saying a mea culpa, while maintaining the larger view that you're competent and the future will be better. That is the single best reality-negotiation strategy."

And it works, once or twice.

Dr. Baron's research looked at criticism from the point of view of managers who have to deliver it. His key question, as he puts it: "How do you give people negative feedback in a way that doesn't drive them nuts?" After reviewing the clearly disastrous effects of destructive criticism (like workplace murder and suicide), his answer is, "Don't criticize someone unless you can see a clear way that your words are going to help him improve."

Dr. Baron conducted that research 15 years ago, but he still profits from it today. "I invite negative feedback in order to get better," he says proudly. "I want to be a better lover, a better father, a better colleague. There's only one rational reason for criticism—to help someone improve. I've realized that, and it's changed my life."

NEED TO KNOW

Manage Stress

Every day, Craig Burzych has to "watch a lot of things at once while making quick decisions." No, he's not playing Metroid. Burzych is an air-traffic controller at Chicago O'Hare, directing more than 200 planes in an hour at the busiest airport in the world. Burzych, 46, has learned a few secrets about handling stress in 18 years on the job.

Head off turbulence. "Unlike in a lot of jobs, I can't just get up and leave anytime to take a break. To head off stress, I've learned to recognize it early. If I'm speaking faster, with a rising voice pitch, and sweating, I know I'm under pressure and need to do something about it—now."

Catch some O_2. "The planes keep coming no matter what, and I can't lose it and walk away, so when I feel tension, I take a deep breath. Then I tell myself to slow down."

Use your copilot. "In the tower, it's a team effort. We work in very close quarters, and it's very busy. But we talk to each other, and as one controller's load gets heavy, others know it, and we share the work. If you see a coworker who's overwhelmed, take some of the load; then, when you have too much on your plate, you'll get some help."

Find your runway. "Federal regulations require that we work only 2 hours at a time. On breaks, I'll hit the treadmill for a mile or two, and it cleans out my system, and I'll go back relaxed. After work, I'll run about 6 to 8 miles. Running knocks out the physical and mental stress. A run winds me back to normal and lets me sleep better."

Don't tower talk. "After work, we limit shoptalk. We make it a rule not to rehash daily events; we've all been there, and there's no sense in talking about those things. But if anything unusual happens, we'll bring that up."

Raise the Stakes

Waiting for a pay bump is self-defeating. What boss wants to reward a man who won't take the initiative? When you do go in, be clear and concise without ruffling feathers, says Peter B. Stark, author of *The Only Negotiating Guide You'll Ever Need.* He also suggests these strategies.

PERCENTAGE OF MEN WHO PLAN TO HIT THE BOSS UP FOR A RAISE THIS YEAR: 10

PERCENTAGE WHO WOULD RATHER JUST HIT THE BOSS AND FIND A BETTER JOB: 35

Role-play. You know what the boss will say, so practice your responses. If he tells you "it's not in the budget," ask how you can be considered when finances change. If he tells you to wait for your next review, set a firm date.

Do your homework. Ask for the wrong raise and you could lose credibility and cash. Research the salaries of other people in your position. Industry associations can be a great source, says Stark. And be specific about how you saved and earned the company money.

Get hired. "Go out and get another job offer that pays more," Stark says. "And don't try to bluff, because if you do and your boss calls your bluff, you're never going to be in a situation to seek a competitive wage." Companies often reevaluate the bottom line to keep an employee out of a competitor's camp.

Think long-term. "I recommend asking people in advance what you need to do to earn a raise this year," Stark says. On new projects, ask the boss what a great job would look like, so "you can get input up front."

Back to School

Hitting the books could increase your brain—and earning—power. Before you start daydreaming about coeds, answer these questions.

Is it free? If the boss will bankroll tuition, you should enroll, says Bill Coplin, author of 10 Things Employers Want You to Learn in College. Also, look for tuition-relief programs through your state's higher-education agency. Find them at www.ed.gov.

Are you free? If you spend evenings watching reruns of Monster Garage, you have time for classes. Many professional master's programs have night and weekend courses.

Do you need to network? Grad school can ease the transition into a new career or help you develop contacts in your current one, Coplin says. Talk to recent grads to see if the program helped them.

Are you alone? Don't be the only dunce at work who's not learning the latest methods or developing management-track skills.

Career Switch

Jim Koch did the unthinkable when he was in his mid-thirties—he quit a lucrative gig to make beer. "When I started Sam Adams, I was at a high-powered management consulting firm," he recalls. "I flew first class, stayed in nice hotels, got paid a lot of money; but it reached a point at which I knew this was not what I wanted to do for the rest of my life." Nice idea—but that first step is a doozy. Here's how to brew your own start-up.

Don't be afraid. "When I was starting the beer business, I called the guy who originally hired me—who had become one of Jack Welch's top guys at General Electric—and told him what I was doing. He said, 'Frankly, Jim, you're not taking any risk. I'd sooner hire you with 3 years of a failed entrepreneurship on your résumé than 3 more years of management consulting.' So the downside of risk taking is a lot less than you think."

Share the love. "I 'run' Boston Beer Company, but there are only a couple of things I do well: make great beer and work hard to sell it. They happen to be the things I like. I focus on doing the things that I enjoy. Things I don't enjoy, like accounting, somebody else can do better."

Use hire power. "We don't hire someone unless he's better than the average person we currently have. Also, hire slowly, fire quickly. If you take your time in hiring someone—four or five interviews—you really get to know him."

Let talent show. "I don't think we've ever hired a bad person. But we have put people into the wrong jobs. The worst thing you can do is put talented, intelligent people in the wrong jobs. You spend forever trying to teach them to be good at it, but they never enjoy it. You're better off moving them or letting them go to find something they can enjoy."

Have a train schedule. "We give new people 2 to 4 weeks of training every year. A friend of mine once asked me, 'Jim, what if you train someone and he just leaves?' I said, 'Well, what if I don't train him, and he stays?'"

Remember what's real. "A company doesn't exist. A corporation is a legal fiction that lawyers have created. What does exist is a collection of great beers and a group of people who come together for a part of their lives—people who have common goals and objectives. The company can never be better than the people."

NUMBER OF MEN WHO THINK ABOUT CHUCKING IT ALL FOR A NEW CAREER A FEW TIMES A WEEK:

4 in 11

Turn Ideas into Dollars

Starting a business is the most exciting thing a man can do with his career and money. Reed Hastings, 43, famously launched Netflix (www.netflix.com) after racking up late fees at Blockbuster. Enter the no-late-fee, mail-order DVD-rental business. "In 1999, we did $5 million in revenue and thought, Well, that's a pretty good start. This year, we'll do about $500 million," Hastings says, despite new competition from Blockbuster and Wal-Mart. Try a few of his stay-ahead secrets.

Important versus urgent. "Most good management isn't day-to-day. It's a lot of investment in things, say, over the next 2 years—investments in relationships, in management. So most of my time is spent making sure that the day-to day-urgent doesn't take over for the important. If you keep working on the important, you'll have to do some of the urgent, but as little as possible."

The business trifecta. "Americans love convenience, and they constantly choose convenience over almost every other thing. Think of [a great business model] as a triad of convenience, selection, and value relative to what people are used to. You nail all three, then you take off."

Mapping unseen dangers. "The most difficult thing is anticipating the threats ahead of time. We've got a great head of steam, fast growth, big earnings, customer growth, all kinds of good things, but we've watched a lot of companies rise and then fall, especially in Silicon Valley. So we work very hard to kind of game-theory it out: what could happen if all of these things happened, how we'd react in that scenario, strategic planning, anticipating what will come up."

Coping with fear and derision. "Fear because we're fighting Wal-Mart, which is the world's largest company, and Blockbuster, which is much bigger than us. Derision in that we've been competing with them for more than 2 years already, and we have a 95 percent market share. Our service works better, and we continue to invest to make it better than theirs, so we keep a steady eye on them. But we have so much more momentum and are so focused on a better consumer proposition that we're not too worried."

PERCENTAGE REDUCTION IN A MAN'S HEART-ATTACK RISK IF HE TAKES AN ANNUAL VACATION: 30

PERCENTAGE REDUCTION IN HIS OVERALL RISK OF SUDDEN DEATH: 20

NUMBER OF WHITE-COLLAR MEN WHO
DREAM ABOUT DOING BLUE-COLLAR
WORK INSTEAD: **1 in 2**

Pair Up at Work

Nice guys finish last? Not in Jonathan Tisch's company. Tisch, the CEO of Loews Hotels, lays out his strategy for working with business partners in his book *The Power of We*. His rules for finding the perfect partner:

Find common ground. "Think through who you're going to do business with. It's not going to be successful without a common goal. Find out what you want and find out what they want. Usually that's to look good in the eyes of their boss."

Know what you're bad at. "When you see a weakness in your organization, bring on a partner who complements your strengths. At Loews, we formed a partnership with the chef Emeril Lagasse, whose style matches exactly with the fun and casual image we've tried to build into our brand."

Give to the needy. "You have to have respect from all levels of your organization. It will be a lot easier for people to work for you if they feel you have an understanding of what they need. When the partnership isn't working, I sit down and say, 'Look, we're veering off course. I need you to work with me and work harder in this area.'"

Take a joke. "I appeared on a reality TV show and spent time making beds, toting luggage, cooking eggs, and handing out towels by the pool. To win over the Miami Beach City Council on a zoning vote, I dressed in drag and got them to chuckle. Don't take yourself so seriously. Create an environment where people can laugh while they do their jobs. That means laughing at yourself and laughing with others."

WHAT'S NEW

PAIN RELIEVER

Become a South Paw

Using your computer mouse with your left hand may reduce the risk of pain, according to a recent findings by Canadian researchers. For 27 study subjects, mousing on the right side if the keyboard resulted in potentially pain-causing posture 75 percent of the time, compared with 46 percent on the left. The numeric keypad to the right of the QWERTY keys makes righties reach farther. For lefties, "the posture of the arm is more neutral," and that can help relieve pain, says study author Alain Delisle, MD, PhD.

COOL TOOLS

In a Flash

A new flash drive lets you do whatever you want—personal e-mail, naughty Net surfing—on any PC without fear of anyone tracking it. All surfing history and cookies are saved onto the thumb-size StealthSurfer, leaving no trace. (The surf protection doesn't work on a Mac, though.) It's also a regular flash drive (for PC and Mac). The USB 2.0 connection makes for fast document transfer, and it's tough—it can survive a washing machine. 128 MB, $100; 1 GB, $300. www.stealthsurfer.com

Push Fewer Buttons

Tapping out text messages on a cell phone can degenerate into a thumb-wrestling match, and the keypad has home-court advantage. Give your thumbs a break with the Samsung p207, the first cell phone to take dictation. Other phones might dial a person's number via voice command, but the p207 can also translate your spoken words into text. After "teaching" the phone your voice, you can IM or text things like "Julie, sorry I'm late. The meeting ran long," with just one button push. Now, if only it could manufacture better excuses. $100 to $150. www.samsungusa.com

THE COST OF . . .

. . . Being a Workaholic

Skipping vacation actually takes a toll on your wallet and your health. Here's what becoming a slave to the man can cost you.

You'll need . . .	The research shows . . .	It'll cost you . . .
To give up 2 days' worth of your salary	The average American loses 1.8 vacation days a year because he or she feels too busy to use them.	$284
Math and English tutors for the kids	Goofing off with Junior helps him do better in school. A New York University study found that children who play with their dads develop early cognitive and language skills.	$4,160
Two cardiologist visits, daily aspirin, and a home defibrillator	A British study shows that workers who don't take time off when they're sick double their risk of heart disease.	$2,000
A personal trainer and weight-loss shakes	Less downtime means fewer Zzzs—which leads to weight gain.	$2,080
A marriage counselor and Prozac	Time spent outside of your normal routine improves your ability to cope as a couple. Lack of leisure time leads to depression, according to a study of Japanese white-collar men.	$1,830
Weekly massages	Austrian researchers have found that aches and pains decrease after a vacation.	$3,120
To wait longer for a promotion	Taking a vacation boosts productivity. According to a survey, 95 percent of men feel that taking time off improves their performance.	$1,380
TOTAL		$14,854

FAST FIXES

It's your first day on the job. Your new peers can't wait to rip you to shreds; subordinates are looking forward to hating you. Here are eight ways to take command and be perceived as a strong leader, even if you haven't a clue.

1. Be a little weird. The image you want to convey is "I'm just like you, but better." Eccentricity is respected as long as it doesn't go too far. Try a retro tie with your black suit—you respect tradition, but you're independent. Or try a solid primary-color shirt (red, green, blue)—it's bold, just like you.

2. Take ownership. Even if you plan to observe for months before making any big decisions, it's important to take control of something early: meeting times, lunch hours, travel requests, the bathroom key. It doesn't matter what, just that you make others come to you.

3. Know what you want. Newcomers often make the mistake of trying to be inclusive, so they'll say things like "We should consider . . . " Instead, say "I want us to consider . . . " Remind them who's in charge.

4. Stand tall. You'll think better on your feet and force others to look up to you. Studies show that tall people are perceived as better leaders.

5. Put others in their place. A person with low self-esteem is more persuadable, so throw subtle barbs at potential naysayers: "Great shoes—you ought to have them shined" or "Have you ever thought of shaving your beard?" The reverse also works: One-up them by sporting your new shoes, briefcase, or BlackBerry.

6. Change your eye color. Steel-gray eyes are considered the most commanding, followed by blue, which are also seen as warm. Brown does nothing for you.

7. Or wear glasses. Glasses put up a barrier—bad for building relationships, but excellent when you're marking your territory. Make others squirm by looking at them over the tops of your lenses; they'll think they're under scrutiny.

8. Memorize the agenda. Working without paper will make you seem smarter and more certain of your department's direction.

OUR FINAL ANSWERS

Office No-mance

I asked one of my coworkers out, and she said no. How do I avoid looking like a jerk now?

—B.T., Austin, Texas

Don't *be* a jerk. Don't talk about her, don't sabotage her, don't avoid her, and don't seek her out any more than you would anyone else in the office. Most important, don't go back to the well again (and again and again), or you may find yourself facing a harassment complaint. Simply treating her with respect will keep your reputation—and job—intact.

Tune It Out

Are there any stress-relief tricks—besides meditation—that I can use at work?

—J.S., Hermosa Beach, California

Burn some Beethoven. In a 2004 study at the University of California at San Diego, researchers irritated people by giving them a difficult task, then nudging them to go faster. Afterward, the subjects listened to classical music, jazz, pop, or total silence. Silence was least calming; their blood pressure spiked almost 11 points. Jazz and pop relieved stress a bit more. But the BP of the classical-music listeners rose only 2 points. Jesse Kornbluth, *Men's Health*'s cultural concierge, suggests this starter kit: Bach's six unaccompanied cello suites; Beethoven's Concerto for Violin in D; Brahms's Violin Concerto in D, op. 77; and Mozart's symphonies 35 through 41.

PERCENTAGE INCREASE IN A MAN'S RISK OF BACK PAIN AS A RESULT OF WORKING IN A CHRONICALLY STRESSFUL JOB: 80

Price of Promotion

I need to network, but I can't afford to take a business contact out to a decent dinner. How can I tactfully ask him to split the bill?

—T.J., Terre Haute, Indiana

The person asking always does the paying. But if your company won't cover it or the tax write-off isn't enough compensation, your only other option is to lower your sights to an affordable lunch, a happy-hour drink, or breakfast at a coffee shop.

Hire Powers

A form I signed at my new job says I'm an "at-will employee." What's that mean?

—Milo, Santa Fe, New Mexico

"At-will employee" means you are out of luck if your boss wants you out. Basically, you can be dismissed at your employer's will. Some states are "at-will" states, where most workers fall in this category. Unless you have a contract, you're an at-will employee. An employer can dismiss an at-will employee hired for an indefinite term at any time for any nondiscriminatory reason.

Keep It to Yourself

I just heard that one of my coworkers is being fired. Should I tell him?

—D.M., Tacoma, Washington

Keep your mouth shut. For one thing, false rumors are always circulating. And management could change its mind. What's more, you're butting into a critical personnel issue that could put your own job on the line if management discovers that you spilled the beans.

Unpopular or Paranoid?

When I see a group of people at work having a meeting or gathering in an office, I worry that they're talking about me. Is this normal?

—G.B., Reston, Virginia

No. If you also have these feelings in different settings, you might have "social anxiety disorder"—an obsessive fear of being judged in social situations. And if worrying about people liking and respecting you keeps you from enjoying social interaction, you might need therapy and medication. But if this happens only at work, you probably have too much free time and need to focus on your job instead of what other people discuss.

Parting Gifts

Are employers required to give you a severance package when they let you go?

—G.V., Carson City, Nevada

Dream on. Imagine if you got fired for stealing. Why should an employer be forced to reward you with a severance package?

Family Business

I work for my dad, and he's becoming impossible to deal with. How can I handle him without losing my job or ruining our relationship?

—J.W., Yardley, Pennsylvania

Maybe it's simply a bad fit. If you and your dad can't separate your working relationship from the more important one, you'd better dust off your résumé. You can find another job, but not another dad.

NUMBER OF MEN WHO FANTASIZE ABOUT TELLING OFF THEIR BOSS, AT LEAST A FEW TIMES EVERY WEEK: 1 in 4

NUMBER WHO THINK ABOUT SAYING "TAKE THIS JOB AND SHOVE IT" AT REVIEW TIME: 1 in 23

Does It Pay to Put Up with the Boss?

I'm well paid, but just how much crap should I take from my boss?

—A.M., Provo, Utah

Define "crap." If you're well paid, as you say, your position might demand more, in which case your boss just wants his money's worth. That's legit. Susan Futterman, author of *When You Work for a Bully: Assessing Your Options and Taking Action*, suggests this test: Attempt to discuss the problems with him. If he reacts arbitrarily or angrily, refuses to listen, or intensifies his demands without hearing what you have to say, then he's over the line. "To have someone chipping away at your self-esteem can be debilitating," says Futterman.

Once you've explored every avenue of communication with your employer and the problem persists, it's time to figure out how much that nice paycheck is really worth.

E-Gads

I mistakenly sent an e-mail to my boss, complaining about how he handled a project. It got very awkward. What should I have done?

—G.W., Syracuse, New York

Owned up immediately. In person. Before the boss came to you. Your opening lines: "I can't believe what an idiot I am. I'm so sorry." Since your comments were more about frustration than about gossip, you could have used this as a chance to discuss the problem. If it was gossip, you'd need to apologize profusely and get the word out to everyone who received it that you, and not the target, are the idiot. Follow this simple rule: If you can't post your message on the bulletin board, don't e-mail it.

No Wining

Should I give my boss a bottle of wine for her birthday?

—E.S., Seattle, WA

No, that would be a double mistake. Never give anyone higher up the ladder a gift. It'll irritate colleagues because it will look like you're kissing up. Instead, give a group gift. Second mistake: Don't give alcohol in a business situation. Safe gifts are theater tickets, a plant, an antique print featuring a favorite activity, or a restaurant gift certificate. Keep it to $5 to $10 per person.

EIGHT

LOOK
YOUR BEST

READ UP ON IT

Change Your Clothes, Change Your Body

Five shape-shifting strategies for fine-tuning your image

Styling by Brian Boyé and Jessica Fischbein

DRESS TALLER

Muted, dark-toned ensembles blur your silhouette, creating a long look. Let pinstripes stretch your frame even further: They fool the eye. "When the eye is directed along the stripe, the body appears more vertical," says Marilyn DeLong, PhD, who teaches design and aesthetics at the University of Minnesota. Make sure your suit jacket covers your butt without extending much farther down: A shorter jacket will emphasize the line of your legs, making you appear taller. Conversely, a jacket that's too long will shrink your legs. (Remember Tom Hanks's character in that scene from *Big.*)

Hugo Boss navy pinstriped suit ($900), checked dress shirt ($85), and silk tie ($85), (800) 484-6267, www.hugoboss.com, Hugo Boss stores, NYC and LA. John Varvatos brown toe-edged brogues ($400), (212) 965-0700, www.johnvarvatos.com, John Varvatos stores, NYC, LA, Las Vegas, and Short Hills, New Jersey.

DRESS TRIMMER

Okay, you've logged the gym time, and you want to show off what you've built. Just don't go too crazy flaunting your musculature. "It's a turnoff for most people," says Mark-Evan Blackman, chairman of menswear design at New York City's Fashion Institute of Technology. "It's the same reason Speedos aren't popular and board shorts are: A little mystery goes a long way in a physique." Dr. DeLong suggests "supple textures that conform to the muscle shapes." Fine-gauge fabrics such as linen knits, lightweight cashmere, and high-quality Egyptian or pima cotton will show off your upper torso;

boot-cut jeans, which are slimmer through the seat and legs, are great for the lower body.

Perry Ellis Signature V-neck sweater ($175), www.perryellis.com. Michael Kors five-pocket jeans ($90), www.michaelkors.com, Filene's stores. John Varvatos leather military lace-up boots ($600), (212) 965-0700, www.johnvarvatos.com.

DRESS SMALLER

Imposing men can loom a bit less if they contrast colors on the top and bottom, visually splitting the body—the opposite of the single-color effect. So, unlike the man who's trying to appear taller, you can effectively wear a white or colorful shirt with darker pants. You can also create a wider frame with horizontal stripes or patterns, which add perpendicular lines to your verticals. Stay away from tops that button up high at the neck; you'll look like the Washington Monument.

Michael Kors linen button-down shirt ($80), www.michaelkors.com, Robinson's stores. Canvas bomber jacket ($150), www.michaelkors.com, Lord & Taylor stores. Nautica drawstring pants ($60), (877) 628-8422. J.M. Weston suede trainers ($375), (877) 493-7866, J.M. Weston stores, NYC.

DRESS THINNER

The strong contrast in a black-and-white outfit draws the eye to your face—and away from any out-of-control flesh that might be gathered around your middle. "You can organize the viewer's perceptual pattern—how she takes in the body—through the surfaces you place on your frame," says Dr.

DeLong. "A tuxedo is a good example of contrast at the upper torso—the body is covered in a dark value, and the contrasting white shirt makes the eyes skim the body and focus on the upper portion." To achieve the same effect every day, wear a white shirt under a black sweater or jacket, with black pants. Wearing a single dark color on top and bottom shaves off a few pounds and lengthens you. If you have a full face, wear open-collared shirts or V-necks, which add an angular look. Crew collars and turtle-necks only add to the jack-o'-lantern effect.

Perry Ellis Signature mesh-collar snap shirt ($110) and snap-front cashmere cardigan ($425), www.perryellis.com. Giorgio Armani pants ($600), www.giorgioarmani.com. Sergio Rossi leather ankle boots ($590), www.sergiorossi.com, Sergio Rossi stores, NYC and Beverly Hills.

DRESS BIGGER

If, to paraphrase the song, your physique is less than Greek, create more mass on your upper body with layers. Wear a T-shirt under an open-collared dress shirt and vest and put a sport coat on top of that. A range of jackets, including natural-shouldered tweeds in earthy colors, is also a must-have for the man who wants to look beefier. Thin men tend to have very sharp shoulder pitch: "Their shoulders aren't squared out; they slope a little more," says Blackman. "So a blazer or suit jacket would help create the illusion of width and bulk where there isn't any."

Also, if you have a narrow build, horizontal stripes will broaden your chest and shoulders and look good on you, adds Dr. De-Long. But beware of baggy. "Do not think baggy clothing makes you look bigger," warns Justin Shafran, cofounder of the Social Climber clothing label. "You just look like a pencil in a sleeping bag."

Nautica striped dress shirt ($45) and long-sleeved V-neck pullover ($80), (877) 628-8422, www.nautica.com, select Filene's stores. Victorinox By Swiss Army Toba Hydration vest ($200), (866) 997-9477, www.swissarmy.com. John Varvatos dark stonewashed jeans ($255), (212) 965-0700, www.johnvarvatos.com, John Varvatos stores, NYC and LA.

Men with Style

Eight men we admire, eight distinctive answers to the only style question that matters: How can a man's look reflect what's most important about him?

By Hugh O'Neill

What the hell is style? We'd been grinding away at that question for months, but at last the answer came—with bourbon, at close of day. Watching the sun slide down behind the lake, we could suddenly taste each distinct ingredient of the liquor—the corn, the barley, and yep, some rye, the oak sugar, hints of vanilla, and traces of wood smoke. That's when we realized that we'd been asking the wrong question. The question isn't what is style, but what is it made of? It's not a thing but an anthology of traits, a whiskey made of many spirits. With help from notable men who are themselves icons of timeless style, we've distilled style into eight founding principles: strength, intrigue, mischief, defiance, poise, confidence, command, and smarts. Of course, it would be great to actually have these traits. But, no worries. Even working on them will make you look good.

STRENGTH

The mission behind the muscles. Strong need not mean big and muscled—though we're all for lean beef. Strong need not mean aggressive, though we think that boldness is underrated these days. Strong means being comfortable in simple, unadorned styles; no fussy patterns allowed. Strong means walking with shoulders back and head high, as though you have power you might deploy at any moment on behalf of your team. Strong knows that even being a mouse means going forth and being a mighty one.

Classic clothing: _Khakis._ Many of the classics of male style—our much-loved khakis included—have military origins. A British officer, billeted in India during Queen Victoria's reign, had the stain-hiding idea of dyeing white uniforms with a mix of curry powder and coffee. The resulting color, khaki

THE STRONGEST SUIT

The pinstripes in suits are most likely an homage to the columns in old ledgers of the London stock exchange. Don't choose widely spaced, prominent stripes—called chalk stripes. There's no way around their mobster connotation (though there's a certain strength to that, too). Choose faint stripes that aren't visible from 15 feet away.

(from the Hindi word for "dusty"), christened these pants, and some Hall of Fame trou were born.

The rules: Khakis are barging into formal events where they don't belong. They're perfect for a neighborhood cocktail party on the deck, for parent-teacher night, or when you're tieless and wearing a blazer. But they are not for moments when you're trying to impress people who might give you money. Don't let khakis become your default pants for every occasion just because you don't own anything better.

Peyton Manning

Field general. We're not much for making athletes into heroes, but Indianapolis Colts QB Peyton Manning is strong enough to test our skepticism. Sure, there are the passing records. But by our lights, his iron-man gene is even more impressive. He's started 96 straight games and taken every single snap in all but eight of them. He's got heart, too. His Peyback Foundation (all right, it's a bad pun—he's human) helps poor kids by supporting youth organizations. Plus, the man can work a suit. To him a road trip is business. "I always wear suits," he says. "I figure I'm representing my family, the fans of Indianapolis, the league. Besides, looking good helps you play better." Given his record, he must look really good on the road.

INTRIGUE

Make them yearn to know more. Style is at once superficial and deep. Sure, it's about appearances, about fabric and color and proportion and texture. But style is also the seductiveness of things unseen. The stylish man appears to know something the rest of us don't. He seems to come stocked with answers, where the rest of us just have questions. But he's not a know-it-all, because he doesn't always feel the need to share; that's part of the power of knowing. He hums with promise and embraces his own ambiguity. Style calls us forward, to seek the wisdom it withholds.

Classic clothing: *White dress shirt.* The white dress shirt is a five-tool player. It throbs with crisp and clean, and it can do just about anything. Paired with blue jeans, it shouts wholesome and strong, at once cowboy and cosmopolitan. Under a suit, it sings of honesty. A white dress shirt is a pristine backdrop against which to play with necktie color, a blank slate on which she can write her fantasies. How does white do all that? That's the mystery.

The rules: Don't miss a chance to add some intrigue at your wrist. French cuffs and the cuff links they demand are an instant class transfusion. But most men wear them only at very formal or black-tie events where every loser and his brother will be sporting shine. Break out some glint or some silk knots when nobody else will dare, and you'll lift yourself above the drones.

This doesn't mean at the PTA meeting; but the office Christmas party will do just fine.

Sir Ben Kingsley

Master of mystery. His film performances flicker across the screen, but rather than vanishing when the lights go up, they're seared into your memory. The proud military man in *House of Sand and Fog,* the gangster who won't take no for an answer in *Sexy Beast,* his Oscar-winning Gandhi—all of them have an arresting and unforgettable clarity.

Sir Ben Kingsley, who was knighted in 2001, uses all his acting arrows— his expressive face, his singular voice, his mastery of gesture and inflection— to create intriguing characters with something compelling going on beneath the surface. Sir Ben brings the same attention to his personal style. From his choice of clothes to his manners, everything about him suggests depth.

MISCHIEF

Laugh first, last, best. Stylish men are entitled to have more fun than everybody else. Often seen with a glint in his eye, a mischief maker is never content with the mundane but aspires to polish up even the plain moments— just a bit. He won't surrender in line at the DMV; he cocks his head in search of the angle that saves the day, that turns everything into play. He's a glass of champagne—dignified but effervescent. Remember the wisdom of Sebastian the Crab in *The Little Mermaid:* "Life is de bubbles."

Classic clothing: *Parka.* An Aspen ski instructor named Claus Ober-mayer often gets credit for coming up with the first insulated jacket, circa 1949, and from the start, the ski jacket has pulsated with outdoor energy. But when the heralds of hip-hop brought the parka to the pavement, it earned street cred, too.

The rules: Off the slopes, always partner jackets that have outdoor DNA with jeans or cargo pants and with footwear featuring enough sole, enough gadgetry (metal, eyelets, and so on), or laces fat enough to suggest a working-man's shoe or hiking boot.

LL Cool J

The classy clown. A founding daddy of hip-hop, LL Cool J (born James Todd Smith) has worked a joyful, smooth groove for 20 years. His style—at once edgy and easy but always authentic—helped rap make its way into main-stream hearts. Now, 10 platinum albums later and still young at 36, LL Cool J has managed a neat trick: He's become a music legend (he won a Lifetime Achievement Award from *Soul Train*) and yet remains a promising new acting talent (honored in 2003 at ShoWest as the Male Star of Tomorrow). That's our idea of career planning.

"I developed my style imitating NBA ballplayers and street hustlers. To me, if a man had money and style, it meant he had options." Just as he does now—from his cop role in *Edison*, a thriller starring Morgan Freeman and Kevin Spacey, to his LL by James Todd Smith clothing line that recently hit stores.

DEFIANCE

The right move breaks rules and remakes them. Like all things artful, style requires balance—in this case, between respecting the rules and blowing them off. Style believes in principles of color and cut but would betray them in a flash to claim the room. And there's a reason why this is especially true of men's style: We become most exciting when we set our own course. When Fred Astaire used a necktie as a belt, he knew it wasn't done, except for the fact that he did it. Style requires both a sense of custom and a sense of "screw you."

Classic clothing: *Leather jacket.* We love everything about leather jackets—the way they feel, the way they smell. Hell, we love the way they sound—the soft creak as she shoves it off us in the leaf pile. Wear one and you're ready to rebel against whatever they've got, or take back Europe from the Axis. Any garment that speaks of both flyboys and hoodlums has to be the ultimate guy gear.

Jerry Bruckheimer

The defiant one. There's a reasonable case for this claim: Nobody has more influence on American pop culture than Jerry Bruckheimer. Once he got growing up in Detroit out of the way and learned a few skills in the advertising business, he became synonymous with having a good time at the movies—no matter how many critics sniffed: *Top Gun, Armageddon, Black Hawk Down, Pirates of the Caribbean.* What's that? You don't like action, adventure, gunplay, fireballs, and fast vehicles? J.B. also produces *CSI* and its sophisticated spin-offs.

Bruckheimer's style is the rewrite—be it a rule or a script. But his sartorial style came from his father. "He worked in an exclusive women's clothing store, and I got an interest in quality goods and style from him," he says.

POISE

Be the go-to guy when the game is on the line. Style can't be rattled. It treats both triumph and disaster as what they are: parts of the great story. In darkness, style finds its way. In a flood, style swims. In a drought, it recalls the taste of cool, clear water. Style doesn't shout, except when nothing softer will suffice. Style knows that he who rules others has power, but he who rules himself is mighty.

Classic clothing: *The blazer.* According to style legend, a 19th-century commander of the British battleship *Blazer* ordered his men to wear jackets in honor of a visit from Queen Victoria. True or not, the blazer has evolved into a go-to garment for the well-dressed man.

The rules: Show your colors. Navy blue flatters lots of complexions and lets you add different colors with ties, shirts, pocket squares, and other accessories. "But the black blazer is an option for slightly higher style, a more arty, downtown look," according to Lloyd Boston, *Today* show style expert. Camel-hair blazers look great on darker men, but the color can wash out very pale guys.

Isiah Thomas

The pressure player. Isiah Thomas is the point guard your father dreamed you'd be. Aggressive but never reckless, quick but never hurried, he found that sweet balance between forcing the play and caring for the ball. He always kept his head—hence one championship of the NCAA variety (Indiana University, 1981), two others in the NBA (Detroit Pistons, 1989, 1990), and a spot on the list of the 50 Greatest Players in NBA history.

The same poise that distinguished him on the court has marked Thomas as a coach, businessman, broadcaster, and, now, president of basketball operations for the Knicks. He emanates a sense of soft-spoken authority, a feeling that though others may panic, this man has a plan.

"I went to Catholic school and learned early about the power of wearing a jacket and tie," he says. "And I had a big brother who taught me the importance of looking good."

According to Thomas, there's another asset that point guards need, on top of peripheral vision and quick hands: "When you're talking to your teammates in the huddle or your office mates in the conference room, you'd better have clean teeth and fresh breath," says Thomas. "People can't listen and hear unless your hygiene is perfect." Good advice whether you're a two-guard in the rec league or a guy who's getting too big for his cubicle.

CONFIDENCE

How the winners got that way. Sure, you want her—as in, right now, yeah, in the produce section. But, key point: You don't need her. Kids need their mothers. She's not your mother. And even if this particular sweetness doesn't come to pass behind the bananas, something else urgent will, soon. Style knows life is bursting with opportunity, that there's plenty to go around. Sure, you want this deal. And you'll work to get it. But guess what? Style doesn't need this particular deal. There's always another one. Something even better, perhaps. Confidence is born of faith.

Classic clothing: *Jeans.* Levi Strauss often gets the credit for inventing jeans. Wrong. Back in the 1870s, miners out San Francisco way needed heavy-duty pants for fortune hunting, and a guy named Jacob Davis came up with an early version of jeans (brown, not blue). He reinforced the pockets with rivets so they'd be strong enough to hold ore samples. This is where Levi comes on the scene. In one of the great investments in history, he gave the tapped-out Davis enough money to apply for a patent, and so became both a partner and synonymous with the most celebrated garment in the history of men's style.

The rules: No pair of pants looks better on a man than blue jeans that were stiff and dark when they came home from the store and have been soft-ened and sculpted and battered against his body by life. Buy a single pair that starts out looking like something Potsie wore on *Happy Days*. Over time, they'll mature into your favorite pair. Hers, too.

Classic clothing: *Denim jacket.* It's an American classic that prob-ably appears more often in clubs in our great cities than it does out on the range. Even so, it still hints of a can-do man, a guy who knows how to string barbed wire.

The rules: Just avoid the cardinal sin, warns Michael Bastian, men's fashion director at Bergdorf Goodman: "Don't ever wear a jean jacket with a pair of jeans. No denim leisure suits." You'll also want to avoid mixing rough-hewn with elegant—unless you're pairing a cashmere sweater with jeans. For some reason, this works.

Peter Gallagher

A man for all stages. Sure, it's easy for Peter Gallagher to project an air of confidence. We'd have it too, if we'd mastered stage, film, and television. Gallagher currently plays the hunky father Sandy Cohen on the tube's hottest show, the Fox series *The O.C.* When he steps offstage, Gallagher wears low-key stuff from Dolce & Gabbana, Hugo Boss, and Armani and devotes him-self to small style touches. "I resist clothes that scream 'Look at me,' and I like working with high-quality accessories," he says. "I agree with Mies van der Rohe's thought that 'God is in the details.'" Gallagher recalls a lesson in style from a meeting with a legend. "When I met Cary Grant, I suddenly knew why God invented the blue suit," says Gallagher. "He looked fantastic, formi-dable—but it didn't stop him from being accessible."

COMMAND

To be the boss, look the part. Style is in charge, even if it's not the boss. Its authority isn't hierarchical but gravitational. Objects fall into orbit around it. Its force derives from impeccable taste and an imperturbable sense of direction. Style knows which stripes will work with which checks, and it also knows that a man needs a mission. The mission needn't be grand, but it had better be all his. Style doesn't wobble but has clear eyes. Find this clarity—through ease of confidence and a few choice items—and they'll salute the man, not the rank.

Classic clothing: *Wool overcoat.* Fashion man Lloyd Boston puts it best: "Your overcoat is the first thing anybody sees. If you invest in a high-quality wool coat, you'll get back the money many times over." He recommends camel hair: "It's classic and works well with all colors."

Classic clothing: *Wool trousers.* If you're over 40, the phrase "wool trousers" may give you sweaty-in-church flashbacks. Well, times—and fabrics—change. Wool trousers are now available in every conceivable weave and weight, from heavy flannels to light summer wools that are as cool as Glavine with the bases loaded.

The rules: Buy high-quality wool trousers and pair them with sport coats, blazers, or casual jackets. Wool drapes beautifully and will add an immediate sophistication to your look. Check for these signs of quality, says clothing expert Andy Gilchrist, of www.askandyaboutclothes.com.

- X-stitching pattern on the buttons, indicating that the pants were hand sewn
- Lining in the crotch
- Extra fabric inside the crotch and seat—to allow for alterations

Dylan McDermott

Man in charge. Dylan McDermott's sense of style dates to his days in high school. "We had to dress up, and my father bought me a blue velvet suit. I loved it, and I wore it for years," he recalls. He credits New York City, too. "I was a teenager in the postpunk period, and the streets of Manhattan had a strong fashion vibe. You had to be aware of how you looked."

He's come a long way since velvet in homeroom. As passionate defense attorney Bobby Donnell on the Emmy Award–winning series *The Practice*, McDermott invoked his client's constitutional protections in killer designer suits. He always looked better than the prosecutor—even when she was Lara Flynn Boyle. "The clothes are a great fringe benefit of being on TV," says McDermott.

SMARTS

Be a "more than meets the eye" guy. Style doesn't exhaust itself choosing clothes but has other projects—business ventures, work-free enthusiasms—in mind. Style needs grist for the mill between its ears. It's curious about the world. So the notion that wheels are turning works for the stylish man. He's not accepting things at face value. Rather, he's drawing conclusions, altering his life—maybe history, even—with the power of his thought. That quality can make him irresistible—a puzzle that everyone wants to solve.

Classic clothing: *Dark suit.* The dark suit has been making us look taller and smarter for centuries. You need one (black). No, make that two (blue). Or three (charcoal). Precisely because they appear so plain, dark suits are great canvases on which to splash some personality. Flash nonconformist color with a necktie. Show flair with a pocket square. Its color should refer to your tie, and its fabric should match it, but its pattern never should. Thrifty tip: Work's done, hang the suit. You'll extend its career.

Classic clothing: *Peacoat.* The hip-length double-breasted woolen jacket is commonly called a peacoat—most likely after the first letter of "pilot": one of the guys who first wore it. In the '60s, poetry-swilling intellectuals snapped them up from vintage-clothing stores and donned them against the winter on MacDougal Street and in Harvard Square. This coat is a great split-the-difference addition to a guy's wardrobe—more casual than an overcoat, warmer than a barn coat, and less ski-lodgy than a down jacket. The navy blue works on sailors of all hues.

Russell Simmons

Jam mastermind. When Russell Simmons was still just a teenager, he had one of those life-changing moments. In a club called the Charles Gallery in New York City, he saw a proto-rapper named Eddie Cheeba seize the crowd by shouting out rhymes. It was a new art form that would touch the masses, and he had the cultural intelligence to know it instantly. Soon after, he started promoting concerts and managing performers, and he eventually cofounded Def Jam Records, producing some of the earliest stars of rap, including the Beastie Boys, LL Cool J, and Public Enemy.

Now, almost 30 years later, the godfather of hip-hop is not only among the most successful entrepreneurs of his generation but also a force in reshaping our culture, both musically and in terms of style. In 1992, Simmons started Phat Farm, a clothing company dedicated to mixing classic style with the flavors of the inner city. "Hip-hop helped Tommy Hilfiger and Ralph Lauren. We're adding our energy to those traditions," says Simmons. "We're offering the Nu American dream, classics with an edge."

His wisdom on how hip-hop performers achieve success might well be a mantra for finding your own style: "The secret is to tell the truth about yourself. You have to be authentic."

Handsome Like Me

He was tired of chasing women. So he made a few upgrades designed to get women to chase him, instead

By Colin McEnroe

I fell in love with Maud. She appeared none too happy about the whole thing.

"I'm in love with you," I'd say.

"You're not. You're besotted with me," she would counter, warily.

"What's the difference?"

"I don't know, but there is one."

Maud never offered to be in love—or even besotted—with me. "I like you well enough," she'd say.

I had been separated from my wife for almost a year, and I was in the process of a divorce. A 49-year-old man, newly single, reasonably attractive, able to hold down a job and cut his own meat, is, by some weird quirk of Malthusian dating theory, the equivalent of George Clooney. Lots and lots of women—better-looking women than I had any right to expect—wanted to go out with me. I didn't want to go out with them. I wanted to go out with Maud.

"Hmmm," said Maud.

I was permitted to hang around Maud's house sometimes. Occasionally, she would go out in public with me, but not very often.

We began having sort of a relationship.

"How do you feel about me?" I would ask.

"I like you well enough."

This started to drive me a little crazy. I know what it's like to move a woman's needle, and I wasn't moving Maud's.

"I'm perfect for her," I told my friend Peter. "She loves my cooking. We have the same sense of humor. I know the words to her favorite songs. Her dog loves me. Her mother loves me."

"You sound like her favorite gay friend," said Peter.

"Arrrgh."

THE LIST

I began to think maybe I wasn't handsome enough. I had reason to think I was decent looking, but Maud's most recent, very long-term relationship had been with a fabulously attractive man. A great guy (so there was not even the luxury option of hating him), very accomplished, and drop-dead handsome, in the manner of an aging J. Crew catalog model.

Was I handsome enough? Should I try to become more handsome?

I made a list of what could be improved. My posture was lousy. In prep school I had experimented with a kind of William F. Buckley slouch and never emerged from it. And my teeth were not exactly sparkling white. They were kind of . . . an earth tone. My skin occasionally blazed up in odd bouquets of rosacea and extended-stay adolescent acne. And there is nothing really wrong with my hair; it's just very fine. It takes 20 strands of my hair to produce the same crowded effect that a fat-haired person sees with five or six strands. Maud's ex-boyfriend has fat hair.

This review of my quirks makes me sound like Quasimodo, I know.

That's the way it is when you start thinking about your liabilities, said Wendy Lewis, sometimes known as the Knife Coach.

"It's like a car or piece of furniture with a scratch or mark on it. You know it's there, so it bothers you, and whenever you look, your eye goes right to it," she said.

Lewis specializes in telling people what kinds of cosmetic surgeries they need and where they should have them. We were sitting in her Manhattan apartment, and she had just finished telling me I didn't need any plastic surgery. I should probably just have the little red spider veins lasered off my nose.

And, said Lewis, I should consider veneers, the Dom Perignon of teeth whitening, at $1,500 to $2,000 per tooth. "In other words, it's a car," said Lewis.

A car that lives in your mouth. And chews your salmon.

In general, Lewis said, it's better to change a little than to change a lot. "My ideal client is someone who wants to look a little younger, a little better, a little fresher, a little more polished . . . not someone who wants to make everybody yell 'Oh my God!' the way they do on those extreme-makeover shows."

"Do you mind the little spider veins on my nose?" I asked Maud a day or two later.

"What veins, honey?"

I decided not to do the nose thing.

PEARLY WHITES

"If you're going to invest in anything, invest in your teeth," Elena Castaneda told me. She is a famous image consultant. She told me I needed whiter teeth so that I could smile at people.

"Marla Maples taught herself to smile 24 hours a day," Castaneda told me firmly. "The main reason anyone is interested in you is because they think you like them."

It's a strange thought that begins with, *If only I had Marla Maples's discipline* . . .

The veneers were too expensive, but I got a whitening system, the kind in which your dentist takes impressions of your teeth and makes little mouth-pieces into which you squirt a bleach solution. And then you have to wait for your girlfriend to go on a business trip, because you don't want to hop into bed looking like Gerry Cooney staggering back to his corner after round three.

When Maud returned from her business trip, I waited for her to notice my white teeth. Nothing doing. I smiled idiotically, like Ryan Seacrest on Ecstasy. Nope.

A CUT ABOVE

I decided to have my hair cut by somebody really good. For most of my life, I've gone to people whose idea of a precutting consultation was three words of David Lynch dialogue.

"Show the ear?"

This time, I arranged to be cut by Joseph Boggess, a stylist of such magnitude that he ordinarily doesn't take private clients. Boggess cuts and styles a lot for photo shoots. He did Norah Jones's hair for the cover of her first CD, *Come Away with Me.*

The "show the ear" guys have always cut my hair in 20 minutes, and sometimes that included time out to watch Pokey Reese leg out a triple on the barbershop TV. Joseph spent about an hour, and, during that hour, he told me a lot about my hair.

I shouldn't wash it every day, because that takes out all the stuff that makes it look healthy.

If I insist on washing it anyway, I should take hair gel and mix it with hand cream to make my own "product." Joseph put a lot of product in my hair and then began shaping it into a state of disorder, a storm-tossed sea of follicles with little peaks of waves and stingrays and squid poking their snouts to the surface. Maybe I was not George Clooney, but I now had hair that looked like a perfect storm. Joseph also redesigned my hair so that it could flop to my right. My hair needed flow, it needed movement, he said.

Also, by flopping to the right, Joseph added, some of my hair could become a plucky rearguard unit, covering the retreat of my actual hairline, especially in that right-of-forehead area, which was shaping up as a coiffure Fallujah.

Of course, the minute I got home and tried to re-create this effect, my hair refused my attempts to urge it into little dolphin leaps. But left on its own, my hair went out of its way to prove Boggess's point, looking its best an hour or two after I got up, before I had showered. At that time, it would gather its spindly strands together and, guided by the underlying wisdom of the Norah Jones–affiliated haircut, move and flop itself over in a becoming way, as long as I didn't touch it very much. So, at 8:30 many mornings, I looked pretty hot (while being, perhaps, a trifle smelly). Unfortunately, Maud is a very late sleeper.

AN ATTEMPT AT STRAIGHTENING UP

The one thing that actually did seem to matter to Maud was my posture. "Stand up straight," she snapped at me every time my spine settled forward into the protective curvature it so deeply enjoys.

I decided to do yoga.

Yoga combines the disadvantages of exercise class (an instructor making you do strenuous things in a peer setting, where you don't want to publicly wuss out) with the disadvantages of religion (people who don't feel any need to be reasonable).

Age 49 is probably the wrong time to start bending. If you left Gumby in the same position for 49 years, he probably wouldn't bend either.

So, if you were to watch me, you might conclude that I am a conscientious objector to yoga, refusing to do the postures out of some deep-seated moral opposition to them. In fact, that's just how I look when I'm doing yoga: not that different from when I'm not doing yoga.

My shoulders, however, started to unkink and bend backward, so that now—if I am mindful or if Maud snaps at me often enough—I'm less likely to resemble some hunched-over minor pirate in *Treasure Island*.

A HEALTHIER COMPLEXION

The last stop on my handsomeness tour was a visit with Nicholas Perricone, MD, the Donald Trump of dermatology. Dr. Perricone is the author of several best-selling books, including *The Wrinkle Cure* and *The Perricone Prescription*. He has his own line of high-end skin-care products, sold at Nordstrom, Sephora, and other nice places. He appears on the big-time morning news shows, and half of Hollywood is slathered in his skin toners. (In his office, I noted a picture of the Doc being hugged by Heidi Klum.)

At his corporate headquarters in unglamorous Meriden, Connecticut, everything, even the leather placemats and coasters in the meeting/dining room, is embossed with "Nicholas Perricone, MD."

If that sounds like vanity, Dr. Perricone would have you make the most of it.

"Vanity can save your life," he says.

Dr. Perricone's main idea is that if you follow a very strict diet designed by him, your skin will look great. The dirty secret is that everything he's pushing also helps fight cancer, heart disease, diabetes, and other deadly ills.

"Can I interest you in a little *noni?*" he said, as we sat down in his conference room.

"That depends on what noni is," I said cautiously.

It turns out to be a Polynesian fruit whose juice contains unique phytonutrients and enzymes. There's a whole cult of noni that believes that it shrinks tumors, improves mental function, boosts immunity, bestows x-ray vision, and grants other life-altering benefits. Noni is the new pomegranate juice.

I drank noni. I ate a Perricone lunch. I got his books and some of his products. I kind of jump on and off the diet.

THE NEW ME, SORT OF

So what's the end result of my quest for better aesthetics? My skin looks pretty good, most of the time. Better than it did, anyway. And my shoulders are back and straight; my teeth are within biting range of white; my hair . . . well, my hair is my hair. I have cool glasses. Frankly, although I shouldn't be the one to say it, I'm borderline bootylicious.

In the midst of all this, I had a conversation with my best friend, Luanne.

EXTREME GROOMING

Four looks upgrades—no scalpel required

Colorizing your head. Dust the snow off your roof by coloring or blending your hair. "Men's colors are cooler in tone, as opposed to the warmer tones that many women have," says Walter Roman, color specialist at DopDop Salon in New York City. Start with a semipermanent color, so you can shampoo away mistakes. Select a shade close to your natural color, not what you wish it was. Roman recommends L'Oreal for men. $10. www.loreal.com

Get some face a-peel. Though it sounds more painful than a lava bath, a face peel won't make you scream. But it will remove dull, weather-beaten skin and reveal the smooth, healthy layer underneath. Just let a cream or gel with mild acids dry on your face for a few minutes. When you peel it off, the old skin goes with it, says dermatologist Dennis Gross, MD. Look for a product with alpha and beta hydroxyl acids, which you can use every day. A safe all-around peel: Alpha Beta Daily Face Peel. $70. www.mdskincare.com

Banish unwanted hair. For your initial foray into hair removal, try a sugar-based wax solution so you can wash it off if you accidentally slather on too much, says Audra Senkus-Lemma, co-owner of Haven Spa in New York City. Spread on one coat in the direction of hair growth; if you wax an area more than once, you'll end up skinned and bruised. Try the GiGi Sugar Bare Microwave Formula Hair Removal System. $8. www.sallyhansen.com

Paint on a smile brightener. "Most of these whiteners dissolve in 15 to 30 minutes, keeping the teeth from being exposed to peroxide too long and causing irreversible damage," says Jonathan Levine, DMD, a cosmetic dentist. We like Dr. Levine's 2-week GoSmile System Starter Kit. $75. www.gosmile.com. (Preliminary research shows that the hydrogen peroxide in teeth-whitening kits may cause oral cancer, so use sparingly.)

"I've always thought you were handsome. Very handsome. Craggily handsome," she told me in a best-friendly tone. "There are different kinds of handsome. Your kind seems very effortless, and women like that. Women like that you don't care. It's more appealing than a pretty boy."

Wendy Lewis said the same thing. "We don't want you to seem interested in your looks. And we certainly don't want to be competing with you for bathroom mirror time."

Great. The one thing I ever had going for me was my lack of interest in grooming, and now I was turning into George Hamilton.

But the conversation with Luanne made sense. Some of my confidence began to flow back in, and it made more difference than any of the treatments I did or didn't get. Confidence, said Elena Castaneda, is the hottest thing going.

Something, anyway, made a difference.

"You know, you're cute," Maud said to me one night.

"Thank you."

"You're really cute." She couldn't stop saying it. "You're a cutie-pie. You're *cute*."

"I'm going to get you the best neurologist money can buy," I told her. "Something is very wrong with you."

"I just like you, that's all," she said. "Stand up straight!"

"I like you too," I told her, throwing my shoulders back in Mountain Pose. "That is, I like you well enough."

NEED TO KNOW

Color Your World

One of the simplest ways to look your best is to wear colors that flatter you. Shades that are too close to your skin tone tend to wash you out. Tanned or olive skin looks delicious with contrasting bright colors and whites. Soft pastels and earth tones add an appealing creaminess to fair skin tones. Here's a tip that women notice and love: Wear a shirt that matches your eye color.

That's a Good Point

Is your shirt making the right point? There's an infinite number of shirt collar combinations, each for a different body type. It's best to choose a collar based on the shape of your face and the length of your neck.

Wide face: If your face is round like a basketball or wide like a football, choose a straight-point collar 3 inches long, which will lengthen your appearance. Stay away from spread collars, which will only accentuate the width. For the best examples of this style, look for shirts by Perry Ellis, Girogio Armani, Claiborne, and Hathaway. With a narrow collar, keep your tie knot small.

Narrow face: A spread collar with a half-Windsor tie knot balances a narrow face. Try Tommy Hilfiger, Robert Talbott, and Banana Republic. Spread-collar shirts are increasingly the shirt of choice for businessmen and are best when worn with a tie. Woven, as opposed to printed, ties make thicker, chunkier knots.

Long neck: If your neck is long, wear a high collar, such as one from Dolce & Gabbana. These shirts stand up well under a jacket when worn without a tie; they won't creep down below your lapel as the day or evening wears on.

Off the Cuff

Should you wear cuffed pants? That depends. If you're under 5-foot-10, go without cuffs. They break up your height and make you look even shorter. And skip them if you're wearing khakis, cords, microfiber trousers, or flat-front pants, or if you're dressing for a casual evening out. When *are* cuffs called for? They're a polished look that will serve you well in the boardroom. "Sophisticated men wear cuffs on their pants, and other sophisticated men notice," says Andy Glichrist, author of *Andy's Encyclopedia of Men's Clothes*. "Cuffs are de rigueur with pleated pants, especially suit trousers."

Don't Be Tied Down

For too many guys, tying a tie goes like this: flip, flip, flip, stuff, pull, slide, good enough. Wrong. You must check the dangling ends before giving yourself the all-clear. The tip of your tie should fall in the middle of your belt buckle. Too short conveys cluelessness and looks stumpy. Too long and you look like a sloppy 14-year-old. If you always come up short, try a different knot or buy longer ties; they come in lengths from 52 to 58 inches. Now then, if the skinny end extends below the wide end, just tuck the excess into your waistband, says Alan Flusser, author of *Dressing the Man*. Nobody will know— as long as you use the tie's keeper to hold your look together.

Travel the Beltway

You need only one belt on the road, and this is it: Salvatore Ferragamo's leather belt travel set. It's reversible, with interchangeable gold and silver hardware. $295. (800) 628-8916, www.ferragamo.com

Battle of the Bands

That reliable old Ironman watch may have seen you through hundreds of workouts, but it shouldn't be seeing you through your workday or a night on the town. "Wearing a plastic-strapped sports watch with dress clothes is like wearing a brown belt with a blue pinstriped suit," says Andrew Block, senior vice president of marketing for Tourneau. He recommends that when choosing a dress watch, you pick a shape you like and then make sure your shirtsleeve fits over it comfortably. Or invest in a watch with a strap rather than a metal bracelet. That way, you can change the strap to match your wardrobe, and the watch can be dressed up or down, depending on the occasion.

PERCENTAGE OF MEN WHO SPEND LESS THAN 2 MINUTES A DAY PICKING OUT THEIR CLOTHES: 53

Time Saver

Whether you've inherited Grandpa's ticker, bought an antique, or decided to clean up one of your cruddy old watches, here's how to restore its former glory.

Stem: Use cotton swabs and a commercial cleaning solution (preferably one that's waterless) to brush away grime that's collected in the scoring and behind the crown.

Casing: To shine it, use a polishing cloth (look for a red rouge type) to avoid gooping polish on the small surface.

Watch face: Yellowing can indicate moisture within. Have a watchmaker look at it; watch-face repairs start at around $30. Go to www.awi-net.org to find a reputable watchmaker in your area.

Armband: A weathered band is usually irreparable. A jeweler can match a new one to the old watch.

Out, Out Damn Spot

Here's an instant fix for stubborn coffee stains. Wet the stain from the underside of the shirt with cold water while rubbing a bar of Ivory soap on top. Rinse with cold water. Air-dry. Proceed to your board meeting.

WHAT'S NEW

Don't Dye Young

French researchers studying hair follicles found that hair turns gray when follicles lose cells that produce pigment. If scientists can identify what causes the cells to die, gray hair "could be prevented or even reversed," says one of the study authors, Bruno Bernard, PhD.

Keep It Casual

Somewhere between casual Friday and the gym, the lines of fashion get blurred. Thanks to Puma's new casual-clothing line, 96 Hours, we have a clear vision of what makes stylish weekend wear. Designer Neil Barrett looks to motorcross styles to inspire this urban-themed collection. www.store.puma.com

We'll Be Brief

Our short list of quality underwear brands is, well, short. There's $2^{(x)}$ist, Calvin Klein, and Jockey. Now add a fourth: C-IN2. Why? Experience. Gregory Sovell, the creative force behind $2^{(x)}$ist, used his design skills to create this new line of supercomfortable briefs, boxers, T-shirts, and swimwear. The fabrics and fit are spot-on. Coming soon: sportswear and denim. www.c-in2.com

THE COST OF . . .

. . . Not Looking Your Best

Every guy's done it—let stubble turn into a winter beard, ignored laundry for weeks, watched the love handles spread. Seems as if you're saving money on clothes and razors and detergent, but research shows you're losing in the long run. Here's what a few months of Unabomber living can cost you.

You'll have to . . .	The research says . . .	It'll cost you . . .
Pay extra for big-ticket items	Salesclerks, car dealers, loan officers, and others in service industries are more willing to make deals with nicely dressed men than with those in more rumpled attire.	$1,630
Forget about that promotion	Employers consider hygiene and appearance when handing out promotions or pink slips. One study concluded that overweight men are 3,610 percent more likely to be passed over for a corner-office spot.	$2,238
See a dentist for gum work and a doctor for a talk about a Prozac prescription	People with poor oral health are more likely to suffer from anxiety and depression.	$80
Schedule visits to a dermatologist	Not using sunscreen will likely lead to skin problems and the need for removal of suspicious moles.	$150
Start taking Viagra and seeing a couples therapist	Guys carrying extra pounds are likely to have erectile dysfunction and be mistreated by their wives.	$3,150
TOTAL		$7,248

FAST FIXES

Too much of a good thing can be a problem when it comes to styling and grooming products. It's noticeable when you have too much goop on. How big a blob should you use? Let the coin be your clue.

Moisturizer
Dollop size: Nickel
How to use it: Use it after shaving and spread it in an upward motion. Men tend to go for squeaky clean and dry out their skin with bar soaps, says Joe Venezia, marketing manager for Nivea for Men skin-care products. We like XCD for Men, $15. www.xcdskn.com

Hair Gel
Dollop size: Dime
How to use it: Guys often go wrong here. Too much gel leaves your hair looking like a plate of fries—crispy and greasy. Always apply gel to wet hair and work your style into place. We suggest John Allan's Texture, $15. www.johnallans.com

Aftershave
Dollop size: Quarter
How to use it. Coat all shaved spots and the back of your neck and side-burn areas. If you're going to apply moisturizer or a sunscreen, wait about 5 minutes for the balm to be absorbed. We recommend Nivea for Men Fresh Cooling Balm, $6. www.niveausa.com

Shaving Gel
Dollop size: Quarter
How to use it. Wash your face to soften your beard, but don't dry it. The moisture makes it easier to spread the gel, says Venezia. Massage it into your skin so the moisturizers are absorbed. We use Gillette Complete Multigel, $7. www.gillette.com

Pomade/Hair Wax
Dollop size: Penny
How to use it. Glide your fingertips over the wax and apply it to dry hair as if you're scratching your scalp, advises Vaughn Accord, a men's stylist for Bumble and Bumble. We like Jack Black High Definition Hair Pomade, $16. www.getjackblack.com

ADDITIONAL TIMES A MONTH THAT MEN WITH MESSY SOCK DRAWERS HAVE SEX, COMPARED WITH GUYS WHO FOLD THEIR SOCKS: 3

Facial Cleanser

Dollop size: Nickel

How to use it. Wash twice daily, once before you shave and again at night. Lather the cleanser in your palm, then work it into your skin. We recommend Biotherm Homme Detoxifying Cleanser, $16. www.biotherm.com

OUR FINAL ANSWERS

Dating Duds

What do women like a man to wear on a first date?

—M.R., Wheeling, West Virginia

If you want to make it to date two, the key is being comfortable (if you're fidgeting, she'll take it personally) but also dressing for the occasion (if you look sloppy, she'll take it personally). On casual daytime dates, wear chinos with a fitted T-shirt and a lightweight cotton sweater. With Puma sneakers, it's irresistible. Just drinks? Try stylish jeans like Seven; a cool button-down striped shirt, untucked; and calfskin ankle boots. A classier night of cocktails or fine dining means suit pants, a black cotton slim-fit shirt (no jacket or tie), and your most stylish black shoes and belt.

Tie Your Look Together

Is it okay to wear a tie without a jacket in more relaxed formal settings?

—O.G., Laredo, Texas

If you want to look like a used-car salesman, sure. There's nothing wrong with taking off your jacket on certain occasions. But leaving the house without one makes you look like you left your style at home, too.

Scratch That

Wool is so itchy, it drives me crazy. What's a good, warm alternative?

—O.E., Aurora, Colorado

Cashmere! It's half the weight, twice as warm, and infinitely less itchy. A quality sweater will be at least two-ply and about three times the price of wool, but worth it. Cashmere is a magnet to women's hands.

Jean Code

I know you're not supposed to wear a jean jacket with jeans. So what looks best?

—S.D., Rochester, New York

You're right, the full-denim outfit is a little too country for most gals. Instead, add a buttery suede or leather jacket. You'll love it, and so will she.

Shoe Clues

What color shoes go with navy pants?

—D.Y., Gary, Indiana

Black pants require black shoes. Navy slacks require caramel or chocolate-brown shoes. Just as in boxing, being black and blue is never a good thing.

Match Game

How important is it that the leather of your belt, shoes, and jacket matches?

—D.H., Arnold, Maryland

Very. The colors don't have to match exactly, but they should be similar. Jackets can be slightly different. And never combine black with brown.

Sticking to It

How can I get rid of static?

—V.O., Newton, Massachusetts

Carry a dryer sheet in your pocket and periodically rub it on the underside of your sweater or pants. And wear natural-soled shoes (like leather) to make sure the only spark you feel is from mutual attraction.

Handle with Care

Does "Dry-clean only" really mean dry-clean only?

Yes. Go against the label at your own risk. There could be repercussions—shrinkage, fading, changes in fabric texture, or more, according to Jay Calleja, a spokesman for the International Fabricare Institute. Yes, going to a dry cleaner is a pain, but if a garment needs dry cleaning, chances are it was expensive. Think about the cost. Adjust attitude accordingly.

The Tooth Hurts

Do teeth whiteners weaken your teeth?

—T.B., Madison, Wisconsin

No. Tooth bleach weakens enamel about as much as paint weakens drywall, says Jay Neuhaus, DDS, a dentist at Gramercy Dental Arts in Manhattan. "The only downside is that for about 7 hours after the process, your teeth will be more sensitive to cold air and water."

Banish Bacne

Should I treat my body acne the same way I treated my face zits as a teen?

—L.P., Little Rock, Arkansas

Yup. Clearasil. Oxy 5. Neutrogena. The standard antipimple army you used as a teen is still your best bet to fight adult body acne, says John Romano, MD, a dermatologist in New York City. Look for products like Neutrogena's Body Clear Body Wash, made for your body instead of your face. Whatever product you choose, make sure it has benzoyl peroxide; but you may need to use a moisturizer like Cetaphil after you wash, since peroxide dries your skin. Be aware that it can take months or years for your body acne to go away. In extreme cases, you may need a prescription medication such as Retin-A or Tazorac. "Adult acne is a genetic issue. You can be predisposed to it even if

Mom and Dad didn't have it," says Dr. Romano. If the acne appears on your lower abdomen or thighs, see a dermatologist, as this could indicate a skin infection.

Gray Matters

What's the best way to cover gray hair?

—B.R., San Mateo, California

Women love the salt-and-pepper look. But if you insist on dyeing, consult a professional colorist at a salon. If you must do it yourself, start with a semi-permanent mixture so any color catastrophes can be shampooed away. Just for Men and L'Oreal make excellent men's dyes.

A Hairy Situation

I've got a hairy back. Do those hair-growth inhibitor creams really do the job?

—G.M., Butte, Montana

Yes. While they're often advertised for use after shaving, they're most effective on less bristly arm and back hair, says Zoe Draelos, MD, a dermatologist at Wake Forest University medical center. But for coarse beard hair, you'll have to stick with shaving.

Excess Baggage

How do I get rid of the seemingly permanent bags under my eyes?

—J.G., Vancouver

Prepare to travel lighter. Having bags under your eyes is largely genetic and very treatable if you're willing to go under the knife, says Albert Kligman, MD, PhD, a professor emeritus of dermatology at the University of Pennsylvania School of Medicine. Caused by a protrusion of fat through the muscle under the eye, bags "are very common and respond well to surgery," says Dr. Kligman. "It only costs a few hundred bucks, and you can get rid of them permanently."

The outpatient procedure—called transconjunctival blepharoplasty—involves an invisible incision under your lower eyelid, leaving less baggage and no visible scars. You can't say that about your last wife.

INDEX

Underscored page references indicate shaded text. **Boldfaced** page references indicate photographs.

A

Abdominal fat
  from alcohol, 82
  cortisol and, 46
  dangers of, 28, 34, 72
  liposuction and, 35
Abdominal muscles
  strengthening
    with Abs Diet Workout (*see* Abs
      Diet Workout)
    general guidelines for, 50
  types of, 61, 64
Abreva, for cold sores, 136
Abs Diet
  dining out guidelines for
    Chinese restaurant, 22
    diner, 20–21
    fast-food restaurant, 19–20
    Italian restaurant, 21
    Mexican restaurant, 21–22
    sandwich shop, 18–19
    sports bar, 21
  foods allowed in (*see* Abs Diet
    Power 12)
  food shopping for, 22–25
  guidelines for, 4–5, 17
  recipes for, 12–13, 25–29
  results from, 3, 72
  snacks in, 16
  success stories, 8, 11
Abs Diet Power 12
  almonds and other nuts, 7
  beans and other legumes, 7–8
  dairy products, 9
  eggs, 10
  extra-protein (whey) powder, 15
  icons describing, 6
  instant oatmeal, 9–10
  olive oil, 14
  peanut butter, 14

raspberries and other berries, 15, 17
rules for using, 5
spinach and other green vegetables,
  8–9
turkey and other lean meats, 11, 14
whole-grain breads and cereals,
  14–15
Abs Diet Workout
  components of, 62
  exercises in
    bent-leg knee raise, 66, **66**
    bicycle, 71, **71**
    corkscrew, 70, **70**
    crunch/side-bend combination, 70,
      70
    figure-8 crunch, 65, **65**
    hanging single knee raise, 71, **71**
    medicine-ball torso rotation, 67, **67**
    modified raised-feet crunch, 65, **65**
    stick crunch, 71, **71**
    Swiss-ball pull-in, 67, **67**
    Swiss-ball superman, 69, **69**
    traditional crunch, 65, **65**
    twisting back extension, 68, **68**
    two-handed wood chop, 68, **68**
    two-point bridge, 66, **66**
  guidelines for, 61, 62–63
  schedule for, 63–64
  starting, 62
Accutane, depression and, 236
ACE inhibitors, safe use of, 188
Acne
  body, 295–96
  in teens, 236
Acupuncture, for erectile dysfunction,
  121–22
Acupuncturist, for back pain treatment,
  145–46
ADD, treating, 229, 234
Advil, for joint pain, 140

Gastric bands, for weight loss, 37
Gas-X, 138
Genetics, muscle mass and, 79
Genital herpes, 117
Genital warts, 117
Germs, office, 160, <u>160</u>
Gifts
  to bosses, 266
  lingerie, 89, 125
Grains, whole
  in Abs Diet, 14–15
  buying, 24–25
  weight loss from, 45
Gray hair, 289, 296
Greenfield, Jeff, <u>242</u>
Grilling, food safety and, 161–62
Grocery store, best food choices at,
  22–25
Grooming, costs of ignoring, <u>290</u>
Grooming products, how to use,
  291–92
Gum disease
  heart disease and, 197
  from wisdom teeth, 155

H
Hair
  coloring, <u>284</u>
  dyeing, 296
  graying of, 289
  removal of, <u>284</u>
  styling, 282
Hair gel or wax, how to use, 291
Hair-growth inhibitor creams, 296
Hand washing, <u>160</u>
Hanging single knee raise, 71, **71**
Hanks, Tom, <u>242</u>
Hawk, Tony, <u>246</u>
Headaches
  identifying types of, 159–60
  medications for, 138, 139, 154
  migraine
    medication for, 139
    preventing, 164
    symptoms of, 159
  sinus, symptoms of, 159
  tension
    medication for, 154
    symptoms of, 159–60

Heart. *See also* Heart attacks; Heart
  disease
  exercise for, 189–90
  medications and, 135, 188
Heart attacks
  aspirin during, 193
  from bitter-orange extract, 33–34
  medications increasing risk of, 163
  syndrome X and, 172
  vacation reducing, <u>258</u>
Heartburn, medications for, 139
Heart disease
  C-reactive protein and, 194, 196–99
  diet reducing, 34, 192
  erectile dysfunction from, 119
  from vitamin D insufficiency,
    177, 180
Heart surgery, aspirin and, 188–89
Heat wraps, for joint pain, 140
Hemorrhoids
  medication for, 140
  from weight lifting, 85
Herpes virus, 117
HIV vaccine, 117
HMB, for muscle building, <u>59</u>
Hormone-replacement therapy, prostate
  cancer and, 191
Horniness. *See* Sexual interest
Human papillomavirus (HPV), 117

I
Ibuprofen
  for nasal congestion, 137
  topical, for pain relief, <u>136</u>
Ice, for muscle soreness, 77–78
Ice cream
  as binge food, <u>25</u>
  buying, 25
  soft-serve, as snack, 59
Imodium A-D, for diarrhea, 138
Impotence. *See* Erectile dysfunction
Infertility, male, 222–23
Infidelity, <u>104</u>
Inhalers, asthma, 165
Insect stings, 161
Insulin
  cholesterol and, 172
  intensive therapy with, 190
  role of, 171